D1550516

Performing Women

Also by Alison Oddey

DEVISING THEATRE

Performing Women

Stand-ups, Strumpets and Itinerants

Introduced, Interviewed and Edited by

Alison Oddey
Senior Lecturer in Drama and Theatre Studies
University of Kent

St. Martin's Press
New York

St. Martin's Press, Scholarly and Reference Division, 175 Fifth Avenue, New York, N.Y. 10010   ˙

First published in the United States of America in 1999

This book is printed on paper suitable for recycling and made from fully managed and sustained forest sources.

Printed in Great Britain

ISBN 0–312–22909–7

Library of Congress Cataloging-in-Publication Data
Oddey, Alison, 1954–
Performing women : stand-ups, strumpets and itinerants / Alison Oddey.
p.   cm.
Includes bibliographical references and index.
ISBN 0–312–22909–7 (cloth)
1. Women entertainers—Great Britain Interviews.
PN2597.O23   1999
791'.082'0941—dc21   99–39867
                                                CIP

In loving memory of the actress Susan Leong (1955–1993), and for my son, Oliver Williams, whom I learn from daily and love very much.

Acknowledgements

I wish to thank the University of Kent, School of Drama, Film and Visual Arts Research Fund for a grant towards this book; Val Oswald and Sue Sherwood for assistance in transcribing some of the interviews. Special thanks to Dr Nicola Shaughnessy, Jill Davis, Jessica Naish, and my mother, Patricia Oddey, for reading parts of the manuscript and for generously sharing their own thoughts, insights and criticisms with me. I would also like to thank Professor Christopher Baugh and my editor, Charmian Hearne, for their advice, support and constant encouragement.

Thanks are also due to Ruth Young, Ali Day, Sue Hunter, Kathleen Earl, Cathy Edis and Sylvia Morris (The Shakespeare Centre) for their reliability and efficiency during the research process. I want to thank particular friends, Dr Louise Naylor, Alison Kirkpatrick, Jos Kirkvliet, Phil and Claire Poole, Alison Packer, Paula Hamilton, Doris Dodd and Alison McCloud, who have supported and encouraged me in various ways. Finally, special thanks to Ben for all his continued in-house support, love, patience and wisdom, and most of all, to the 'performing women', who have shared something of themselves with me.

Every effort has been made to contact all of the copyright-holders of illustrations included in this book but if any have been missed we would be happy to make appropriate acknowledgement in future printings.

Contents

List of Illustrations		ix
Acronyms		xi
1	PERFORMING WOMEN	1
2	HISTORICAL AND CULTURAL CONTEXTS	5
3	STAND-UPS, STRUMPETS AND ITINERANTS	13
	Jenny Eclair	15
	Niamh Cusack	24
	Imogen Stubbs	35
	Josette Simon	45
	Meera Syal	55
	Jane Horrocks	66
	Kathy Burke	76
	Marianne Jean-Baptiste	89
	Heather Ackroyd	98
	Jo Brand	106
	Imelda Staunton	118
	Juliet Stevenson	130
	Kathryn Hunter	143
	Fiona Shaw	153
	Dawn French	165
	Miranda Richardson	176
	Victoria Wood	185
	Penelope Wilton	198
	June Whitfield	208
	Sheila Hancock	218

Brenda Blethyn   232

Alison Steadman   244

Julie Walters   254

Bobby Baker   266

4 WHY PERFORM? Themes Arising from Interviews   279

Selected Bibliography   294

Index   295

List of Illustrations

Alison Oddey and Oliver Williams, September 1994   xii
Jenny Eclair Photo: Chris Frazer-Smith   15
Jenny Eclair, aged 7   18
Niamh Cusack Photo: Fatimah Namdar   24
Niamh Cusack, 'I don't want to be on Aideen's pony!'   28
Imogen Stubbs Photo: Carole Latimer   35
Josette Simon Photo: Carole Latimer   45
Josette as a child   51
Meera Syal Photo: Geoff Shields   55
Meera pretending she could ride her uncle's motorbike
    Home, Essington, 1972, aged 9   58
Jane Horrocks Photo: Alan Strutt   66
Kathy Burke Photo: Jackie di Stefano   76
Kathy Burke, London, January 1976, aged 11   81
Marianne Jean-Baptiste Photo: Lisa Linder   89
Heather Ackroyd in *Desert Grass*, Joshua Tree National Park,
    California, 1991 Photo: Heather Ackroyd & Dan Harvey   98
Heather Ackroyd, aged 10   101
Jo Brand Photo: Trevor Leighton   106
Jo Brand, aged 6   110
Imelda Staunton Photo: Brian Aris   118
Imelda Staunton 'when she was small', London   125
Juliet Stevenson Photo: Brian Aris   130
Juliet in Paderborn, Westphalia, 1958, aged 2   135
Kathryn Hunter as King Lear in Shakespeare's *King Lear*,
The Young Vic, 1997 Photo: Stephen Vaughan   143
Fiona Shaw Photo: Neil Libbart   153
Fiona as a senior infant at the Mercy Convent, watching Mother
    Patrick cutting a toffee with a blunt knife for those infants who
    were 'good', aged 4   161
Dawn French Photo: Trevor Leighton   165
Miranda Richardson Photo: Brigitte Lacombe   176
Victoria Wood Photo: Brian Moody   185
Penelope Wilton Photo: Sasha Gusov   198
June Whitfield (Photographer unknown)   208
Sheila Hancock Photo: Amanda Searle   218
Sheila Hancock as a child   222
Brenda Blethyn Photo: Michael Mayhew   232

Brenda Blethyn, aged 6   234
Alison Steadman Photo: Jillian Edelstein   244
Alison Steadman as a child   247
Julie Walters Photo: Brian Moody   254
Bobby Baker in *Take a Peek!*, Royal Festival Hall, London
International Festival of Theatre, 1995 Photo: Andrew Whittuck   266
Bobby Baker, Swanage, 1954, aged 4   275
Alison Oddey, Bristol, August 1959, aged 4   278

Acronyms

BAFTA	British Academy of Film and Television Arts
BBC	British Broadcasting Corporation
ICA	Institute of Contemporary Arts
LAMDA	London Academy of Music and Dramatic Art
LIFT	London International Festival of Theatre
RADA	Royal Academy of Dramatic Art
RNT	Royal National Theatre
RSA	Royal Society of Arts
RSC	Royal Shakespeare Company
RTS	Royal Television Society

Alison Oddey and Oliver Williams, September 1994

1
Performing Women

Original intentions

Early in September 1994 I stood holding Oliver, my three-month-old son, and my first published book, *Devising Theatre*,[1] cradling a sense of both wonderment and achievement. Returning to work in October as a full-time academic at the University of Kent, my life as a working mother began with this research project investigating and pursuing further my longstanding interest in contemporary performance, and in women performers in particular. There has been a proliferation of work in the broad field of gender and theatre, which has attempted to address the issue of women and marginality. I wanted to foreground the voices of performing women within the process of research and writing; to place this research work within the context of a wider feminist project, building and developing out of previous pioneering books, whilst contributing to a new theatre history/her-story. It was within this context that the book was conceived in 1995.

Performing Women has a gender, theatre, history orientation, looking at women performers across three generations and identifying the issues that have engaged these performers. The content of the book was based on a perpetual preoccupation with the question: why perform? It seemed to me that it would be fascinating to talk to women performers in theatre whom I had admired for a long time, and investigate their reasons and motivation for performing. I was also interested in creating a different kind of book from those I had previously read.[2] Previous books, including collections of interviews, have revised history, studying the representation of women in Shakespeare or Restoration Comedy, as well as reclaiming and repositioning women alongside their male counterparts. The form of this book originates in the secondary pragmatic practicalities of being a working mother with a young child. I needed to devise a project which would allow me to work in stages: interviewing, transcribing, editing and writing. The interviewing took place between February 1996 and September 1997. In every case, the interviews were conducted in London or Kent, with the exception of that with Julie Walters, whom I interviewed in Brighton.

Choosing the performers

At the beginning, I wanted to include as diverse a list of performing women as possible, but it became clear that I would have to set my own parameters for the choice of the interviewees. I was conscious of a restrictive hierarchy of familiar figureheads of the female performance tradition, created by male theatre critics. I chose not to invite a particular list of acknowledged, renowned women, who have always been revered by the London critics, but to focus predominantly on a distinctive middle generation of performers whose body of work excited me.

I interviewed a cross-section of performing women from different generations, cultures, perspectives and practice. In selecting the final list, it was important that I liked their work, and could relate to them in some way or other. These interviews tell various stories collectively. It is a dialogue between stand-ups, 'classic' actresses, film and television personalities/character and comedy actresses, and performance artists. It has been the most fascinating and stimulating experience to interview these performing women, and I have felt extraordinarily privileged to discuss with them how their personal history has contributed to their desires to perform. It has felt like a group of friends, sitting down in comfort, eating and drinking up the conversation. Interviews usually lasted 90 minutes, but sometimes extended to three hours. I warmed to the generous spirit of these women, to their friendly, open manner of discussion, and to their kind hospitality often inviting me into their homes, or buying me lunch at a pre-arranged venue.

As the interviews progressed, the nature of my research changed, incorporating film and television performance into the discussion, as well as unearthing an important sub-text of motherhood, and the problems and particularities of being a working mother. Of the twenty-four performing women interviewed sixteen are mothers,[3] and thus, inevitably, the theme of 'Identity: performing, motherhood, being' emerged. In conjunction with this, in April 1996, I devised a solo performance work, 'What Shall I Do With My Amstrad?', which I toured and performed in various venues until July 1997.[4] This meant that 'practice as research' fed into the underlying questions of my enquiry, whilst developing and contributing my own 'stand-up, strumpet, itinerant' interests to this research experience.

Presentation of material

These are women performers speaking at the end of the twentieth century, and in a particular performance context, time and place. For this reason, I have chosen to highlight the specific performance context of the discussion within the brief commentary prior to the start of each interview. It provides a background situation to the work that they had recently completed or were currently doing, and what they were about to do in the immediate future. This simply sets the scene for the interview and is in no way a substitution for a description of their careers.

These performers are very difficult to present in any kind of category, but for clarity's sake I recognise four types of performer – the stand-up comic, the 'classic' actress, the film/television character/comedy performer, and the performance artist. I want to define the stand-up comic as being funny, owning her own identity through the words that she has written and speaks. The 'classic' actress, however, having had a conventional drama school training, including Greek drama, Renaissance and European naturalism, loves to become a character in a play, investigating and telling a story. These characters are fictional creations, often created by men, and are therefore not 'women' characters, but projections of masculinity. In the essay 'Performative Acts and Gender Constitution: An Essay in Phenomenology and Feminist Theory', Judith Butler argues that 'Gender reality is performative ..., that it is real only to the extent that it is performed.'[5] Thus, the 'classic' actress embodies and substantiates such fictions as real, tricking the audience into seeing 'women' on stage, where none really exist. The category of film/television character/comedy performer covers the diversity of roles undertaken by these performing women. They are working in all the mediums, and may have established themselves particularly in one of these areas of work. The performance artist is involved with making work, which is often concerned with the analysis, exploration and presentation of the 'self'. It is visual, physical and often focuses on the body as a primary site for performance.

Categorising and labelling these performers by definition goes against the overall tone of the collection. I sensed a yearning from many performers to be allowed to play parts outside of their recognised abilities and talents, and the difficulty of having that opportunity to do something completely different. The edited interviews selected in this volume only represent a part of the dialogue that took place between 1996 and 1997. It was felt important to present these interviews as closely as possible to the original conversations, offering a distinctive and unique voice to each one.

The process of researching this book has not been easy, entering a world of theatrical agents, personal assistants and photographers – endless telephone messages, endless faxes, and endless repetition of the same information. Scheduling interviews proved difficult at times: juggling the different responsibilities as working mothers; compromising in terms of timing and venue; being sensitive to particular personal circumstances of performers; respecting privacy and confidentiality. Every interviewee was sent a first draft of the transcript, and invited to make revisions, changes or cuts as desired. When faced with the mirror of the interview transcript, some performers made alterations in light of changed circumstances, or feeling that what they had said at the time was no longer relevant. Only one contributor has made major changes to the original text.

Title of the book

I want to distinguish the difference between the terms 'Performing Women' and 'Acting Women' to describe this collection of interviews, so that it is clear from the start how I perceived and approached the project. Performing subsumes different types of performers, including the stand-up, actress and performance artist, whereas acting consists of actors, who perform 'characters', written by a playwright and interpreted by a director. Acting is conventionally associated with a written script whether for theatre, film or television, whereas performing embraces the wider context of devised[6] work, which does not necessarily focus on the written play script of a single author, but embraces the roles of both entertainer and artist.

Acting is about impersonation and mimesis. It is about interpreting and representing a character. Michael Kirby states that to act '... means to feign, to simulate, to represent, to impersonate'.[7] However, he argues that '... not all performing is acting'.[8] Performing does not have to include 'acting', in that performers can be themselves, and are not pretending or representing anybody else. This is certainly true of the stand-up comic who stands in the same time and place of the audience. This can equally be true of the performance artist, as she does not impersonate others or play a particular role, as opposed to my earlier definition of the term 'classic' actress. Kirby calls this state of performing 'not-acting', and argues that, 'Acting can be said to exist in the smallest and simplest action that involves pretense'.[9] Performing contains dance, performance art, live art, stand-up, all of which may not include any acting.

Various performance theorists, including Herbert Blau and Marvin Carlson,[10] have defined performing as having a consciousness to it, and my title simply implies that these 'Performing Women' are consciously performing for someone, for an audience of some kind. The actresses are performing characters, created by playwrights, in a dramatic action, but the stand-up comics' and performance artists' work becomes 'performative' (in the sense of particular skills being publicly demonstrated) when they consciously display them for an audience. The 'self' is expressed through the performing, even though there is a different emphasis of language, via word or body, between the stand-ups' performance and that of the performance artist. Both use few conventional theatre trappings, such as set, props or costumes. In stand-up and performance art, the performer's personal contribution fronts the performance, playing with the boundaries of reality and imagination. Marvin Carlson writes about the 'double consciousness' of the performer and audience:

> Within the play frame a performer is not herself (because of the operations of illusion), but she is also not not herself (because of the operations of reality). Performer and audience alike operate in a world of double consciousness.[11]

2
Historical and Cultural Contexts

The female stand-up comic

Of a comedian: performing by standing before an audience and telling a succession of jokes.[12]

the figure who stands apart in a public place and invites our laughter.[13]

Victoria Wood is, in her use of song, her Northern accent, and her jolly-sister persona a throwback to music hall.[14]

Stand-up began with Music Hall in the nineteenth century,[15] growing and developing out of pub entertainments in back rooms, where the only women present were prostitutes. It progressed to the solo woman on the bill and a tradition of singing songs in character, such as Marie Lloyd who represented 'respectablility' on the one hand, whilst being viewed as a sexual object within the context of a male-defined sexuality on the other. In *Women and Laughter*, Frances Gray suggests that the ambivalence of the female performer meant being 'engaged in the task of transforming the prostitute–client relationship, simultaneously trading on her sex appeal' and 'defamiliarising it'.[16] Gray argues that Lloyd offered 'an image of what the single woman might achieve', raising 'questions about female desire and sexual freedom that the "legitimate" theatre of her day hardly dared to handle'.[17] Gray suggests that:

the female comic presence in music hall and vaudeville has been seen as an early sign of change in the position of nineteenth-century women, evidence of at least a few women who managed to come out on top despite the enormous obstacles to their freedom and independence.[18]

Oliver Double in, *STAND-UP! On Being a Comedian*, argues that stand-up as 'the transformation of funny singing into funny talking' was the case by the

1930s, 'but singing and even dancing remained an important part of the art of stand-up comedy right up until the variety circuit collapsed in the early 1960s'.[19] Since the 1980s the nature of female comic performance has changed from simply telling jokes to incorporating specific gender problems via an integral autobiographical process, which is then transformed into a public performance. The female stand-up comic asserts her sexuality, is the subject rather than the object of laughter; she controls and creates her own material, challenging body image, domesticity and patriarchy. There is no doubt that despite personal preference, there is an acknowledged list of female stand-up comics, which includes Victoria Wood, Jo Brand, Jenny Eclair, Donna McPhail, Hattie Hayridge and Rhona Cameron in the 'top ten' list. It is a short list. It has remained a short list for some time, which begs the much wider question of why there are still so few women stand-ups.

Strumpet: the first English actresses

An unchaste woman, a prostitute.[20]

The analogy between actress and prostitute begins after 1660, when the first English actresses were introduced and welcomed in the public theatre. Prior to this date, however, women actors at court or in private houses were not generally accepted, and were viewed as whores. Elizabeth Howe in *The First English Actresses: Women and Drama 1660–1700*, confirms the low social standing of actresses, and the general assumption that 'the word "actress" stood for "prostitute"', which soon 'became a self-fulfilling prophecy'.[21] Howe states that:

> ... no woman with serious pretensions to respectability would countenance a stage career, and yet the profession demanded more than women of the brothel class. An actress had to be able to read and memorise lines at speed, to sing and dance to some degree and to emulate a lady's behaviour. This left only a 'narrow middle stratum' of society from which actresses could be drawn.[22]

In 1662, it became law that women should play women's parts, and companies exploited the sexual availability of the actress in order to attract audiences, 'the actress's sexuality – her potential availability to men – became the central feature of her professional identity as a player'.[23]

Actresses continued to be exploited as sexual commodities throughout the nineteenth century, living 'a public life' and consenting 'to be "hired" for amusement by all who could command the price'.[24] In *Actresses as Working Women, Their Social Identity in Victorian Culture*, Tracy Davis argues that the association between actress and prostitute persisted in the Victorian period

'... because Victorians recognized that acting and whoring were the occupations of self-sufficient women who plied their trades in public places'.[25] Davis claims that 'the actress and prostitute were both objects of desire whose company was purchased through commercial exchange'.[26]

How far has this image persisted into the twentieth century? In terms of my own research, I wanted to discover whether the seventeenth-century image of actress as prostitute or 'strumpet', or the nineteenth-century image of actress as a public commodity to be purchased, had changed in the opinion of late twentieth-century women performers. Although this has been a fascinating area of enquiry, I have only been able to include a small selection of responses to this debate. However, it is clear that many interviewees considered the actress to have a more serious image than previously. Many have argued that the glamorous, trivial, 'showing off and posturing' (Marianne Jean-Baptiste, p. 96), looking gorgeous and taking 'their top off at some point' (Josette Simon, p. 53) has been '... taken over by supermodels ... and that sort of other world of immediate showing off'[27] in the 1990s. Dawn French suggests that it is fashionable 'to be slightly strumpetty, to pout, to be angry, not care and be slightly tarty' (p. 174). There is something rebellious about the image, 'It is somebody who doesn't give a toss about how she is seen' (Meera Syal, p. 64).

Imogen Stubbs believes that the actress is being 'pimped' by television for high ratings, which '... reduces actors to strumpets, because you are selling yourself for ratings' (p. 43). There is an overall sense that the younger actress, coming into the profession, may have to prostitute herself by gratuitous nudity, particularly on television. However, for performers making their own work, such as Heather Ackroyd or Bobby Baker, it is *not* 'carrying your sexuality at the forefront as a way of proving yourself',[28] but an empowering experience, which makes use of sexuality to communicate ideas: '... so it's taking back that image, owning it and making use of those associations rather than avoiding them' (Bobby Baker, p. 276).

Itinerant

A person who travels from place to place, esp. as a preacher, actor, etc.[29]

The search for historical origins reveals that women have had a longer history as performers in theatres of low status and informal organization and as travelling players performing often without script on makeshift stages in the open street, than in the high status theatres equipped with permanent buildings and royal patronage. Women have therefore performed in a number of spaces and in a number of ways which have been invisible to theatre historians and literary critics.[30]

Katharine Cockin argues that the history of the female performer is perceived differently when the focus is no longer on 'script-based performances and permanent theatre buildings' and the emphasis is on 'what has become known as "illegitimate" theatres, in unregulated performances'.[31] Cockin makes the point that theatre historians have often disregarded women performing devised performances in non-theatrical spaces, or in their public performing role as preachers.[32]

Itinerancy is integral to the female stand-up comic's desire to perform. Victoria Wood feels that 'it's part of a job travelling around being a comedienne in different towns', and 'having a different audience in each place makes me able to do it' (p. 186). She states that she 'would never make a joke about a town I had never walked around' (Wood, p. 187). Similarly, Jo Brand loves 'staying away and wandering about' (p. 116), and Jenny Eclair is 'almost nostalgic for this tour before it's over' (p. 17).

Part of the appeal for many performers is that it takes them away from domestic preoccupations, giving them space and opportunity to focus completely on the work. Some performers love to explore new places, touring to different kinds of audience abroad, 'just observing the way different people appreciate theatre',[33] seeing how different audiences respond: 'To go and see is when I come alive ... I don't like nests – horrible. To go back, like the bird who has flown, then you can go back and that's quite cosy'.[34] Amongst these women performers, there is a sense of restlessness and a desire to be always moving on: '...I'm always wanting to just get on a plane and go. Maybe that's in the blood of actors, that sort of gypsy thing or whatever it is, the wandering spirit that you want to move from point to point endlessly.'[35] Alison Steadman would hate to do the same thing in the same place, and Jo Brand is 'quite happy living out of a bag' (p. 116). Julie Walters likes the fact that she could be anywhere, not quite knowing where she is going, 'Travelling in some escapist way', and that 'you are not mapped out for the rest of your life' (p. 262). For others, they see themselves as itinerants in terms of their sheer love of travelling from role to role.

Cultural perspective

In the late 1990s, a 'quick fix' and 'instant' culture exists, 'demanding quick satisfaction for consumers as they move from one new product to the next'.[36] It is a culture of instant gratification interspersed with leisure and dominated by work. This fragmentary, ready-made culture focuses on the individual rather than the group. The notion of a company does not exist any more in an economic and cultural climate, which places emphasis on funding theatre that can pay for itself, justifying the costs of every play production. Amongst these women performers, there is a general desire to work within a company and to be part of a team. Historically, this appears to have been the case for those performers devising theatre in the 1970s, and especially for those working at the Royal Shakespeare Company in the 1980s. It is the organic process that appeals to these women, the intensity of the experience, and the developmental nature of the work. More than anything, it is the desire for a collaborative, working experience, which involves everyone in the process from the start.

I detect a strong yearning to be part of a team, and a certain kind of performance pleasure to be gained from performing as a company – together – not independently alone. This is particularly highlighted in the experiences of Juliet Stevenson and Imelda Staunton, who describe the sheer pleasure of being part of an ensemble in the Theatre de Complicite production of Brecht's *Caucasian Chalk Circle* or Richard Eyre's production of *Guys and Dolls* at the Royal National Theatre in 1997. I perceive a dominant theatrical culture of West End musicals and canonical 'classics', and the continuing re-visiting of traditional female roles. This theatre is 'safe' and respectable in the interests of commercial success. Risks are rarely taken and I detect a lack of courage in deciding what can and cannot be put on. The status of women in theatre has changed over the last few decades, notably in administration, with greater opportunities for female artists to be integrated into mainstream culture. Despite new writers and new writing, there is still a demand for roles that express the realities of being a woman in the late 1990s. Much more diversity is needed. Performers have discussed a certain kind of work for actresses in their thirties, followed by a disappointment with what is available in their forties, and a real lack of good parts for women in their fifties, particularly in television. Consequently, women are choosing what they want to perform, making the work happen that they want to do, and that is relevant to them.

There has been a rise in solo women performers over the last two decades, including stand-up comics and performance artists, who are creating their own material and production projects. Dawn French has her own production company, which focuses on particular projects that she wants to create. The choice to perform 'male roles', such as Fiona Shaw in *Richard II* at the Royal National Theatre (1995–96)[37] and Kathryn Hunter in *King Lear* at the Young Vic (1997)[38] has been an exciting development in recent times. As Shaw points out in the foreword to *The Routledge Reader in Gender and Performance*:

I had no sense that this experiment would work, but I knew that the idea excited me enough to go to the next stage. ... The experiments in gender, both socially and artistically, can remind us all of the constant bravery necessary to force the universe of the imagination outwards. It is a reminder that freedom is vigilance, that one sometimes has to play what one isn't suited to play. … Gender (and its experiments) and performance are merely another metaphor for the unknown.[39]

Notes

1 *Devising Theatre*, Routledge, London and New York, September 1994 (hbk), October 1996 (pbk).

2 Rutter, C., and Evans, F., *Clamorous Voices: Shakespeare's Women Today*, The Women's Press, 1988. Woddis, C. (ed.), *'Sheer Bloody Magic' Conversations with Actresses*, Virago Press, 1991. Juno, A. and Vale, V. (eds), *Angry Women*, Re/Search Publication, 1991. Tushingham, D. (ed.), *Live 2 Not What I Am, The Experience of Performing*, Methuen, 1995. Goodman, L. (ed.), *Feminist Stages, Interviews with Women in Contemporary British Theatre*, Harwood Academic Publishers, 1996.

3 It is now seventeen at the time of writing, January 1999.

4 This show explored the theme of 'Identity: performing, motherhood, being', examining multiple identities with particular reference to being a working mother, which was fundamental to the performance. This work has been written about in the following articles and books: 'What Shall I Do With My Amstrad?' in *Studies in Theatre Production*, No. 13, June 1996, pp. 105–8. 'SHOW AND TELL: The Delights of Devising Theatre' in *Studies in Theatre Production*, No. 15, June 1997, pp. 43–50. Chapter 10, Viglen's Revenge, Donnell, A., and Polkey, P. (eds), *Representing Lives: Women and Auto/biography*, Macmillan Press, 1999 (forthcoming). Goodman, L., *Sexuality in Performance*, Routledge, 1999 (forthcoming).

5 Butler, J., 'Performative Acts and Gender Constitution: An Essay in Phenomenology and Feminist Theory' in Case, S-E. (ed.), *Performing Feminisms, Feminist Critical Theory and Theatre*, The Johns Hopkins University Press, 1990, p. 278.

6 'A devised theatre product is work that has emerged from and been generated by a group of people working in collaboration.' Oddey, A., *Devising Theatre*, Routledge, 1994, p. 1.

7 Kirby, M., 'On Acting and Not-Acting', Zarrilli, P. (ed.), *Acting (Re) Considered*, Routledge, 1995, p. 43.

8 Ibid.

9 Ibid., p. 46.

10 Blau, H., *To All Appearances: Ideology and Performance*, Routledge, 1992. Carlson, M., *Performance: A Critical Introduction*, Routledge, 1996.

11 Ibid., Carlson, p. 54.

12 *The New Shorter Oxford English Dictionary*, Volume 2, Clarendon Press, Oxford, 1993, p. 3030.

13 Gray, F., *Women and Laughter*, Macmillan Press, 1994, p. 117.

14 Ibid., p. 133.

15 In *Women and Laughter*, Frances Gray traces stand-up comedy to the figures of 'Fool', 'Joker', or 'Trickster', but argues that women were denied the opportunity to be part of a female comic tradition. Gray informs us that Mary Tudor had a woman fool called Jane, 'but history has preferred to mythologise her father's fool, Henry VIII's Will Somers', p. 117.

16 Ibid., p. 125.

17 Ibid.

18 Ibid., p. 118.

19 Double, O., *STAND-UP! On Being a Comedian*, Methuen, 1997, p. 23.

20 *The New Shorter Oxford English Dictionary*, Volume 2, p. 3104.

21 Howe, E., *The First English Actresses: Women and Drama 1660–1700*, Cambridge University Press, 1992, p. 32. Howe informs us that 'the first time that the word "actress" was used with the meaning "female player on stage" was not, as the OED states, in 1700, but directly after Queen Henrietta Maria's first court performance in a French pastoral on Shrove Tuesday, 1626: ... as a "principal Actress"', ibid., p. 21.
22 Ibid., p. 8.
23 Ibid., p. 34.
24 Davis, T., *Actresses as Working Women, Their Social Identity in Victorian Culture*, Routledge, 1991, p. 69.
25 Ibid., p. 100.
26 Ibid.
27 From an unpublished part of the interview with Penelope Wilton.
28 From an unpublished part of the interview with Heather Ackroyd.
29 *The New Shorter Oxford English Dictionary*, Volume 1, p. 1430.
30 Cockin, K., in introduction to Part One: 'The History of Women in Theatre', Goodman, L., with de Gay, J. (eds), *The Routledge Reader in Gender and Performance*, Routledge, 1998, p. 20.
31 Ibid., p. 21.
32 When the theatres were closed to women as performers (under pressure from Quakers), both Protestants and Quakers allowed 'the role of public performance as preachers', ibid., p. 22.
33 From an unpublished part of the interview with Marianne Jean-Baptiste.
34 From an unpublished part of the interview with Kathryn Hunter.
35 From an unpublished part of the interview with Imogen Stubbs.
36 Oddey, A., Chapter 19, 'Devising (Women's) Theatre', Goodman, L., with de Gay, J. (eds), *The Routledge Reader in Gender and Performance*, p. 119.
37 Cottesloe Theatre, 2 June 1995–1 January 1996; directed by Deborah Warner.
38 Haymarket, Leicester, 25 February – 15 March 1997 and Young Vic, London, 25 June – 2 August 1997; directed by Helena Kaut-Howson.
39 Shaw, F., in 'Foreword', *The Routledge Reader in Gender and Performance*, p. xxiv–xxv.

3

Stand-ups, Strumpets and Itinerants

Jenny Eclair

'Look at me, look at me!'

Performance Context

Born: 1960, Malaya.

Prior/current commitments: Tour of stand-up show *Prozac and Tantrums*.

Post-interview (selected): In May 1997, West End debut as Josie in Nell Dunn's *Steaming*. In October 1997, she hosted *Jenny Eclair Squats* for Channel 5 Television. In 1998, the third series of BBC Radio 4's *On Baby Street* was broadcast, co-written with Julie Baloo. In the 1998 Edinburgh Festival, she starred in her new one-woman play *Mrs Nosey Parker*.

Other: In 1995, her stand-up success was acknowledged when she became the first ever woman to win the prestigious Perrier Award, for her show *Prozac and Tantrums*.

Interview

I laughed heartily at the outrageous comments of Jenny Eclair in her dressing-room at the Marlowe Theatre in Canterbury on 19 February 1996, prior to watching her perform the Perrier Award winning stand-up show Prozac and Tantrums.

Alison Oddey: *You're performing the 1995 Perrier Award winning show here at the Marlowe Theatre in Canterbury. How has that award made a difference to your working life?*

Jenny Eclair: I'm getting huge amounts of dosh wherever I go! It gives venues confidence to book you and give you stupid advances, guaranteeing big wads of cash. So this is two weeks in Antigua – it's a jag – it's a whole new spring outfit. I'm thinking in terms of boots and shoes every night. It's a bit of a treat. I don't know how tonight's going to go, but most of them, especially up in the north, have almost been the justification of all the crappy times. Up to this point I've enjoyed 96 per cent of them. There have been two dodgy ones, where one audience was dull and the other one was a bit thick. I do think there are thick audiences and I don't think there's any truth in that old crap – no such thing as a bad audience – because there are. Sometimes you look out at the audience and you just think – collectively very stupid. Of course, I always want to be loved by everybody, which means that I always go down to the lowest common denominator. It's a managerial kind of thing, we'll shove out the Perrier award winner, and let's make everyone a pile of dough, which I'm quite happy to do. I'm almost nostalgic for this tour before it's over, because I think what if this is as good as it gets? I like this position of being where I am now, and being treated nicely. Diet coke and low-calorie sandwiches in the fridge on my arrival.

Is that your idea of heaven then?

Well, it is. A calorie-counted heaven must exist somewhere. It makes a change from what I call the four carpets, bed and breakfast days. Every room has four different carpets in, and it's basically a flophouse. Now, we stay at posh hotels. I love touring. It takes you away from all the domestic rubbish. This is complete freedom.

Performing is a kind of escape then? Is that why you perform?

I always knew I was going to perform, from the age of about four. It's just a totally natural thing, a natural state. I think that I have performed naturally on and off stages for most of my life. It's a sort of pathological need for attention. The classic army upbringing is quite prevalent in a lot of performers. The changing school malarkey: you change schools – all your best friends move away – and you've got to do something to make new friends, so it's just as easy to be an idiot really. It's high-class idiocy that I managed to get myself into!

So becoming a performer is related to an army upbringing and moving around a lot?

I've met a lot of people who've come from similar backgrounds, who end up in this kind of profession. I had the shyness and all that kind of nonsense knocked out of me at a very early age, because there was never any time. If you go to a new school, there's no time to be shy. You've got to get on with it, and I have an absolute antipathy towards shy people to this day, because I think it's lazy and dull. I feel that everyone's got to make an effort to entertain each other.

Does that tie in then with you being a comedienne?

Yes, I think so. As a child, I did have a streak of humour, but I thought it would be much more balanced to be a proper film star. I would have made an ace silent movie star, you know – rolling eyeballs and all that kind of thing, because I'm far too over the top for the naturalistic sort of stuff that was around. There's this sort of comedy persona, which I've created and is very easy to slip into. People often don't know that there's a difference between that persona and myself, because they expect me to be badly behaved all the time, which is rather exhausting. I can't do it. People are quite shocked that I actually say please and thank you. It's a healthy schizophrenia. I'd recommend it to all. It's a sort of cathartic kind of thing every night – just letting it all go – which I hugely enjoy.

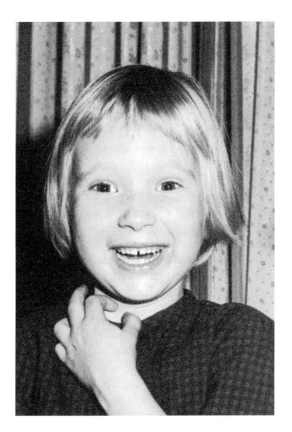

Aged seven

Is your stand-up material always autobiographical?

To some extent, yes, because I can only write from the angle of being a thirty-five-year-old woman with one child. So a lot of that comes into it, because that's what my natural interest is. However, in the last few months, I've been writing with an older bloke because I don't want to get too labelled, or too pigeonholed into purely female comedy. The biggest criticism of female comedy is that we ghettoise our material – we're all very genitalia orientated and that sort of thing, because – let's face it – we are ruled by our hormones, so you tend to have tunnel vision down to your fanny really. It's quite liberating and healthy working with someone who pushes me into other kinds of areas. I'd like to be able to perform at fifty, entertaining a huge crowd, as well as doing other things, such as acting, writing comedy drama for radio, or guest editing for magazines.

Has anybody inspired you particularly?

I'm not a comedy anorak at all. The first bit of television I saw, when I was about eight, was Lucille Ball. I was struck by her looking fantastic and being very over the top. I suppose John Cooper-Clark was influential in some respects – he was the punk poet at Manchester. I kind of got the punk poet thing by osmosis … if you hung round Manchester long enough, you became a punk poet. So poetry in the early 1980s sort of kick-started my performance; it was a way into performing and was something to do on stage. French and Saunders were already amazing by this point, but I never saw them live on stage, doing their thing. By the time that I was doing the London clubs, there were three women comics – Helen Lederer, Jenny Lecoat and me. We were all very different. Jenny Lecoat was very femme – sort of power to women kind of stuff – Helen Lederer had this sort of apologetic kind of style, and I wasn't very good particularly. I didn't really hit my stride until I was nudging thirty. Seeing Jo Brand for the first time was a bit of a kick up the arse for me, because there was a woman on the London circuit, who claimed the stage as her own without being mealy-mouthed about it. She seemed to have every right to be there, and stood solidly on the stage. Up until then, there had been a lot of girlies faffing around, skipping on and skipping off. I remember thinking that I'd got to get my act together, that there was going to be a spate of new birds like this one. I'm very competitive, and as soon as I see a new girlie name in the listings, a wave of nausea sweeps over my body – they're going to be the next female Perrier award winner, younger and cuter with better legs, and I don't want it. I would never have a female support act or a woman driver either. I'm an old-fashioned girl.

What does being a performing woman mean to you?

I think it's a huge privilege, but I think it does take a long apprenticeship. I do deserve a good time now. I still get slapped in the face. You do 750 people one night, then you're down to 80 with the next. So you're constantly being tripped up. I've never contemplated giving up and changing tack. It's some sort of dogged belief that this is right. I have quite a lot of energy on stage, more than in any other aspect of my life. I feel most alive on stage. I do need that adrenalin. I like it, I get off on it. It's very much the girl in the playground, hanging upside down without pants on, which is sort of 'look at me, look at me!' As a comedian, I'm not interested in all these comedy classes, where you learn to be a comic, because apart from learning how to take the microphone out of the stand, it's got to be innate. The rest is just practice and experience, and nobody now can take away my experience, which is very nice. Even on a bad day, I've got about thirteen years of performing skills behind me.

Is there any therapeutic value to being a stand-up?

I think that's a bit too 'up it's own bum', but I know it makes me happy, even though I have fear and loathing about the whole thing. I'm very scared, particularly with this new show last year, when I was trying to get it together. I went through misery and hell, because the act didn't have a natural flow, and now it has turned into a greatest hits album. It's a regular sort of fix of that kind of triumph. I can't thing of anything else that makes me quite as happy. It's the most satisfying work I've done. I love my daughter Phoebe so much and I physically miss her terribly but I couldn't swap it.

How do you cope on tour as a working mother?

I have a good bloke, although he let her pack her own bag to go away for five days to my mum and dad's house near Blackpool in February. She's six. She'd packed summer clothes, no pants or socks – just sequined shorts. I went into 'Dixon' mode and just started shrieking. It's a lot of juggling. The worst thing is when she's ill; you dread those calls – 'Don't worry, but she's got a temperature, an earache, a rash' … I'd cancel without blinking. This country's very small, but you can always get home.

Has it been a constant balancing act since you had Phoebe?

Yes, but the work got better as soon as I had her. I became a lot more focused. I stopped fiddle-arsing around, because I realised very quickly that I couldn't bear to be an 'at home' mother. So work had to justify being away from her, be of a better standard and better paid, so I could afford to pay people to help me. However, it does get easier as they get older. She writes notes to me now – 'Dear Mummy, I love you, but I hate your job.' It is written evidence of what she feels.

How does that make you feel?

A bit rubbish, but I tell her that she wouldn't have food, clothes or toys – she'd be barefoot and naked. You can win them round with Barbies and stuff like that. She's lucky that I'm with an older bloke, who is quite happy to do a lot of babysitting, and they have a really strong relationship. She misses me, but it's a way of life. It will backfire when she's a teenager; she will hate me. She'll be embarrassed about me. The public image of a sort of wildcat blonde from hell – that's my mother. Horrible, isn't it? Poor Phoebe – start saving up for therapy now!

Do you have a particular way of making a stand-up show?

Oh, yes. I need loads of time. Every word is totally scripted. It's a clumsy procedure. What happens is you write material, you try it out, if it works you keep it in, and then you edit. You find themes and shape it until it has a movement of its own. It's basically a collection of one-liners and little stories, which you try to give some kind of shape. I've got a couple of lines, which are probably five years old, but I haven't used them for ages, and I feel like doing them again. Then there are lines that are two weeks old, and some that are a year old. This is the final run of work that's been going on for nearly a year. It's a sort of annual thing, after this the hard work starts.

Are you performing an aggressive humour?

I think that I've mellowed in performance style. Certainly, when I used to get very tense about it, I got a bit shrieky and a bit shrill. I think it could grate quite a lot. However, I'm more confident – not the panicky creature I used to be – because I was just desperate to get through it and get to the bar. It's got more base, and I trust most of it. It is very dirty or some people think it's dirty, but I just think it's silly toilet humour. We are medically designed to laugh at ourselves because otherwise we wouldn't be able to fart – if the human race didn't fart we probably wouldn't have a sense of humour. It's a sort of design fault that's created a sound and a smell – fantastic – you've got to be able to laugh when your body can do that, that's funny. It's been a quick route to notoriety in some respects, and it's worked. I will have to watch it, because those things can become very tired and the knives will be out this year. If I just churn out more smut, they will turn round and say that they're bored of women talking about their vaginas. I'm going to have to be terribly clever in the coming months, tempering it with other stuff that will make them say that I'm clever as well. You've got to have some sort of sense of irony about it really. I'm very shocked when people are shocked.

Do you think you put yourself down in the material at all?

A little bit. I admit to things I'm not good at, I admit to being a bit desperate – ageing stuff: the make-up and the hair. In order to enjoy a woman on stage, it's easier to watch a comedy grotesque than a young, attractive woman. Being a sort of Les Dawson invention makes it more of a pantomime dame figure. I think that's why I've had more success in my thirties, because people are more confident of me. I think there was a lot of nervousness around watching me when I was in my twenties, in case I failed and couldn't cope with it. Now, they know that when I'm on stage, whatever happens, I can probably hack it, which makes them a bit relieved.

Can you describe the image of yourself on stage?

I would say that it's a sort of celebration of every tragi-comedienne there's ever been. It's one of those over the top, there but for the grace of God go I, creatures of the night. It's a sort of back alley cat with delusions of grandeur slinking around, ricocheting from disaster to defeat, to triumph to whatever. The character has become more and more based on an old poet called Don Marquis, who is dead now. He wrote a book called *Archy and Mehitabel*.[1] Mehitabel is a cat, who thinks she is the incarnation of Cleopatra and all sorts of princesses and queens. She's basically an old moggy, who has sex with all sorts of tabbies and drowns her kittens. She's very like Mehitabel – little things that Mehitabel says are very Eclair. It's a very camp image, very queeny. It's Joan Crawford crossed with the local supermarket check-out woman – the shrieky one. It's a combination of Elsie Tanner and all those larger than life soap opera people.

How does gender make the work different?

I think that when comediennes do write and perform from the heart, they have a sort of consciousness of their lines, whereas men tend to be much more surreal or physical, and not so personal. It will be very interesting to see if there will be a new wave of women comics this year, doing the Lee Evans, Harry Hill, or Jack Dee kind of slightly impersonal, maybe deadpan style. Hattie Hayridge does deadpan, but leaving out the 'my boyfriend, my weight, my body, my life stuff', it's very interesting. I'm sure that whoever it is will be very successful, because it will be a big novelty. There must be some clever little minx somewhere, thinking, 'I'll show the bitches.'

It's quite hard to imagine what kind of act that would be.

There isn't a female Lee Evans – why not? I'm too old now, I can't do all that … I can't sweat on stage to that degree.

That is what is amazing to me about the Perrier award; it takes years of performing before you get the credit.

Yes, it was nice. It was a surprise for a lot of people. I think it was popular, but I think it was a shock. It was a great, great moment. I really like to relive the moment. I can remember it all. I saw some footage of it, and I've never seen anyone look quite so smug.

What is the state of women comedians?

There's not much room at the top for women comedians, so they allow one through every five years. I think that by contrast we probably get paid a lot less, and we don't have the kudos. I don't think we're taken seriously, and we're not considered such pulling power, although in the North, I am quite popular. I can sell out in Nottingham, Birmingham, Manchester, Leeds, and those kinds of places. Surprisingly enough, Oxford as well. I didn't think that we would get 600 in Oxford, but we did.

Who are the top women comedians?

You can't count Victoria Wood or French and Saunders, because they're just in a different league. Jo Brand is almost in that league now as well, but I would say that she's still a jobbing comic. So, Jo Brand at the top, I'm second, Donna McPhail third, Rhona Cameron fourth, and then you're struggling. There are probably about six others that have sort of come through, taken their time and might surprise us, but it's slow. Jo is on huge amounts of money, but she's almost the league now. The rest of us are getting nowhere near the Jack Dee or Lee Evans kind of ratings. Maybe we're not as good. I don't think we appeal as broadly. I appeal to a smaller audience, but there are very few male comics that can actually hold my interest for a whole hour. I get fed up with the untruth of it – the sort of surrealism. I know it's funny to talk about cheese, but come on now, I need to know a bit more. I want some sort of heart and soul here. I think that is the genuine difference, that women are very aware of the messiness of life – all the stains and soiled bits falling out – so it's sort of what we deal with on a daily basis, which I don't think men do to the same extent.

What do you really care about?

Apart from Phoebe, I care about proving night after night that I'm good. I care about my position in the echelons of comedy. I care about historically being there, and making a mark. I do want to have made some kind of impact.

Notes

1   Marquis, D., *Archy and Mehitabel*, Faber & Faber, 1958.

Niamh Cusack

'I'm a working actress.'

'I'm just beginning at the age of thirty-seven to discover
that I'm not a child and that I can make a difference.'

Performance Context

Born: 1959, Dublin.

Prior/current commitments: 1996/97 Royal Shakespeare Company season in Stratford and London.

Post-interview (selected): Claire in Genet's *The Maids*, Donmar Warehouse/tour.
Fran in Peter Moffat's *Nabakov's Gloves*, Hampstead Theatre.
Bridget Paterson in Catherine Cookson's *Colour Blind*, Festival Films Production for ITV.

Interview

I enjoyed my conversation with Niamh Cusack in her kitchen on 11 April 1997, surrounded by toys and young children's books. A juggling act of work and motherhood; a juggling act from her role in the television series Heartbeat[1] *to leading the company as Rosalind in* As You Like It *at the RSC's Stratford season during 1996/97.*[2]

Alison Oddey: *You've just completed a year's work in Stratford and London with the Royal Shakespeare Company, playing Rosalind in* As You Like It *and Armande in* Learned Ladies *by Molière.*[3] *So it's about ten years since you played Desdemona in* Othello *and Juliet in* Romeo and Juliet.[4]

Niamh Cusack: Yes, this is my first time back after ten years, but I've always loved Shakespeare. I just love the language and the thought that it provokes. So I'm really glad I went back and did Rosalind. It was hard, not least because the RSC is somewhat in the doldrums at the moment and getting a lot of bad press. I think the way the RSC is run at the moment means that there is not the same frisson in London because the plays have already opened in Stratford. Also, Stratford is a really magical place and it's very difficult to feel the same way about the Barbican, particularly when the directors are generally onto new projects. You don't see them very often. I think what was good for me was that I felt I was leading a company for the first time. Although I played Juliet, I was there playing the juvenile lead, even though it's a heavyweight part. With Rosalind, I felt I made a difference and I think that is something I love about playing leads. I love being in a position where I can actually make a difference to the way the company feels. It's quite a discovery for me because I think being the junior in my family (I am number four), I've always felt a bit like a child in any sort of work situation as well. I'm just beginning at the age of thirty-seven to discover that I'm not a child and that I can make a difference. As the lead, I can suggest something that someone who has got nothing to say, can't. I was lucky with the director I worked with in that he did generally listen to me. Steven Pimlott is an open man, so it was a good working relationship.

Did you notice anything different in terms of working at the RSC now to previously?

It seems to be cyclical … in the 1980s you felt that you were in a place that was really buzzy, with fine actors that had done a lot of Shakespeare, a lot of classics and we seldom had empty seats in *Romeo and Juliet* or *Othello*. Absolutely opposite was the case when I came to do *As You Like It*. Not so much at Stratford, because Stratford has loyal audiences that come every year, but it was hard in London and you were aware that everybody in the building also knew that we were not as successful a company as we were. The thing I love about Stratford is that the same personnel, who were there when I first came, are still passionate and loyal to it within the building. I think that is wonderful and has always been something that has made the RSC special, and will continue to do so. Our particular company was full of families, which was a very positive, bonding thing.

Presumably then for that length of time you took your son, Calam, and your partner?

Yes, I did. In fact, it was a very tricky time for me because my partner, Finbar Lynch, was with the RSC in America playing Puck in *A Midsummer Night's Dream* for five months. That was when I was rehearsing *As You Like It* and opening, which was very hard even though I had a full-time nanny who was wonderful. It was much easier when I got to Stratford because I didn't have the travelling to do. We were living up the road. He used to come in to watch things like dance calls, or go to wigs and wardrobe. Everybody in the wig room knew him and he had his own set of toys there. There was a great sense of community there. The hardest time was when I was travelling and rehearsing Rosalind. I was leaving here at nine and getting home at about nine at night, which was pretty hard and I felt torn about it. I found it a very difficult decision to make, to decide to do it, but I really did feel that Rosalind was a part that would never come again and this was my chance. Fin was very keen that I should do it and very supportive about it, but you can only be so supportive when you are thousands of miles away! I don't know quite how I did it. I was very tired because Cal wasn't sleeping through the night, and if he woke up at six I felt I had to play with him because that was our time. Calam is the son of two actors and there were things in Stratford that happened for him, which he will treasure and always value. Whether he knows that or not, I think theatre people are a bit like travelling people, they are very warm and they rejoice in children. What we do is childish, so in a way we have a lot in common, both the grown-ups and the children. I think I'm giving him good things in that respect, but I'm aware that when I'm away he would much rather I was at home and he suffers to some extent. He says, 'I don't want you to go to work' and I have to wrestle with that, but I said to him, 'This is what I do', and to me that is actually the answer. I make choices in terms of the kind of work I take on, which will be most accommodating for my home life. So I'm really pleased that Stratford was so conducive to having children and I would go back for that very reason. I would also now choose to do a play in London rather than a play in Manchester or Glasgow.

It's interesting because you have repeated the pattern of your own family's theatrical background.

Yes, although my parents had more or less split up by the time I had any real awareness and my mother had stopped acting. The three older ones – Paul, Sinead and Sorcha toured with my parents, having a much more peripatetic life, but my little brother and myself had a very ordinary upbringing – we didn't do the touring. We were very aware of my father being an actor, but my mother had fallen out of love with the profession because to some extent the profession had made the difficulties in her marriage, and she did not encourage us to dabble in anything theatrical. We were given every other lesson under the sun but not drama. I never did a school play. I never went to elocution lessons, but I did go to see my father act. I suppose theatre was very much part of my world, but I didn't do the kind of travelling that Calam has already done and indeed that my older siblings did.

So did you grow up in the same household as both your parents?

Not really, it was a bit complicated. My parents were both Catholic and so they didn't divorce, and he continued to come out to the house but he didn't actually live with us. I was pretty hazy about the whole thing. We lived in Dalkey, which was ten miles outside Dublin. I remember saying that my father lived in Dublin, because he was rehearsing there. They weren't together any more, but because it was a less modern society then, it was left unspoken. Children now will say, 'My dad's picking me up and I'm going to stay with Dad for this weekend', but where I was brought up, that wasn't the case, people didn't acknowledge it.

'I don't want to be on Aideen's pony!'

You trained as a musician, a flautist, originally, and then went into acting. What are your first memories of wanting to perform?

Well, I wanted to be a ballet dancer from as soon as I could walk. I loved music. I auditioned for the Royal Academy of Dancing when I was about eight and they did a medical examination, which I failed. Some squiggle in my back, which meant that I couldn't become a professional dancer. I think it was very clear to people around me that I was a performer. I liked to perform, so did my brother. We were excruciating really, we would do songs together and my mother was very proud of this. I suppose my mother thought that I had an ear for music, so I got started on the piano. I also had asthma. Someone told my mother that if I played a wind instrument it would help my asthma, so I chose the prettiest one – the flute. Both my music teachers were wonderful. They also got me involved in the recorder and I played in consorts. I did a lot of dancing with the consort, playing and touring. When I was thirteen or fourteen, we went to Italy a few times. So that's when the music took off. I was at music college here for three years, and during that time I lost my love of playing. I don't know why. My mother died in my first term so that might have been a contributory factor. Also, the technical side of being a musician really got in the way of instinct, which was very dampened in music college. I didn't like it, it was a very narrow world. It was a lonely existence. I came out of there, worked a little as a musician in Dublin, and then came back to London for personal reasons. I went to an adult education centre behind everybody's back. I didn't tell anyone what I was doing. After my first day at that adult class, I knew acting was what I wanted to do. I had seen a production of Chekhov's *Three Sisters* in Dublin with my ex-husband and told him, 'I know how Irene feels, I could be Irene.' I used one of Irene's speeches for my audition for drama school, and eventually went to the Guildhall School of Music and Drama.

That moment of recognition about being Irene came to fruition when I saw you perform in Three Sisters *at Manchester Royal Exchange in 1985.[5] You had found an identity, and performing enabled you to be and do.*

It's got harder as I've got older. It seemed very easy then. As I get older, I'm more aware of my failings technically, so that makes me more self-conscious, more nervous. I find it harder to do, but I still adore doing it, and when it works I wouldn't be doing anything else. I don't want to do anything else.

Your eyes lit up when you said that. Can you describe that feeling of when it works?

I think you really feel it on stage because it's to do with fusing with the character and the audience. It's what you would be like completely if you were this person. The antennae of this creature, which is you in character, is reaching out to all the little antennae in the theatre, and they are all going 'ping'. It's a moving experience and you feel like your heart is really full. It is a little bit like being in love, I suppose, or moments of being in love when you feel a profound connection with another human being, and where being human is a shared thing as opposed to a lonely experience. I felt that a few times, and it really is wonderful.

Would Imelda Staunton's performance of Adelaide in Guys and Dolls *at the Royal National Theatre reflect the kind of experience you've just described?*

Yes, I thought it was exactly that. Adelaide is the character, but you felt it was Imelda as Adelaide, which I think is what great acting is. It's when someone infuses the already sterling character that's written with their own uniqueness and energy, and the audience meet it. You have to have confidence for that to happen, and Imelda has it. You do feel it in the audience, when you are in the presence of something like that, you feel the same sort of perfection.

So performing is a way of discovering these moments of perfection. Is there a need to fulfil something, and what motivates you?

I really don't know, in fact the best part is always getting the role, I find. Sometimes I do wonder myself. I adore rehearsal and the discovery that you make in rehearsal, and I'm always very excited about the fact that you meet new people and new imagination. I love all that. I love the fact that suddenly I'm introduced to a period of history or a country, and of course, a person that I then have the chance of living with for a while. I do really love that and I would find it very difficult to give up, although it's not what I think when I take on a job. I just think I'm a working actress. I think well, I've finished doing *As You Like It*, what will I do next? I presume that I'm going to work. It's what I do – back to that again – and I think I do love the chance of living as somebody else for a little while. Ralph Richardson said that every character you do lives with you for the rest of your life and I love that idea. I love the idea that everybody gets a life to lead and I get millions of lives to lead, I get off on that. But I'm terribly scared of the whole thing and I dread press nights. I hate them, and I hate being criticised. I don't want people thinking, 'How does she do that, it's not as well as so and so did it twenty-five years ago.'

Have you ever turned down a part thinking that it has been done by someone great in your eyes, or because it was supposedly the definitive performance?

No, only because I haven't seen someone do it. For instance, I knew there were a fair few fine Rosalinds, Vanessa Redgrave being one! But that didn't put me off, because I thought well I haven't seen that. I had seen the play a few times but it hadn't really worked for me. I took that part because I thought I'd do it my way. I remember seeing someone playing Nora in *A Doll's House*, which I did about four years ago,[6] thinking that it was wonderful but that I couldn't do it. However, when it came to it, I had to give it a go, because it is one of THE parts, and again it's a chance to live with someone.

Does performing enable you to enact Niamh Cusack personae, which may not be visible in a daily context?

I do find it easier to act people who don't seem like me at all. I find that great fun, liberating, and I'm often better at playing those than I am playing characters that are closer to myself. I don't know whether that's because they liberate a part of one of my personae that people don't see, or whether it's that they are so different that I find it easier to be them, I don't know. Everybody has got all of these things in them so it is a bit of me, but a persona seems to me to be something which you show, which you fabricate and you put there in front of the real you.

You're cast in certain parts immediately – how are you perceived as an actor?

Well, sadly, people to a large extent label me as someone who has a quality of goodness, people try to think of me as very conventional and I find that irritating.

Why do you find that irritating?

Well, because I actually think that nobody is conventional and it's such a patronising thing to say that someone is. It's not astute, nor does it recognise people's variety, whoever they be, and I find it makes me angrier as I get older.

What kinds of performance challenge would you like to be given?

I'm really pleased with recent work. Rosalind is all things. Some of the characters I've played have such strength in them. It's been a wonderful opportunity to key into that kind of strength, that kind of wit and articulacy which I don't have. I think Armande was great because she was so screwed up, funny and bitchy. They were great contrasts. The part I'm just about to play is Claire in *The Maids* by Genet,[7] which will be really interesting because it's a very difficult and dark play. I think it explores the darker side of everyone and I think that is the sort of challenge I want. I'd quite like to do someone who is funny without knowing it, who is so flawed that they are funny. I want to work with younger directors because I think that is quite a liberating thing to do when you get to my age. It's very easy to just work with people who are older than you, the old masters. I've done a lot of that; I've found it very inspiring and learnt a lot.

What is the satisfaction that you gain from performing? Has it changed over the years?

Yes. When I started I wasn't aware of what the satisfaction was, I just did it and I loved it. As I've got older, I think it is the exploration, the meeting with other minds and imaginations, being fired by that. And the good nights, because let's face it there are a lot of bad nights! I think when you are younger you just do it – you want to show off – you don't realise what you are overcoming to do it, and now I'm much more aware of what I have to get over in order to do it. Having a child gives you a different perspective, because no matter how the show has gone, I'm fine once I get home to Calam. Having a child makes you more tired and it's much more of a mountain to climb to do it. I find that the way to do it is not to worry about me, but to think that it is a wonderful play. The play is fine without me, and there are other people who provoke me to do what I do in the play. As long as I stick with those two things, it will be a good performance. If I start thinking about me and how tired or unsure I am, then I won't do a very good job.

That sounds very disciplined to me.

I think it is. It might be to do with the fact that I was a musician first. I work on my voice and at being an actor, so perhaps I'm not an instinctive actor. I just think as you get older it's less to do with instinct, and more to do with the stuff you've learnt through your instinct and through the chances you've been given. I think that's why people get better or not. It's partly to do with the chances, the people you come into contact with, and then just how you use the past chances. Someone said to me that it takes twenty years to make an actor. I think that's true. I think it's the staying power – being able to develop is what being an actor is about. I think I've learnt more from the failures I've had, and from doing long stints where nobody is watching in the same way as if I had had an award where people would have been coming to see me. I actually think that's a terrible pressure to put on a young actor.

Has the development of television been significant for the young actor?

Yes, because you don't have to have done any training or to have a particularly good voice to get a lead in a television series. However, to stay the course, you are talking about a profession, a craft. I think the media, journalists and television have really undermined the craft of acting. The producers think that the public needs a new face every day, so that's what you get, and that's not what acting is about. Acting is not about being a television star, it's actually about being able to do a lot of television with craft and intelligence. That takes work, but you can get away with it on a one-off basis. Everybody is encouraging people to take those sorts of choices. If one of your students said to me, 'I've been offered the lead in the next BBC drama series', I'd say, 'Take it, for God's sake', but I would also say, 'Go and see Patsy Rodenburg at the National and do some work on your voice.' Take the opportunity of having money for the first time to broaden your horizons. Whilst you are in a BBC series, write to the West Yorkshire Playhouse or Manchester and ask them if you can play a part in one of their plays because you are on the telly, that's the way to capitalise on it. I think very few people do it like that, very few.

Are you looking forward to doing The Maids*?*

Yes, it's a wonderful opportunity, really exciting. However, I actually make the decision without remembering that I'm a mother. I then panic and think, 'How on earth can I do it?' I have woken up so many nights thinking about whether it makes him more insecure if I'm out during the day rather than the evening. He's starting a new nursery school and I'm going out to work. How am I going to juggle all that? I fret about it all the time, and yet not enough not to do it. I remember talking to the actress, Lesley Manville, who thought theatre was easier than television in terms of having a family life, because it's more regular. She thought having daytime was more valuable, and I think that. Often, I'll leave home half an hour later than I should so that I can be with Calam, and not have such a good warm-up. Whereas Fin, who is also an actor, will diligently leave at the right time, because he knows that he is an actor first. In my heart, I think that I am a mother first, but I still get to the job. I cut corners in a way that a man wouldn't, and the person who always comes out the worst is you. You manage the play, manage to give your child an extra half an hour, and you are a neurotic mess at the end of the day because you had no time to refocus. You think laterally in a way that you couldn't have imagined being capable of before you had a child. Once you have a child, you just do the most amazing leaps and jumps in order to accommodate everything, but you do get very tired. What I really can't do now is the glamour actress bit. I tend to rush into work in whatever I'm wearing, Calam's chocolate stains and all! When I go to an interview, I do get changed at the last minute, so there is less likelihood of muck on my clothes. However, I think that's part of the magic for me of theatre and film. I love all that make-believe, which justifies my not putting on my best jacket, when I'm going to have a costume anyway, as well as make-up and wig time.

What about key moments in your life as a performing woman in the widest sense? Are there any moments that you will always remember because they were so stunning? What comes to mind?

It's very odd, it seems like deciding not to do *Heartbeat*[8] any more was very good for me, and gave me great strength to turn my back on that. But it was very lonely as well, and it was a key moment. I could have stayed and decided that I was a different kind of performer, but I think I was true to me. Having Calam is one of the big ones. Doing *Three Sisters* in Manchester was an amazing time, and Casper, who directed it, was terribly influential at that time. I don't see him any more, but I would say he had a profound effect on me. Karel Reisz inspired me both as a man and a director. He was so thorough in his knowledge of the play (*A Doll's House*), and he was utterly concentrated and focused in rehearsal, while having a great sense of humour. Going back to work for the first time after having Calam was a key time. There are quite a few actually. My father dying was a key time as well – I was doing *A Doll's House* when he died, which was both sad and liberating. A time of thinking, 'I'm on my own now' and 'I'm no longer that person's daughter, I'm me.' That was liberating – four years ago – in 1993. Playing Nora was key in that her journey and things she overcame have informed how I have dealt with my life, not that I've copied them, but I think that you do become infected by a person's qualities.

Notes

1   Mrs Rowan in *Heartbeat*, Yorkshire Television for ITV network, various directors, 1st–5th series, 1992–95.
2   *As You Like It*, directed by Steven Pimlott, Royal Shakespeare Company, 1996/97.
3   Both productions were directed by Steven Pimlott.

4 Desdemona in Shakespeare's *Othello*, directed by Terry Hands, RSC, co-starring Ben Kingsley and David Suchet, 1985. Juliet in Shakespeare's *Romeo and Juliet*, directed by Michael Bogdanov, RSC, Stratford and Barbican, co-starring Sean Bean, 1986.

5 Irina in Chekhov's *Three Sisters*, adapted by Michael Frayn for the Royal Exchange Theatre, Manchester, directed by Casper Wrede, 11 April–11 May 1985.

6 Nora in Ibsen's *A Doll's House*, directed by Karel Reisz, Gate Theatre, Dublin, 5 October–27 November 1993.

7 Claire in Genet's *The Maids*, directed by John Crowley at the Donmar Warehouse and on tour, 1997.

8 See note 1.

Imogen Stubbs

'One of the great things about acting is you can be so
many people, or you find so many people within you,
and you never have to think, "This is me."'

'Why should one need people who you don't know to
say you are great … it's something very strange to me.'

Performance Context

Born: 1961, Rothbury.

Prior/current commitments: Yeliena in Chekhov's *Uncle Vanya*, Albery Theatre.
Stella in Williams' *A Street Car Named Desire*, Haymarket Theatre.
Rosalind in Shakespeare's *As You Like It*, BBC Radio.
Post-interview (selected): Anna in Marber's *Closer*, West End.
Emma in Pinter's *Betrayal*, Royal National Theatre.
Other: Plays and Players Award, 'Most Promising Actor (female)', RSC Stratford season, 1986.
The Jailer's Daughter in Shakespeare and Fletcher's *The Two Noble Kinsmen* and Hellena in Behn's *The Rover*.

Interview

My interview with Imogen Stubbs took place at her London home on 8 July 1997 against a scene of constantly ringing telephone, a loud answerphone message repeating endlessly, the chatter of nannies and children playing.

Alison Oddey: *How are you perceived as an actress?*

Imogen Stubbs: Unfortunately, I'm perceived by many people as Anna Lee,[1] which isn't something I particularly want to be identified with. Most people think of me as a classical actress. I remember being labelled as a Shakespearian actress early on in my career when I had only played Queen Isabelle in *Richard II*.[2] That's the only Shakespeare I had done professionally, but for some reason I was considered a Shakespearian heroine. It must have been the photos of me – I looked like one. Now, I'm probably perceived as the wife of Trevor Nunn. On stage, I'm probably perceived as someone who is quite passionate and quite a daring actress. On screen, as someone who looks quite young and prettyish, but also comes across as relatively shallow and not so confident. I find stage easier than having a camera pointed at me.

What is it about performing in theatre that you love?

On stage, I love the fact that you start the first day of rehearsal and three weeks later (eight weeks at the RSC), you look back and have learnt so much, discovering so many things, solving riddles, getting to know this person and enjoying working off that person. In that sense, I love theatre because of rehearsal. I don't like it for the sheer grind of eight shows a week, which I find very gruelling, but for its loyalty to actors, nothing beats theatre. Television and film are very fickle and very hard on women. We are living in a time when it's of no relevance to a lot of film or television whether you've proved yourself as a capable actress or not. Much of it depends on a look or a modern youthfulness, and in that sense it's neither here nor there whether people have accrued any experience for coming at a role in an interesting way, or being able to show emotions in a way that's more complicated than the obvious. It's hard enough dealing with the onset of middle age in your own life, but the horror of acting is that it continually reminds you that you are no longer young. If you move on to the more interesting roles that come as you get older, then emotionally you get to play something much more complicated and interesting.

Are you from a theatrical family background?

No, not really. My grandmother (Esther McCracken) wrote plays, *Quiet Wedding* and *Quiet Weekend* being the most famous. I think one of them was on for years in the West End during the war, which is incredible, and they were comedy. She was very funny, but other than that, Robert Eddison was a relative of mine and Ralph Richardson was my grandmother's cousin. My father was in the navy and my mother wasn't anything to do with the theatre.

Where do the roots of your desire to perform originate from?

I'm not somebody who has always known, since they were six, that I must be an actor. I'm actually somebody at the age of thirty-six who is still trying to work out whether that's something I want to be. I was a younger sister with a shy brother, and quite a show-off from an early age because I got a lot of attention. I was rather good at gymnastics and always enjoyed applause for doing a handstand or whatever. I loved singing in the church choir from an early age, which gave me a taste of the excitement of being with a group of people, so you're not doing it on your own, which I never would have done. I remember doing the 'Messiah' at St Paul's Cathedral (with a thousand other people), and it was so thrilling the impact all those voices made. I didn't do much at St Paul's and when I was at Westminster Boy's School I had to be in most of the plays, because there weren't that many girls available. I also went to the London Contemporary Dance School in the evenings and at weekends, but I would never have been a great dancer. Then I thought that I'd love to perform, but couldn't be a dancer, gymnast or singer. When I went to Oxford, I did a lot of drama. I did a lot of revue stuff, including a revue with Ian Hislop, so I was often the girl in the revue. I loved that because it was doing accents, characters, singing, having fun and doing everything. I didn't want to do something academic, but I also wasn't too confident that I had any particular talent as an actress. Then I went to RADA, did another three years, and by the end of that thought that I'd have to be an actress because I'd put in so much time.

So what does performing give you that makes you want to continue doing it?

It is a drug and there is something addictive about it, whether it's just nostalgia. In the first place, I said that I quite like showing off and I think it's human nature as children – if you clap, they blossom. If you make someone feel they are wonderful, they become more wonderful. I love the team work. I would never want to do monologues. I like bouncing off people and the investigative side of it. When you are really flying as an actor, it's like taking some kind of drug. You really do float off into some area where something takes you over, and that's a very exciting buzz. Why one should need people who you don't know to say you are great … it's something very strange to me. I find it rather sad that there is some need to perform, and therefore, when actors aren't in work, they feel frustrated, depressed, very unfulfilled. They feel as if there is a huge part of their life missing. When you come down to it, other than being a financial need, it's a very strange, almost sick thing that what's missing in your life is people staring at you or responding to your interpretation. It's like needing to be marked all your life, you're not going to write an essay just for the hell of it. It's a job which seems to be playing to people, who you think care about whether you do it well or not, or whether you will have an effect on them or not. I really don't know what the answer is – it can't just be the sound of clapping.

What motivates you?

It's very hard to pin down, but I find that there are certain characters which are like a riddle. You dream about understanding the whole character and if you take on the challenge of that, the more you confront that character, the more you are drawn into a combat between you and a bit of writing. Suddenly, you find that it's making sense to you and there is something very thrilling about that. You begin to inhabit something, to be able to say the lines so that they are coming from *you* (from a real person), and then the ultimate challenge is to stand in front of people, convincing them, moving them in some way or pulling off the riddle of that character. Almost once you've done that, you want to do something else. It's a real challenge, an academic challenge. Why I do it is very personal, but with classical or complicated characters, it's a challenge to me both emotionally and intellectually. I love modern plays and one of the joys is being associated with an eloquence far greater than your own. That is a great thrill. I just find it a real kick to hear something coming out of me that doesn't originate in me. I love that, I find it really fun and you never feel static. You feel that you're constantly changing. One of the great things about acting is you can be so many people, or you find so many people within you, and you never have to think, 'This is me.' Actors are people who refuse to take life lying down, constantly reinventing themselves to be anything, to go in different directions or live in whatever period. It's a fear of being ordinary and makes you feel like you are constantly in a state of extra-ordinariness. I think that is one of the dangers of acting. So frightened of being ordinary, that just being yourself becomes a terrifying prospect, because it seems so ordinary, limited and static, as opposed to being kinetic. If you say things like, 'From now on, I'm just going to be Imogen, living here and I'll pick up the kids from school', God knows there is nothing wrong with that, unless you have indulged in the fantasy of being an actor and then that becomes a terrifying, banal prospect.

Is performing a heightening of the self?

It can be a degrading of the self. I think actors have to believe it is a heightening of the self. You have to believe you are interesting (both emotionally and spiritually), and that you have chutzpah. I think for actors the biggest illness is that total rejection (the way they look, their soul and emotions), and that's why so many actors are such phenomenally miserable people. You think get a life, just live, you've got enough money, just get on with life. Why do you have this yearning, this tugging towards pretending to be someone else? It's sick. In any other case, it would be called schizophrenia, madness or a licence to behave in a very strange way. I don't know many happy people who are just actors. It seems a terrible waste of life if you're living in constant frustration because that side of you is not being indulged. There's something really odd about the fact that I could play a mother of two living in Hammersmith, married to a director. I could play my life and that would fulfil something, but just to live my life, which could be identical to what I'd be playing (and I don't need the money so I'm very privileged), could be less fulfilling than pretending to be that. It has to all just be an attitude, because literally what I've just said is insane, but there's a certain truth to it too. As a job, you can actually be playing somebody less interesting than the potential of what your own life is. Often you're performing something at night, which you hope never to live through in your life, and you're doing it eight times a week, which is emotionally gruelling. In some ways, you're actually destroying yourself, and that's when you do think – what am I doing?

Can you describe what it feels like physically and emotionally to perform?

The excitement is like throwing a ball between you and the other actors, and if they come back with something else, then you're taking off. I did *Heartbreak House* with Vanessa Redgrave.[3] We were playing opposite each other a lot, and sometimes, a scene that we had been doing tearfully, she would suddenly play it through laughter, challenging me to have to come back on the same level that she was playing. Well, that was thrilling, because I really learned a lot, but she was also pushing me to be more and more adventurous as an actress (never to be complacent in the scenes). So you could never do the same thing with her, and you were really on your toes working with her to live off the moment, which is what I love. It's the only kind of acting, it's the best. Anyone who just repeats the same old thing (which is understandable because it's safe) is very dull, but Vanessa is completely daring and crazy sometimes, and you have to go with her or fall behind. So in that sense it was an adrenaline thing, which was like paragliding. It was really frightening and very exciting.

When you were performing in A Streetcar Named Desire[4] *(playing someone pregnant), you had recently had a baby. Did you find it difficult to reconcile those two roles in reality and fiction?*

I had only just had a baby then and I started to resent the work. At first, you think that it's only at night-time, but then you are on tour or re-rehearsing something because people are endlessly ill. You have the time literally at home, but your emotion and energy are so depleted that you haven't got any for your children. One is coming back from school just when you're going out and the baby is asleep all day. I found that very hard because I felt that I wasn't doing any job properly. I got over that, but at one point (when I was still breast feeding), I was thinking, 'I'm out of my mind, I can't begin to understand this play, I don't know what I'm doing here and I can't think why I'm in it.' That dominated my day. I just rued the decision I had made to do it. That's the worst, if you do something you have to go with it, and that's a life choice I have made. I have to make my life work around that, rather than making a mess on either side, and that's when being a working mother is horrible. There you are, it's a drug. What can be more fun than having a baby, and yet I still went back and did two plays. If you are being truthful to yourself, it isn't going to satisfy you enough just to be at home with that baby, and you know that then you are going in some way to be less interesting and therefore take it out on the baby that you are being boring or whatever. I hate to think that I'm like that (but I am like that), therefore, I don't think it would be a solution for me to say, 'I must not be an actress because I'm a mother now.' I can't reinvent myself like that. I could as a character, but not as me. I'm not like that, I would explode.

Isn't that one of the attractions at one level of having several identities?

Yes, but I have the privilege of having somebody to help me enormously, and therefore, I feel I can have the best of both worlds. I don't think the children suffer, they have people who adore them – one person who is paid to be in a good mood with them, and one person who is always in a good mood with them because it's always the good stuff without the bad. I'm almost always in the situation where I know that I have help, I don't ever have to be at the end of my tether, and I'm never so exhausted that I can't deal with them. I'm lucky that I don't have to do school runs and all that stuff, so I've no excuse whatsoever to be anything other than at my most vivacious and fun as a mother when I'm with them. That isn't necessarily realistic (maybe it isn't necessarily a good thing that they only ever see me at my best), but certainly for me it's a great joy that I can do both. In my selfish way, I think it's wonderful to be socially whatever I need to be with Trevor, serving my function as a hostess or whatever we are meant to be at the National. Doing all different sorts of things, and bringing bits from one area to another to stimulate them.

So why does anyone do it?

The hardest thing is to understand why anyone should subject themselves to an arena which is so dependent on other people's approval. Maybe at a certain age in your life you become more circumspect about what you share and what you keep for yourself. Maybe when you get older, you just get more private. I'm actually only thirty-six and I really feel it! That's because I spend a lot of time with older people and I see where it's going. Living with Trevor, and partly the world we live in, I see what's coming ahead of me, so I need to take pre-emptive action, which is learning to play the saxophone, writing screenplays or reviewing for *The Times*. Making sure that the definition of yourself isn't just an actress, and making sure that you are well armed for that ludicrous situation that we are all put through, which I despise people saying – 'and what do you do?' – especially to women.

Why do you object to that so much?

It puts women in that terrifying situation of thinking they have to have a definition of what they do beyond just being a mother, of being themselves, of shopping or whatever else they do – that they actually have to have a job! Being a mother is an achievement in itself, but it's that terrifying question for actors of being asked what they're doing if they're not working. I have this real horror of becoming a sad person. How many actresses in their forties can say, 'This is just the best thing, completely fulfilling, I could never be happier'?

I've met a number actually!

Well, I'll go and quit my saxophone lessons! I am so pathetic I bought a skateboard (a really dangerous one that goes down grass) in this desperate attempt to stay a child forever. I have found myself going along on this skateboard thinking that at least I can put this on my curriculum vitae, that I can skateboard on grass, play the saxophone, and I've perfected my Geordie accent.

Having children must have taken you on another journey of enlightenment?

I think if having children gives you any gift, it gives you the gift of wonderment because you are going through childhood again, and you are going through it vicariously. Having children is so incredible, and maybe, it just becomes more important as an actress that you have something to defend when you are acting.

Do you think that the word 'strumpet' has any resonance for the profession in the late 1990s?

I think it's thought of with a slight smile on your face – strumpet is such an old-fashioned word. I played Cressida once in *Troilus and Cressida* and there is that famous bit when somebody says 'the trojan's trumpet', but it's always said like 'the trojan's strumpet' and the word strumpet hangs in the air. Cressida – the strumpet! It all sounds rather cosy to modern people, because it sounds like crumpet.

I'm thinking here in terms of an actress prostituting herself.

When I left drama school, if you wanted some experience you almost always had to accept a job which involved gratuitous nudity as a way of getting film experience, and that felt like producers and film companies taking unnecessary advantage of girls, because most girls have no desire to do that at all – it wasn't at all why they went into acting. I was always written about because I'd taken my clothes off in *The Rainbow*,[5] which actually was one of the few areas where there was a justification to it in the sense that you know what you are letting yourself in for. Everything I was in, somewhere along the line, a scene would suddenly appear where for no reason at all you had no clothes on. It gave people a sort of superiority over me – interviewers – journalists – the public – the crew – there was some sense of smugness that they had had an intimacy with me that I hadn't had with them, and it was one that they also knew was associated with something slightly risqué or rude. It's an awfully English thing and it meant that people felt superior to you in some way, and that you were somehow prostituting yourself, or by the very fact that you have been naked you were at a disadvantage because it cheapened you. I still feel that the public look at some actors as their property, because they have made themselves public actors, and therefore, it's the right of the public to be fairly disparaging. Something like ratings on television reduces actors to strumpets, because you are selling yourself for ratings. You are being pimped by the BBC or ITV for high ratings, which gives actors selling power, and therefore, they compromise in order to get into a position where they can call the shots and be a something. I think that the pimping that goes on does relate to the word 'strumpet'. A lot of agents are pimping and a lot of young actors go into it with absolutely no idea. They are pimped by agents very wrongly, because it makes quick money, which gets them a quick satisfaction but not a long-lasting one. Then it tosses them to the side when they are of no use any more, and they are no longer sellable.

Can you identify any key moments in your life as a performing woman in the widest context?

When I was at St Paul's in *Oh What a Lovely War* aged fourteen (with fourteen-year-old boys) and in *Three Sisters* at Oxford, where at the end of the show instead of what you expected, (and in each case I was quite naïve as an actress), which would be applause, there was complete silence because people were so moved. I've only ever come across it those two times – I've never even been in an audience where it's had that impact. Maybe we've become more cynical, but people just didn't clap for ages and it was just a quality in the atmosphere where you had realised that the whole audience was deeply moved – fourteen-year-old children doing *Oh What a Lovely War* without really understanding what it was about or the impact. Then this extraordinary production of *Three Sisters* which, no thanks to my own performance, was devastating and when people came round afterwards to try and talk about it, they would just break down and burst into tears. Grown-up people! I've seen things that are moving, but twice in my life I've been witness to the real power that theatre can have, even unexpectedly. When you know it can be like that you hang on in there. I remember doing a viva at Oxford. I'd done my finals and got through all that and I had a viva with sixteen people in the room. I remember when I went in feeling so young and ill-equipped, and really performing and acting my way through this viva. I was pretty sure I was being viva'd for a first and not a third, so I wasn't desperate but rather cocky. I had a very good memory at the time and I remember quoting bits of Anglo-Saxon at them. I had really worked hard that year but I was also using bravado, which I'd used enormously in the exam to try and seem to know more than I did. I remember when I got my result thinking how extraordinary that they should give me a degree at all, when I felt that I looked so young (so inexperienced) and I was so obviously bluffing my way. I remember thinking how extraordinary that I could con sixteen people (all with incredible brains) into thinking that I knew massively more than I did. I remember thinking how did I get away with that, because that was a real performance! That's another moment in my life that's stuck in my mind.

Finally, what do you think is your most significant achievement as a performing woman?

Giving birth to my children and bringing them up. I did a film with a Down's syndrome child and that was the most interesting filmic experience I had.[6] It was in French, and I played a working-class hairdresser in La Borgoyne (the mother of a sixteen-year-old Down's syndrome girl), and I had a husband who beat me up. Everything about it encouraged me as an actor, but also the film itself in a very simplistic way was promoting something I genuinely believed in and wanted to show, which was the whole complicated and riveting side about Down's syndrome and about this particular girl. We had an opportunity to show people and I thought I learnt a lot from it personally and the film taught people quite a lot. At the same time I also got to do the kind of acting I love, which was way away from anything to do with me and very altruistic, because everything was centred on the Down's syndrome girl. I had had my first baby and I was so proud of this, and was fascinated by the whole experience. This film will never be seen here – it was a small French film for television, but oddly it was one of those significant things I had done for my own peace of mind, where I felt fully vindicated in giving up that time and doing the job I do.

Notes

1   Anna Lee in television series, *Anna Lee*, London Weekend Television, directed by Colin Bucksey and others, 1994.
2   Queen Isabelle in *Richard II*, directed by Barry Kyle, Royal Shakespeare Company, 1986.
3   Ellie Dunn in Shaw's *Heartbreak House*, directed by Trevor Nunn, Haymarket, 1994.
4   Stella in Williams' *A Streetcar Named Desire*, Haymarket, directed by Peter Hall, 1997.
5   Ursula in Lawrence's *The Rainbow*, directed by Stuart Burge, BBC Television, three-part serial, December 1988.
6   Marie in *Sandra, C'est La Vie*, a French film for television, TV Suisse Romande, directed by Dominic Girard, 1991.

Josette Simon

'I've been the only one very much in my life. I was the
only one at my grammar school, in my year at drama
school, and the first leading black actress at the RSC –
they'd never had one before.'

Performance Context

Born: Leicester.

Prior/current commitments: Hilary Jameson in *Kavanagh QC*, Carlton Television.
Nadia in *A Child from the South*, Southern Films.

Post-interview (selected): Madam in Genet's *The Maids*, Donmar Warehouse/tour.
Hoskins in *Silent Witness*, BBC Television.
Eileen Chung in *Dalziel and Pascoe*, BBC Television.
Dilys Tring in *Polterguest*, Carlton Television.
Titania/Hippolyta in Shakespeare's *A Midsummer Night's Dream*, Royal Shakespeare Company, Stratford and London Barbican.
Queen Elizabeth in Schiller's *Don Carlos*, Royal Shakespeare Company, Stratford and London Barbican.

Other: Evening Standard Award, Plays and Players Award, Drama Circle Award and London Theatre Critics Award for Best Actress as Maggie in Miller's *After the Fall*, Royal National Theatre, 1991.

Interview

Josette Simon warmly welcomed me into her London home on 29 April 1997. Josette's passion for performing Shakespeare and the 'classics' was apparent throughout the interview.

Alison Oddey: *What is the appeal of performing in theatre, as opposed to television and film?*

Josette Simon: Theatre uses every single part of your equipment in a different way from television and film – physically, mentally and technically. The whole thing about whispering on stage and the person at the back being able to hear you ... you need that sort of discipline – the immediacy of it and the live audience. For me, however, the greatest appeal is in doing the classics, even if it is a modern classic. I love filming – it has its own very different discipline, but theatre is live. As an actor you are living, breathing, feeling, using everything in that moment, exercising all the humanity you have to offer to breathe life into that character in that play. It's very difficult, there's nothing like it. You are transported in actual time like you are not when you go to the cinema, which was filmed a year ago and that particular thing will be the same tomorrow. There has to be some masochism in it because you go through such agony and it's never good enough. You might reach a place that was better than yesterday, but there's always one step further. All that is a great joy to achieve, but it is always such an agony that you sometimes wonder why you are doing it.

So why are you doing it?

I think there are lots of things where the level of pleasure and pain are so closely linked, and they swap places quite subtly sometimes. There's nothing like trying to strive to fulfil all these things. For me, it's one of the things that drives you mad about people denigrating the profession, the whole luvvy thing. It trivialises what we do. People do think that actors are trivial and empty-headed fluffy people, who do nothing other than put on clothes and pretend. However, what you are doing is what Shakespeare says – holding a mirror up to life. I think that trying to look in at human behaviour, and all the many varied aspects of life are amongst many other things about trying to work out or find out what makes us tick. The different ways human beings behave are one of the keys to why one does it. I know that one thing drives you – opening up a window on human behaviour in all its different and varied forms. The most extraordinary thing I've found during the course of my career is the masochistic side of it, standing in the wings and thinking that I would give anything not to have to go on there.

So why push yourself through that?

It's a sort of compulsion (I don't know why), and part of that desire to explore human behaviour. There is a real need to want to do that; it's a driving force within you.

What originally attracted you to the theatre and to performing?

It's weird really, as I was never one of these people that wanted to be an actor from the age of three, who was on the table entertaining auntie, grandad and the neighbours. I was just completely quiet. I was the quietest child and I didn't do drama at school. I was never in any school plays. I'd never been to the cinema or theatre, or listened to a play on the radio. I had nothing whatsoever to do with it. I was studying languages and hoping to get to university to do French, German and English. That was always my goal. I got nine 'O' levels and then did my 'A' levels. What happened was that when I was about thirteen, my friend and I spotted an advert in the local paper for children to appear in *Joseph and His Amazing Technicolour Dreamcoat* in the children's choir. I was living in my home town – Leicester, and we had to go and sing a little song at the Leicester Haymarket on a Saturday morning. We got into this choir and it was a very popular thing, which kept being revived in Leicester over the years. I was then cast in various things, for example, *The Miracle Worker*,[1] and viewed it as a hobby. I had no interest at all in being an actress, but then it was like a 'eureka moment' at school, when I absolutely knew that being an actress was what I wanted to do. I wanted to act and I didn't go back to school. I auditioned at the Central School of Speech and Drama and got in. When I was younger I used to run, first for the school, then for the county, and then in the England under sixteen cross-country team, which I gave up just like that when I stopped enjoying it. I think the connection between those two things was that I was a very silent child, and the last person at my school anyone thought would be an actress. I couldn't really express myself personally and I was very introverted. This was something that I could get on with on my own and express things. I don't think my acting is about exploring myself and being able to express my personality, but I get tunnel vision when I'm working. In fact, there was a director at the Royal Shakespeare Theatre called Barry Kyle (when I played Rosaline in *Love's Labour's Lost*),[2] who said to me, 'Sometimes you are very private when you are working.' I'll always remember that. I'm not private in the sense that I don't rehearse with people or want to talk about it with the director, but I do beaver away on my own and immerse myself in this world.

It's an interesting analogy – the cross-country runner and actor. Both require you to be self-contained, working on your own towards a goal.

Absolutely. It's incredibly disciplined and very hard work, although acting has to involve other people. I cannot stress that strongly enough. You cannot work in a vacuum, although some people do, and they are very frustrating to work with. I would never want to be like that. From the moment I accept a part and start working on it, I feel a massive responsibility towards the character. I use the parts of myself that are applicable to the character and use all sorts of means to fill in the rest. You use as much of your own tools as applies, but that's it. I like losing myself. It doesn't matter who I am or what I do, I am in the pursuit of trying to transform myself into someone else.

Your desire to perform doesn't originate in your family background, so what is the core of your performing identity?

That's a very interesting question for me, the question of identity, as I've had to battle against my colour. For me, my identity is made up of all aspects of myself as a human being. For some people, identity is made up of the most obvious thing they can see, which is that you are black. Therefore, I've had to fight very hard in terms of identity and identifying with a character. My career has been based on playing parts, where it doesn't matter what colour you are. When I was at drama school, I was told that I wouldn't do the classics, which were my big passion. They warned me that I wasn't going to get very good parts in the last year, because they said there weren't many parts written for black people. They then changed their minds and I got very good parts. All lead roles. I was the only one in my year who was black. I've been the only one very much in my life. I was the only one at my grammar school, in my year at drama school, and the first leading black actress at the RSC – they'd never had one before. Being the only one affects your identity, how other people see you and how you see yourself sometimes. It happens on two levels: first and foremost, you battle to be seen as a human being and not a colour, and then you battle to play parts that are not based on colour but are about exploring that person – it doesn't have to be 'that black person'. You have to be resolute in your sense of your own identity, which is very difficult, because you feel a lot of the time that you need boxing gloves on to fight your corner when people say you can't do this or that part purely because of your colour. Every single part I've done, certainly in the theatre, has always had some controversy next to it, including *The Maids*.[3] It's quite astounding that actually for the most part, you are talking about human being playing human being, not about colour playing colour. I've got used to it now because I haven't known any different, but your identity is always up for question in a sense. I remember there used to be a time in reviews when critics wrote, 'Such and such a part played by the black Josette Simon'. You'd think, 'Oh, where's the white one, is there a white one knocking around somewhere?' Always having to be classified in that way, first and foremost.

How would you describe yourself then, as a performer?

One thing you find when you start work is that you feel like a detective. It reminds me of something I once read about Peggy Ashcroft, who used to call it 'digging potatoes' – you are digging up as many aspects of this character as you possibly can, finding out as much as you can, taking it on and breathing life into it. I know how I would describe myself in terms of how I would like to be, whether I get there I don't know. You want to think of yourself as being extremely brave, going as far as it takes to be real and truthful. For people to look at you on that stage or screen and believe everything you say, fulfilling everything the author wanted in character needs and more. I would want to be open and brave. I would describe myself as truthful.

Do you find identities competing, for example, in your professional and personal lives?

I'm very separate in my two lives, I've always been intensely (almost obsessively) private. Professionally, I've always liked people to know about me in terms of my work, but I don't like bringing the private into the public or the personal into the professional. Even getting married, that's been quite separate. As a child, I was a silent person and that need to be private has remained. Whatever is going out to people, I don't like people knowing much about me.

Are you one of several children?

I'm the youngest of four children. I've got two brothers, who are both horribly academic and hugely clever. Not that I wasn't clever, but the theatricality was completely unknown in my family. My sister wanted to be a designer, but she got married and had loads of children, which has been a job in itself. My parents came from the Caribbean, my mother from Anguilla and my father from Antigua. They came over here in the 1950s, when there was a mass influx of West Indians, and they met over here. My parents are very quiet about those years. They both worked for EMI on the shop floor, and we settled in Leicester. Rather than settling in an area where there were a lot of black people, which people tended to do in order to feel safer in a community, my parents settled in an area where there were hardly any black people, so we were one of a few. I said earlier that I've had a very strange life in terms of being the only one, and that started right from there.

Have your West Indian cultural roots contributed to your identity as a performing woman?

It has indirectly, because people expect it to influence your work, and your performing. When I first went to the RSC, there were black actors who didn't like the fact that I wanted to do the classics, and felt as if I was letting them down. Quite a few times, I was admonished for not doing enough black theatre. It's got to be open to you to do as much as you are fortunate to be asked to do, have access to as many things as possible, so concentrating on the classics was a subject not for derision, but for applause. It's about trying to open up the boundaries. You can't just decide to infuse a thing with West Indian culture. When I did *The Taming of the Shrew* with a fantastic Romanian director,[4] it was wonderful. I played Kate. It was an incredibly physical production, and there was a lot of moving in a very particular way. I don't say that's West Indian at all, but there was something you are able to do over

As a child

and above a British thing, I can't explain it. One of the reasons I liked working with this director from Romania was to experience his Eastern European approach and I found that really exciting. It was a definite attraction. So again, it's about wanting to experience many different influences and utilise many different things.

So what makes the act of performing satisfying?

It's momentary, it's not a whole experience. It's about all the many aspects and details of what you are trying to achieve or struggle with, because it's ongoing. You suddenly hit that note, that particular emotion or expression, which you wanted to get *that way*, the nuance had to be *like that*. You get that right, hitting that thing you've been trying to get, which is incredibly satisfying, and that's just great. They are tiny, detailed momentary things, rather than the satisfaction of the whole performance. *This* bit was working very well, but I've managed to make even more of it. There are all these balls …

You are juggling?

Yes, and if you happen to catch this one in the way you wanted to catch it, and you've been trying for weeks to catch it like *that*, then it's fantastic, so that's very satisfying. What is also satisfying is when something you are trying to communicate reaches the audience in some way that they're really transported and moved. People genuinely feel that they just had a wonderful evening. It meant something and they've gone home feeling affected – that's satisfying.

Has this performing satisfaction changed over the years, or is it still essentially the same?

I think it's changed. Quite early on I used to work so hard that the more agonising and tortured it was, the more I felt I was fulfilling what I was supposed to. The strain of it meant I was giving everything, every fibre of my being was taut just with the weight of it all. It was so much about pain and torture. Thank God I've changed. I relax a bit more and enjoy it, which is such a relief. I still work just as hard, but don't suffer as much. Life has become a bit more important. I've long believed that if you are in the business of portraying real life, then if you're not living it you can't use it, so it's all tied in.

Has anybody inspired or influenced you particularly as a performing woman, in or out of the theatrical world?

I was influenced quite early on by *Antony and Cleopatra* with Helen Mirren and Michael Gambon, which was my first thing with the RSC.[5] I was very affected by both of them, particularly by Helen, because she's an actress after my own heart in a sense and she was so wonderful. I admired her so much. Sometimes you get actors who are so technically accomplished and absolutely brilliant at exploring every aspect of a character to within an inch of its life, almost intellectually, but you remain curiously unmoved even though you might admire the brilliance of the technique. Just watching her on the stage was fantastic, it was great to be so newly out and working with her; I just loved it. It was a very important part of my learning experience, because I was like a sponge, soaking up anyone who I admired. I'm passionate about Shakespeare, a huge massive fan. It never ceases to amaze me how this one man can explore so many different aspects of human behaviour in so many forms and in such detail.

Has the word 'strumpet' any kind of resonance for you in the late 1990s?

'Strumpet' – what a wonderful word! I think if you said strumpet quite a few years ago people would have thought of it in a derogatory sense, but in the late 1990s there is something about strumpet that says, 'Good on you girl'. There is something rebellious about it, something devil may care, in your face challenge about it. At the same time, the implications about this word strumpet are not pleasant – if it's used by a man.

I mean strumpet in a sense of morality in the theatre in the 1990s, and also the kind of image of the actor as a performing woman – how much have we moved on?

Well I don't know that we have that much, and I think that's one of the reasons that a lot of people don't want to use the word actress, because it sounds prissy and trivial. The image is a frivolous, sexually available strumpet. Actor has more weight and less of the strumpet quality. Also, you can be wiggling your bottom in Raymond's Revue Bar and call yourself an actress. I think people still tend to think that actresses don't have a lot of grey matter and are just a few steps up from a bimbo. To the general public, actress is rather a diminishing term. In terms of the wider world and especially in a male environment, I think strumpet has all its negative qualities still sticking to it. I think that we've seen more and more trivialising of actresses, requiring them to look gorgeous and take their top off at some point. We are seeing less development of good fully rounded roles, especially for much older women, who are rarely represented in film or television drama. One of the difficulties of the performing woman is that men control much of the industry, and men put on what they want to see. They don't want to see a sixty-year-old woman being sexual because it turns them off, so they won't provide an arena for it.

Can you identify any key moments in your life as a performing woman in the widest possible sense?

The first one was *Love's Labour's Lost*, which was my first leading role in Shakespeare. It came after a lot of talk about whether the audience would accept me as Rosaline. 'What's a black girl doing in Elizabethan times?' That was a key, significant thing, because it taught me that the spotlight was on the 'black actors can't do Shakespeare stuff'. I also felt that you should be allowed to fail, because if you don't take risks you can't try and reach higher planes. A lot of people were looking at me in the first act – you know – black woman and all that sort of thing. There was a very bright light shining on my face as it were and I remember thinking that whatever is going on around you, and however many people have played those parts, you can only concentrate on the thing as it is now. You have to focus on the work and throw away all those things. If I had thought about those things beforehand, I would not have set foot on the stage, but thank God it went down very well. The second one was meeting Arthur Miller. He actually sat in rehearsals for the last two weeks, which was totally nerve racking. Again, that taught me about focusing on the work, because you had to pretend, as far as you could, that he wasn't there, otherwise you couldn't rehearse. He's a very charismatic man, and he is the most extraordinary being I've met. Meeting him was a wonderful experience. The third thing was getting married, because it was not something I particularly wanted to do before. I was very happy on my own, I'd lived on my own for ages, and we lived apart before we got married. I wasn't thinking it would be a tragedy not to marry, in fact most of my friends dropped like flies when I told them the news. It's great. I just wanted to be married to this one person – a very different thing from marriage for its own sake. Marriage is about the two of you, not like turning into a married couple that are supposed to do this or do that. I think it's as individual as you are. My views on marriage have softened! Those are definitely my three key things.

What is your most significant achievement in the performance arena?

Well it's really about being able to play the parts I've wanted to do that a lot of people said I wouldn't be able to do. Even now I get asked to endless forums about integrated casting and black actors in the mainstream. People talk and talk, but in the end you answer all the questions by doing something. People say it's impossible for someone black to play Maggie in *After the Fall*,[6] or to play this or that part in Shakespeare, but you do it and that question is answered. The big thing for you when you are doing those things is that you want to be good. You're not doing it to answer their question, you're doing it to fulfil your own pursuit of excellence. People said, 'You probably won't do much Shakespeare, most of your parts will probably be characters written for black actors.' People talk about endless things, but you do something and see what the problems might be, and you answer all this talk. The achievement is doing them!

Notes

1   Martha in Gibson's *The Miracle Worker*, directed by Michael Bogdanov, Leicester Haymarket, 1976.
2   Rosaline in Shakespeare's *Love's Labour's Lost*, directed by Barry Kyle, RSC, 1984.
3   Madam in Genet's *The Maids*, Donmar Warehouse and tour, directed by John Crowley, 1997.
4   Kate in Shakespeare's *The Taming of the Shrew*, directed by Mihai Maniutiu, 1995.
5   Played Iras in RSC production at The Other Place, directed by Adrian Noble, 1982.
6   Maggie in Miller's *After the Fall*, directed by Michael Blakemore, Royal National Theatre (Cottesloe), 1990.

Meera Syal

'It makes you a better actor to write, because you know from an actor's point of view what is a good line and what isn't.'

'I liked the fact that I was pretending to be someone else, and it still makes sense.'

Performance Context

Born: 1963, Wolverhampton.

Prior/current commitments: Tina in *Keeping Mum*, written by Paul Myhew Archer, BBC 1 Television series.
Carmen in the film *Girls' Night*, written by Kay Mellor, Granada Films.
Goodness Gracious Me, BBC Radio 4 series.

Post-interview (selected): *Goodness Gracious Me*, BBC Television.

Other: British Comedy Award for *Goodness Gracious Me* – 'Best Comedy Series' – December 1998.

Interview

My discussion on being an actress and writer with Meera Syal in her London home on 25 June 1997 was necessarily governed by the time factor of picking her daughter up from school. At the time of interview, Goodness Gracious Me! *was a successful radio comedy show – at the time of writing it was an even more successful television series.*

Alison Oddey: *Can you remember your first conscious moment of wanting to perform?*

Meera Syal: I remember going on a church trip. I come from a mining village where the church was the centre of our community life, so I did a lot of stuff around the Methodist church. We were taken to a pantomime in Stoke-on-Trent and it was *Dick Whittington*. I was about four and they asked for a volunteer from the audience to come and stroke the baddy's head, who had been turned into a dog. I still remember the act. Suddenly, I was on the stage, in the lights with the audience looking at me! I had to go and pat his head to show he was a good dog. I was very frightened as I thought he would bite my hand, but I felt really at home. I don't know why – I just felt at home standing on stage patting his head. I felt very pleased when I sat down; I thought I had done something magical; I liked that feeling. Mum tells the story of when I put on a play for the school when I was four. I was very precocious and a chatterbox! I enacted a potted version of *The Sleeping Beauty* for the Headmaster, then kissed this boy called Peter Woods. I was lying down and he was playing the prince, and I said, 'You've got to kiss me now', and he kissed me, burst into tears and fled out of the room! I remember thinking, 'I like this.' I liked the fact that I was pretending to be someone else, and it still makes sense. But other than that, my actor's urge was very suppressed, because I was an academic at school.

How would you describe yourself?

As an actress and writer.

Yes, and congratulations for getting the MBE, which was for acting and writing, wasn't it?

Well, services to drama, very grand. It's bizarre. The reaction of most of my friends has been, 'You, why?' They are very pleased for me, but, in the circles I move in, people don't set much store by that sort of thing. I feel it's partly a very deliberate, welcoming political move, because it was Blair's first list and I think he's trying to open up the whole honours system – quite rightly. There were quite a few Asians on the list and black people this year. I won't be using it on my curriculum vitae or cast list though.

You did an English and drama degree at Manchester University – did you know that you wanted to be an actor then?

I suppose that I had the bug that everybody talks about. I didn't think women like me did it, because I had no role models and I was the first generation born here. All the women I knew were either getting married, or doing sensible things like medicine or law. I was an oddball doing English and drama, and I wondered how far I could go. I was lucky that the one-woman show (*One of Us*[1]) took off the way it did. I had the offer of a job with an Equity card at the Royal Court and then a nine-month tour; it was difficult to say no.

So that was your first job straight out of university?

Absolutely. I finished university in July, toured the show to Edinburgh in August and started the job in September. The reason for its success was people recognising when you do something from the heart. It's usually somebody's first work, the thing they've wanted to do for years, and they do it with a 'Fuck it, it doesn't matter if this doesn't go anywhere, I have to say it' attitude, and that was the impulse behind doing that. I hadn't ever seen parts that reflected who I was, or how I felt. I'd been in this all-white drama department and never tackled anything that came close to my experiences. I didn't want to be in plays by middle-class white writers about angst in Hampstead; I know what's going on and I live in Britain. So I just put my toe in the water and I wasn't thinking it would go anywhere, it didn't matter to me whether it did. I had a life set up with an MA place at Leeds to do drama and psychotherapy or a PGCE in London. My life was mapped out. It all changed with that show, and I don't think I've done anything as good since!

Do you come from a theatrical family?

No. My uncle in India was an actor and now he's a film producer. When my father was younger, he was offered a film contract as a child star because he was gorgeous looking and had a beautiful voice. My grandad was a fervent communist and thought this was all bourgeois and forbade him to take it up, but he still has a wonderful voice and is a very artistic man. He never had the chance to explore that because he came here in 1961.

Pretending she could ride her uncle's motorbike.
Home, Essington, 1972, aged nine.

Were you brought up in Wolverhampton?

Yes, near there, in a village called Essington, near Cannock. Then we moved to Walsall to be nearer the Grammar School I went to – Queen Mary's.

Where do you think your performance actually comes from? Does it originate in the family history that you've just described?

When you analyse what makes people act, there is very little that we'd all share. If you took it from a sociological background point of view, I've met sons of earls and people from slums who have done as well as each other. Then there are psychological things like, 'Were you a lonely child? Were you a show-off? Did you get neglected by your parents?' I don't know. It's interesting that my writing has focused on who I am culturally. A lot of the best stories come from my community and they are untold. It helps you make sense of who you are. I rarely feel that in acting, maybe because those parts aren't being written yet. I've written a few of them I like to think, which have made sense of my place in the world. I haven't necessarily played them but I've written them, and that's helped me somewhere. I don't set off thinking that I want to communicate to the world what it is to be a brown woman. I often start with characters that fascinate me, and they tend to be people who are wrestling with identity problems, crises or issues – duty versus desire is a big one. Most of the characters I've ever written are in that and I think that it is not only an Indian concern, but it's a Catholic concern, a Jewish concern, and a middle-class female concern. Those things are universal and they may be refracted through an Indian sensibility or a British Asian sensibility. I couldn't just write, I know that. I would feel bereft without the acting. I would feel incomplete if I didn't have the public communal creative process to balance a very solitary process of writing. If you don't live, what do you have to write about?

Has the writing always been hand in hand with the performing?

It has in a way, and I think it is for a lot of comedy performers. Most comedy performers do actually write the material they perform. Dawn French and Jennifer Saunders do it all the time. I've always been doing comedy off and on. I've never done stand-up but I've done a lot of characters, comedy songs or whatever. I didn't feel like a proper writer until I'd actually written a script for someone else to do. Surely the most important thing is to be a creative person. I don't see strict divisions and it's only the British that seem to think that way. Creative sensibility is about communicating, which is the root of it. You want to share a human experience. If you can't act, then you will do something else. However, I have to juggle all that with one small four-year-old who is at school.

In light of your daughter, what would you like to be offered work-wise?

I think working on a new play with a good director, and, realistically, London-based would be nice. I'd work at any London theatre in a new play if it was somebody really good, because I miss that process a lot. I wouldn't necessarily wear my writer's hat because that's what scares some people, and they think I'll go and analyse the script. I'm very good at being an actor when I have to be and vice versa because I performed my own stuff. I know about cutting and keeping quiet when it's the writer's turn to speak and all that. I'd work with Max Stafford-Clark again at the drop of a hat; Declan Donelin; and there are plenty of people I'd like to work with like Phyllida Lloyd or Terry Johnson.

Have you worked with many women directors?

Yes, and I've enjoyed working with all of them. Carole Hayman gave me my first break,[2] but Carole has gone more into writing now, television rather than theatre. It's interesting to me that throughout my career I've worked with most directors more than once, which is a good sign. I like continuity, which is very hard in this business. I like the idea of a repertory company, which is why I was very happy to be at the National. I would go there again because I did like the continuity and that sort of trust you build up with a company over a period, which you don't get so much any more. That's why *Goodness Gracious Me*[3] has been so good, because all of us are great friends and have been for years. We're all comedy performer writers, wanting to promote our skills, and have worked with each other quite a lot on different projects. It came together organically and that rarely happens. We are truly a company, because we know each other so well and we have a history together of trying stuff out. You can't manufacture that; it shows in the work. It reflects in the ease in which we perform with each other. I think that's why it will be a strong project, because we have that backbone. *Goodness Gracious Me* proves that we don't have to explain ourselves, that we are British as well as whatever else we are, and from that springs some extraordinarily creative stuff.

Can you define your multiple identities, how they compete, and the various contra-dictions within them?

I have a lot of practical contradictions. Sometimes when I have had a writing commission, I have had to turn down acting work to honour that commission. That's been hard and generally I tend to put the acting first, especially as it comes up very quickly and maybe it's short. When I was writing *Bhaji on the Beach*[4] I had to turn down a lot of acting work which was painful, but I thought this will be so good if it comes off for all sorts of reasons. I had to try and do it as best as I could. Also, I do worry that being known as a writer has affected my acting career: it doesn't enhance you to casting directors. They don't seem to understand that you can do more than one thing, and they feed each other. It makes you a better actor to write, because you know from an actor's point of view what is a good line and what isn't. I've always tried, even with the smaller parts, to make them interesting, because I know that as an actor I've done them and it's demoralising to walk in, having two lines which are crap. After years of analysing scripts and performing them, you know what works and what doesn't. I bring that in with me when I go into an audition. There is nothing you can do except remind people that you are still very much an actress and that you try and do good work, preferably with a profile. That will remind them you can do it and you don't scare them off. I think that you have to honour the writer that you're working with, and because I'm a writer, I really respect that. I would never think of changing the lines without discussing it with the writer and the director. I would still take their word for it if that's the overall vision they have, because as an actor part of your brief is to be part of a communal vision, it's not just about your performance and what you think is right. It's what you are creating together.

What motivates you? What drives you on?

Somebody once described a good play as being a slice of life that makes sense. For ninety minutes, the chaos that is everybody's lives suddenly has a meaning and a pattern, and for that time you can kid yourself that your life makes sense and has a purpose. I don't know whether anything I ever do will last or be remembered, or considered great. In fact, that doesn't matter to me. What does matter is that I'm part of a journey. Maybe I was meant to start off with the best thing I ever did – the one-woman show – but it's difficult to describe what effect that had on me. To be understood is a wonderful feeling. Similarly, with *Bhaji on the Beach* I got criticism, because I was tackling taboo subjects like violence, sex, women and pregnancy. There was too much packed into the film, but when you don't think you are going to get another chance to say it, you just cram it all in. God, sometimes your acting is frivolous, dressing-up for money, but those moments are really important and I've had a similar feedback with the novel *Anita and Me*,[5] which has been out about a year now.

I suspect that all women performers want to communicate, to share, to have a dialogue with others. However, you seem particularly self-aware and self-conscious in both areas of writing and performing.

I've been forced to be self-analytical, because I've been held up as a repre- sentative so much in my career. I don't want this label of role model particularly. I don't want to do it, it's not my job. I can't speak for everybody. I've been put in that situation of 'Do I represent a whole community?' Whether I want to or not, it's been pushed on to me. I've had to think about it, and I think that's the only reason. That's what has done a lot of Asian actors' heads in, particularly those of mixed race. However, there's a whole generation coming up of young Asians from RADA and Guildhall who can do everything and the parts haven't increased in proportion to the number of actors. In my age group, a lot of people have dropped off because it has been hard. So there are fewer parts for my age group, and fewer people to compete for them. Brown is the new black in more ways than one. It's very cool to be Asian right now.

Are there Meera Syal personae that are not usually visible to us in a daily context, that appear in a performance?

I do like playing vulnerable women, and I like playing women that have not fulfilled their potential because I resonate with them. I don't know why, because I don't suppose people see me like that. Recently, I played a middle-aged Asian divorcee,[6] who has a crush on Tom Jones and was very dowdy. I had to dress up in this awful leopard-skin dress with bad make-up and hair straight back to meet my idol. I loved playing that part. Those are the parts that I'm really attracted to, and I'm often cast as a cool, capable, confident intellectual. A lot of roles I get offered on television are barristers, social workers, or union representatives. That's obviously how people see me, but it's not how I feel and it's not what I think I play best.

Have you become more self-questioning as a performer over the years?

Inevitably you are, which is probably why having children for women like me is very good, because I think it has rooted me in a way nothing else would have done and I was in danger of spiralling off into complete self-obsession maybe. I've seen it, and I do know actresses in their late thirties who are actually doing very well, but for them, the line between the parts they play and their lives is very thin. A life that is about the parts you play and the time off stage is just waiting for the next part where you live your life, as opposed to the other way round when you live your life and the parts are an extension of the experiences you have. That's why having a child for me has been very good, because I've had to step off the careerist ladder and I've had to live. I've had to do all the Mum stuff and the real life stuff that everybody in the world goes through who isn't an actor. That's given me a sort of confidence I didn't have before, because in the end it doesn't matter as much. I can turn stuff down; I know where my priorities are, and it wasn't like that before.

So, in a way, it is to do with establishing what your priorities are, and what really matters. So having a child is the key turning point in being able to do that?

I'm sure a lot of the women you've interviewed with children have said that, but it makes you a better performer. Motherhood opens up experiences you cannot imagine until you have done it. Forceps onward! Then you are a part of this big club, and suddenly you know what true altruistic love is without a shadow of a doubt. I know I could play it now in a way that I probably couldn't have before. You know what feeling someone's pain on their behalf is, it's such a burning passionate thing and it expands you on all levels. It's like the first year, all your nerve endings are on the surface. I cried at anything. Suddenly the world was big and dangerous, and she was a small speck that I was responsible for, and it just turned me inside out really. Also, I lost two children, so she was a very wanted child.

Has motherhood given you anything else specifically in terms of work that you've done in the last four years?

I certainly wouldn't do any nude things now! Piles of stretchmarks are not attractive – then, I wouldn't before frankly, so that hasn't changed. Practically it has informed all my work decisions; I've chosen to do more television, and I've had to do London based things. I can't go off filming for three months, or tour. Rather I won't, I could, but I've chosen not to.

So it's a practical reason that prevents itinerancy?

Ironically, the time when she was little was the time I really could have done it much more easily, but you don't realise that. They are more portable when they are babies. Also, I have a partner who travels a lot, so I don't have the security of a home-based partner. I did a film job[7] in Manchester recently, which was for four weeks and one of those weeks was half-term. We didn't work weekends, because Julie Walters said she wouldn't, because she had a child. It takes actresses with power to put those sort of conditions down, so that was workable and for four weeks my husband gave a devout promise that he wouldn't go away! You can work it out if the job is worth it.

What makes the act of performing so satisfying to you?

To be part of a communal experience, I think. I'm told football fans get the same feeling going to a match, because without an audience it's not a performance, is it? That's the frustration for actors, if you are a writer you can keep writing, you don't need a reader for the act of writing, but as an out of work performer you are absolutely crippled. There's no point doing it to your mirror. You have to have that feedback.

Is the performance satisfaction the same, or has it changed?

I have higher standards, and there are parts I wouldn't do now. I still get the same buzz. *Goodness Gracious Me* is a particular buzz, because we have the added feedback of an audience that is the way we are, it's absolutely their experience. You really feel that. You come off stage feeling ten feet tall. In part, it is nothing to do with being Asian. It's that somebody has been part of your emotional vulnerability, appreciated it, resonated with it, and for a minute you are in each other's skins. It's amazing.

Do you admire women stand-ups or comedians?

Lots. Victoria Wood has been a huge influence, and French and Saunders. Joyce Grenfell was fantastic in her delicacy. Beryl Reid used to make me laugh and Phyllis Diller, because they went for women being mad, barking mad, being silly and looking ugly! I admired Roseanne's earlier stuff, which was edgy.

Have you been influenced or inspired by any notable women?

By Kathy Burke and Julie Walters, because of their ability to move effortlessly from one medium to another. They play that grey area between comedy and tragedy all the time, which I think is the most interesting area to be in, and they make themselves silly or ugly and can also play dead straight classical stuff. Kathy spans farce, comedy and heartbreaking realism. I don't know of a more popular performer. I've never seen either of them give a performance where I didn't believe completely where they were coming from. It was great working with Julie; I was a bit gobsmacked by it all. Watching Julie work on *Girls' Night* was inspiring.

She's greatly admired in the profession. Does the word 'strumpet' have any resonance in the late 1990s?

I like the word, because it suggests a woman, who is not ashamed of her dark side, whereas men think she is a bit sleazy, outspoken or flirty. I know it's used as an insult, but it is one of the words that has probably been reclaimed, quite rightly. I find it quite an attractive word. It is somebody who doesn't give a toss about how she is seen, and it's hard to do that. It's like 'witch' that was used for healers and midwives, or women that didn't marry, so you can reclaim all those female insults if you go back far enough. Strumpet was used in Elizabethan times for somebody whose dress was a bit too low and wasn't married! That's half of us now!

Is the 1997 image of the performing woman a more positive picture?

I think most women in performance would happily call themselves a strumpet. I think it's a great word. 'Trollop' is another one; 'minx'. These new ladettes are reclaiming all these words. There is a magazine called *Minx* and 'Strumpet' is a very good title for a new girl's magazine, because if you read *Minx* it is something like 'Girls Behaving Badly' and not being ashamed of it. I don't go completely down that road, because a lot of it is aping men and that is pointless. We can do better than that, but I think this edginess about it that is, 'We are cheeky, we do get up your noses, but actually it doesn't mean we are not nice people and we can't think or hold down jobs at the same time.' We do have a mischievous and dark side, which is as much about being a woman as being a wife, a mother and ironing your shirts actually. A lot of men are scared of that.

If you had to think of any absolute key moments in your life as a performing woman in the widest possible context, what would come to mind?

Doing *Serious Money*[8] off Broadway in a public theatre was a dream come true, and also being part of *Goodness Gracious Me*, because that's important to me on a lot of levels. And still my first performance ever of the one-woman show in which several scales fell from my eyes – I felt comfortable.

Notes

1 *One of Us*, a one-woman comedy, performed at the Edinburgh Festival and National Tour, directed by Jacqui Shapiro, 1983–85.
2 Bibi in Townsend's *The Great Celestial Cow*, directed by Carole Hayman, Royal Court Upstairs and Joint Stock Tour, 1984.
3 *Goodness Gracious Me*, BBC Radio 4 series, 'Britain's first Asian comedy' (Syal). Won Sony for 'Best Radio Comedy'. Since this interview, it has been performed as a very successful BBC Television series.
4 Syal wrote the screenplay for *Bhaji on the Beach*, Channel 4, December 1996.
5 Syal, M., *Anita and Me*, Flamingo, 1997. Syal's first novel won a Betty Trask Award in 1996 and was shortlisted for the *Guardian* Fiction Prize.
6 Middle-aged Asian divorcee in Channel 4-funded short film *It's not unusual*, written by Asmaa Pirzada, directed by Ksir Yefet, winning BAFTA 'Best Short Film', 1997.
7 Carmen in *Girls' Night*, written by Kay Mellor, directed by Nick Hurran, starring Julie Walters and Brenda Blethyn, Granada Films, 1997.
8 Jacinta Condor in Churchill's *Serious Money*, directed by Max Stafford-Clark, Royal Court, Wyndhams, Public Theatre, New York, 1987–88.

Jane Horrocks

'I like to think of myself as a chameleon really, that people aren't quite sure what I'll come up with next.'

Performance Context

Born: 1964, Lancashire.

Prior/current commitments: Marla in the film *Bring Me the Head of Mavis Davis*.
Lady Macbeth in Shakespeare's *Macbeth*, Greenwich Theatre and UK tour.
Post-interview (selected): Laura Hoff ('L.V.') in the film *Little Voice*, Scala Productions, Miramax Films.
Cassandra in television film *Hunting Venus*, written by Nick Vivian, Yorkshire Television for ITV Network.
Other: Nominated for 1999 Golden Globe Award and BAFTA for 'Best Actress' in *Little Voice*.

Interview

I listened to the frank responses of Jane Horrocks to my interview questions at the Groucho Club in Soho on 22 January 1997, admiring Jane's diversity of performance in theatre, film and television, and afterwards sharing our thoughts about giving birth in water.

Alison Oddey: *You've worked very diversely across film, television and theatre – do you prefer any one medium?*

Jane Horrocks: At the moment I'm very off theatre. I find it quite exhausting to do, and I find the current state of theatre a bit depressing to be honest. The people who have enormous influence in theatre, the critics, are too old for the job now I think. We need new blood, so I've no interest in it at the moment.

You trained at RADA: was that a positive experience?

I enjoyed RADA very much, because I met some great people there and the teachers were lovely. It was like a shop window for casting directors and agents, and they all came there because of the reputation. So in that respect I really enjoyed it. Whether I came away with anything, any wisdom, I don't honestly know. It's a very cosseted atmosphere there, you're well looked after and you are told that you can play any part that's going. Then you leave drama school and you realise that people actually do pigeonhole, and they hear you've got a northern accent, which means that you can only play northern parts. So ultimately it gives you a false sense of security.

Then when you come out, the real world hits you?

Yes, and you have to make your own mark, control your own career. I could feel myself going into maid parts and easily getting trapped in that area! I went to the Royal Shakespeare Company the day after I left RADA. If I had stayed at the RSC, I would still be playing maids or weird little crippled people. It might be quite interesting for someone like me to play Juliet, but they would never ever think of me in any part like that, so I thought I'd move on. I've never had any interest from the RSC since. Whether I've done so many articles in newspapers that they think there's no way she's coming back! I have been massively misquoted on Shakespeare, because I have said that I find it boring. It's more the productions that I find boring, the casting of them, and the direction of them rather than Shakespeare. What I got so cheesed off about when I did *Macbeth*[1] was that Mark Rylance was trying to do something new with that production. Whether it worked or not is another thing; his attempt was very brave, interesting and looking to the future. He was trying to make it more accessible for youngsters who have to study it in school, which I think is important. I think that's what people should be looking at rather than thinking they have to stick to tradition. Why can't the critics stretch their imagination, try to be a bit less selfish, and think about Shakespeare appealing to a new generation? Look at the RSC, all you can see are American and Japanese tourists. It's soul-destroying, but that's who they have got to cater for. They can't do any productions at the RSC that are a bit risqué, because the American or Japanese tourists would not like it. I think that's what is so brilliant about Mark at the Globe, how he tries to bring it to the working class. If you pay £5 a ticket, you may have to stand up, but at least it's available. That's another thing, ticket prices are just ridiculous. Not many people can afford to go to the theatre.

So you enjoy taking risks, changing things, and exploring your role through the performance?

This is what Mark Rylance encouraged us to do, try something different every night, so it kept the performance alive. A man who came to see *Macbeth* eight times said it was always different each time he saw it. To me that was the biggest accolade. It adds an element of danger, and I think things should be dangerous, shocking and exciting. I think Simon McBurney, who runs Theatre de Complicite, does the same. He keeps his performances very much alive, rehearsing and changing things all the time, keeping the actors alive as well as the audience. I can only think of Mark Rylance and Simon McBurney who do that.

Are you from a theatrical background at all?

No – nothing in the family.

What attracted you to the theatre or to performing itself?

Basically, I like showing off. I like the shock value of life, and I like to make people sit and listen. I wasn't massively advanced when I started out. I wasn't producing any great work, but I did like the shock element of what you could do. You could make people think by doing something often quite extreme.

When did you become conscious of a desire to want to do that? Was it as a child?

Yeah – I had a very vivid imagination and still have. It's been quite detrimental in a way, but I just wanted to create drama.

Have you got any siblings?

Two brothers that are older than me, and there are five years in total between us. They would get together and I was the outsider – the pain in the arse.

Where you grew up in Lancashire, were there many opportunities drama-wise?

Not really – apart from the odd school play. My mum paid a subscription to an arts magazine and found out about various courses, such as a weekend course at the Royal Exchange and a foundation course at Oldham Technical College. From there I went on to RADA.

So where did the roots of your desire for performing originate from?

I enjoyed making people laugh. I felt like I could achieve notoriety. I was not exactly a pretty young person, so I was not popular 'looks'-wise, I didn't have boyfriends or anything. I was friendly with a very popular girl who had lots of boyfriends, so I was like the stooge and found I could gain popularity from doing impersonations and making people laugh.

That kind of comedy is reflected in your recent television piece – Never Mind the Horrocks.[2] *It shows your improvisation ability and the whole range of characters you play to be very diverse.*

I filmed it last year. I like that sort of thing, it's like the dressing-up box. I think, 'I can have that hairstyle, and do that voice.' I'm very into voices. When I approach a character it's the voice that comes first, so it was a lovely opportunity to display all that in the piece.

Do you find it attractive to see a woman being funny?

I don't see any problem with it. I don't see why women can't be as funny as men, but I think men have an easier time doing it. A lot of people have great difficulty laughing at women, they don't think women should be funny. That's why we have so few women comedians.

Have you ever been a stand-up yourself?

No, I greatly admire that, but I'd never do it. I actually saw Jenny Eclair when she was at the Comedy Store years ago, and she was superb, really brave. You are totally exposed up there. That's too risky – I like to be surrounded by people. I like the glory but not to be totally exposed! I think Jo Brand is funny and Victoria Wood is superb.

Little Voice[3] *was an excellent vehicle for you to expose your various talents. Was it actually written for you?*

I was friends with Jim Cartwright, because I did his play *Road*[4] at the Royal Court and then on television. We became friendly after that. We chatted about my doing impersonations and I ended up doing them for him in the back garden. He said, 'I'll write a play about that', and sure enough he did! That's what I'm doing in October – the film version of *Little Voice*.[5]

Having done the theatre version, what will it be like to perform it as a film?

I think it will be very different. *Little Voice* was very speechy in the theatre and I don't think that sustains on film. When we did *Road* on television it changed enormously from what it was like in the theatre. It was much starker on television. Alan Clarke, the director, wanted desperately to make it his own instead of just lifting it from the theatre and putting it on film, which is what it was originally going to be. Doing it on location in the north-east was a really good move on his part. When the stage version of *Cabaret* was filmed, the atmosphere inside the theatre never quite transferred to television.

How would people describe you as an actress?

I hope that people would describe me as a character actress. When we left college character actor was a dirty word! Character actors are usually thought of as enormous with one eye here and one eye down there! It's a shame, as I think the best actors are character actors.

So when you perform, do you see yourself always playing a character?

Yes, otherwise I get bored. I hate playing an extension of myself because it's so boring. I like to look into this person's life – how they talk, walk or how they relate to other people.

You worked with Mike Leigh on Life is Sweet,[6] *and played an amazing character. Did you do a lot of research for that?*

Yes. I did a lot of research on bulimia and Marxism, but best skip through that!

Can you describe the experience of working with Mike Leigh?

He doesn't actually give you the character; it's actually based on someone you know in real life. The person is chosen by Mike. You discuss all these people you know, and he chooses a person to be the springboard for your character. You work for several months on improvisation and discussion. It is hard and quite gruelling, and you are rehearsing until you are about to film.

As a company, how did you operate together on and off set?

It's a weird situation because everything is kept secret when you work with Mike, so you never know what the other characters are up to. You have to have lots of private discussions with Mike, and you are not told if another character is going down to Sainsburys unless the character tells you herself! So you're kept in the dark apart from when you are improvising or discussing the characters. You have to discuss quite a lot about the history of the characters; you have to be all together for that. Really you don't have a great deal of time for socialising. It's quite nerve-racking being with the other actors on a social level, because you think that you're going to spill something. For instance, Alison Steadman, who played my character's mother, never knew what my character was up to in the bedroom with David Thewlis. So after the film was completed she asked me what my character was doing in the daytime, and when I told her, she was absolutely horrified. It's good that it is kept secret.

So what motivates you to perform? Is it to be shocking or to discover voices, or to gain attention?

To recreate myself, and to play something that people would not think I could play. As we said earlier, money is involved so a lot of artists can't take the risk.

They have to go for the obvious. For instance, there was a real battle to get me into the *Mavis Davis*[7] film, which I've just done. They wanted quite a big name and they were looking at Debbie Harry originally. They wanted an old singer who could play the part, so that's my big accolade that I managed to get the part. I loved playing that part as I'd never played anything like that before. I think that's what drives me really, doing things I have not done before. I did get into a stage of playing a lot of gloom and doom parts – little miseries. I was so into comedy when I finished drama school, because I'd played so many comedy parts and old women! When I was told that I would be playing a seventeen-year-old in *The Dressmaker*,[8] it was weird because I thought how do I do a seventeen-year-old without a hump on my back or a walking stick! You think you are going to go in a certain direction, and then someone takes you off in another direction.

Did you create the character of Bubble or did Jennifer Saunders?

Originally, I met her for the daughter part. Then we decided I was a lot too old! It was much more sensible to have someone like Julia,[9] because it was more realistic. So she asked if I was interested in playing the secretary. So I read that, and she said, 'Just do it in your own accent, it would be great', and I created something for that. So she did then write it with me in mind. After three series, I think that the character ends up very differently to how she started off! She's much more on another planet in the end than in the beginning!

Did you enjoy making Absolutely Fabulous?[10]

Oh yes, it was great. I think that Jennifer did a great job with it, and the reason for its success was because it was something very different. People were crying out for something different in sitcom, rather than the 'four girls flat-sharing' scenario. They wanted something like women being gross, something they hadn't seen before. Also, there was this great discovery in Joanna Lumley as well, which is a classic example of what I said earlier – you would never imagine that she could have played that role. Jennifer took the risk of having her in that part and she wowed the nation.

You seem to have played a diversity of roles from Bubble to the character of Alison in Some Kind of Life.[11] *I thought that you were fantastic in that. Did you have to do much research?*

Thank you. I interviewed a lot of wives. I also went to a rehabilitation centre, where I saw a lot of brain-damaged victims who were on the road to recovery, but it didn't seem like it to a naïve eye. I found it tough doing that, because

I felt it rubbing off on my life. I needed to get back to comedy to give my life a lighter touch, but I was glad that I did *Some Kind of Life*. Sometimes the hardest jobs teach you the most.

How would you describe your self-image as a performer?

I always think that people see me as that silly daft person from *Absolutely Fabulous*, or that comedy girl, that northern girl. I hope people think more highly of me than that. It always comes as a nice surprise when people come up and comment positively on your work. I like to think of myself as a chameleon really, that people aren't quite sure what I'll come up with next. Hopefully I might surprise somebody.

Are there opportunities for women to realise that potential?

I think that women complain that there aren't enough good parts for women around. I've never found that, I've always managed to find interesting parts for women. I feel that the range of work I've done since leaving drama school has been quite wide and I've played a lot of different characters. I think that's where the character actor thing falls away from the leading actor. I think you'll find that more leading actresses would complain at that than character actors, so it depends very much on how you start out and whether you're prepared to create your own stuff.

You sound like you've known what you wanted, and you've gone out and got it!

Yes, if I've felt I've got myself in a rut then I've tried to change things. I think that's why I wanted to get pregnant really, because I need something else in my life right now. I can't go any further until I have a bit more life experience. I could have toured around the world or had a baby, and I decided to have the baby! Something that would make me less selfish, less intolerable and that would make me develop more as a person.

So that's an identity in creation – becoming a working mother. Do you envisage conflicts of identity in the future?

When I worked with Alison Steadman, I always felt that her children were the most important thing and her career came second. She absolutely adores her children. When she talks about her children, her face lights up and it is really special to her. I hope that happens to me. I've had twenty-odd years of great fun and doing a wide variety of things acting-wise. I've been very fortunate to do that, so I've no regrets about not playing particular parts. I can only move on. This will be a new part of life, which can only be enlightening and enriching. It will take over and switch the balance – a new priority. I think life is a series of lessons and when you stop learning, then you become redundant. I feel that's my next lesson, I can only go forward.

Can you identify any key moments in your life so far as a performing woman in the widest sense?

Little Voice (in 1992) was a real big peak for me, and it encouraged people to see me in a different light. Also, *Life is Sweet*, and *Absolutely Fabulous*. Those are three things that I'm proud of and which were very different. They made people sit up and take note. 1992 and 1993 were really happy periods of my life. Work petered out in 1994–95 and I didn't enjoy those years at all. Then it picked up again last year when I decided to change things. Those were the highlights, although I did not learn a lot from that. I learnt more from being miserable. I learnt the most from doing *Macbeth*, because it was incredibly hard going.

Learnt in the job sense, or about yourself?

Both. Mark Rylance's brilliant way of working meant that I learnt about keeping a performance alive every night, which I will take into future work in theatre. I found it incredibly useful and if I did another theatre piece I would certainly apply that method of working. Life-wise, too. I wasn't very happy touring, and I felt an incredible sense of loneliness and emptiness that I don't want to experience again. That's why I need something else, something much more real and permanent in my life that would always be there. It could be quite humiliating doing that play with people so against it, so cruel about it as well. I got cheesed off to be at the mercy of other people. You would be giving out your soul and it would be trampled over at the end of the evening.

So being an itinerant did not appeal to you?

No, I'd never do that again.

Do you think if you'd been in something where people hadn't been so negative that you might answer differently?

Yeah, I did *Road* about ten years before, and I had a great time doing that. It was a highly successful show, which had a great reputation in London, so it came with good reports to the different places. We were also doing much smaller venues, so it was much more intimate. We did huge venues with *Macbeth* and it got lost. I got a lot of hassle as I did something rather extreme in the sleep-walking scene – I peed on stage – and the tabloids went bonkers over it. It was banned in a lot of places. I got a lot of flack for that. It just didn't suit me. It's like being a rock and roll singer – it drives me mad touring around – I hate it. I'm a home girl; I'm used to being stable and in one place. I also found it incredibly lonely. One week in Malvern and one week in some other place looking for accommodation, and ending up in some dreary little bed and breakfast. Then having to do the play, which was not appreciated, and then coming home miserable.

Is home to you in London now?

Yes, I've lived here for fifteen years now. My roots are in Lancashire. That's why I've never changed my accent or altered who I am, because it still has a very strong hold over me.

Notes

1 Lady Macbeth in *Macbeth*, directed by Mark Rylance, Greenwich Theatre and UK tour, 1995.
2 *Never Mind the Horrocks*, Hat Trick Special for Channel 4, September 1996.
3 Little Voice in Cartwright's *The Rise and Fall of Little Voice*, directed by Sam Mendes, Royal National Theatre (Cottesloe) and Aldwych Theatre, 1992.
4 Louise, Valerie and Claire in Cartwright's *Road*, directed by Simon Curtis, Royal Court, 1987. Louise in BBC Television version of *Road*, directed by Alan Clarke, 1991.
5 Laura Hoff (Little Voice) in the film *Little Voice*, directed by Mark Herman, 1998.
6 Nicola in *Life is Sweet*, directed by Mike Leigh, for which she won the 1992 Los Angeles Critics Award.
7 Marla in *Bring Me the Head of Mavis Davis*, directed by John Henderson, 1998.
8 Rita in *The Dressmaker*, directed by Jim O'Brien, 1987.
9 Julia Sawalha.
10 Bubble in *Absolutely Fabulous*, BBC Television, directed by Bob Spiers, 12 November 1992–17 December 1997 (Three series).
11 Alison in *Some Kind of Life*, Granada Television, directed by Julian Jarrold, 1995.

Kathy Burke

'The buzz for me is working with other actors.'

'... when you are acting you are allowed to be a bit of a
child, and you can muck around, sit around in corners
and be naughty!'

Performance Context

Born: 1964, Islington, London.

Prior/current commitments: Honour in Fielding's *Tom Jones*, BBC Television. Sharon in *Common as Muck*, written by William Ivory, BBC Television.

Post-interview (selected): Val in *Nil By Mouth*, written and directed by Gary Oldman, Twentieth Century Fox Film.

Mary Tudor in *Elizabeth*, Elizabeth I Productions.

Maggie in *Dancing at Lughnasa*.

Linda in *Gimme, Gimme, Gimme*, written by Jonathan Harvey, Tiger Aspect, BBC Television.

Other: For her performance in *Nil By Mouth* Kathy was awarded 'Best Actress' Award at the 1997 Cannes Film Festival 50th Anniversary; the Variety Club of Great Britain Film Actress Award 1997; British Independent Film Award (BIFA) for Best Actress 1998.

For her portrayal of Martha in *Mr Wroe's Virgins*, Kathy received the 1993 Royal Television Society Award for 'Best Actress'.

Interview

I interviewed the hospitable Kathy Burke in her London home on 6 March 1997 prior to her success at the Cannes Film Festival as 'Best Actress' for the role of Val in the film Nil By Mouth,[1] *and was struck by her strength of character and commitment to performing.*

Alison Oddey: *What are you currently doing in terms of performance?*

Kathy Burke: I'm just in the process of costume fittings and stuff like that for Henry Fielding's *Tom Jones* for the BBC.[2] I'm really looking forward to that mainly because I've worked with the director before, and also because *Tom Jones* is not a normal starchy period piece; it's very ballsy and funny. I'm playing a character called Honour, who basically has none! She's a bit of a coward and the maid to the main romantic lead – a character called Sophia. *Tom Jones* is basically a romp, a farce, and I think it was written in 1786. When it was first published there was an outcry and it was banned.

Was working with this particular director a crucial factor in the decision-making process?

Yes, it was, before I'd even read the scripts. I'd met him before as I've just done a series for the BBC called *Common as Muck*[3] and he directed that – Metin Huseyin. It was the nicest experience I've had with a director; he just seemed to have the lot. Brilliant communicator, his own vision, but without an ego. It was just extraordinary and when we finished the job I said, 'I'd do anything for you … one scene in something'; then he got in contact about this so I was really chuffed. He's got the same camerawoman and he likes to work with the same people. He's got a real good team. He's very open to everybody bringing in their own ideas but he knows how to keep a handle on it; it never gets out of hand or control and he manages to let everybody know exactly what he wants. Metin seems to breeze through all the bad stuff and he'll also let you know if he's going through bad stuff himself if he's not able to work something out. He won't keep it to himself and that's what I mean about not having an ego. He's not afraid to ask for help and he relies on his team, his crew, allowing everyone to do her own thing as long as everything is going in the same direction.

In your experience, is working collaboratively – as a team – common or rare in theatre or television?

It's getting better. I don't know if it's something to do with my knowing more about how it all works now, about being older and not having to audition for roles much now. I think it's a combination of things, but I think the main thing is my understanding the way everything works a bit better. Then you know how much you can contribute, when not to contribute, and when to let them get on with it. I've worked with some great directors, but Metin is the one I have felt totally and utterly comfortable with. *Common as Muck* was very much an ensemble piece. It's the same with *Tom Jones*; it's very much ensemble playing. It just seemed perfect for me.

So you enjoy ensemble playing?

Oh, yes. I have been approached to do one-woman shows and I could not think of anything worse really. The buzz for me is working with other actors. I prefer to be fostered by everybody else. I like the fact that I work with Harry Enfield, French and Saunders, or Jo Brand … I don't belong to anybody and I like that.

It doesn't appeal to you then to stand on your own?

No, a lot of people think I've done stand-up comedy, but I haven't. I think I get credit where it's not due a lot of the time when people call me a comedian, because that to me is really hard work and I've never done it. I would not be brave enough. I've done the cabaret circuit with a cabaret act, which was very much part of the alternative comedy scene.

Do you see yourself as a comedy actress?

No, not necessarily. The part I'm doing in *Tom Jones* is a comedy character. She's very funny because she's an idiot, so there's a lot of room for good fun there, but I never go into anything thinking 'this is a funny role'. I'll always try and play the truth of it and then hopefully it will be even funnier.

Is performing comedy just one dimension of calling yourself a character actress?

I think it's a polite way of saying that you don't do the romantic leads; you are there to hold everything up, the foundations. I think the characters that you get are much more interesting than the romantic lead parts. I always thank God that I've never had to do that – the face doesn't quite fit – as the work I've been able to get is vastly more interesting, such as misfits or outsiders. I'm much happier being the person nobody wants to know! I just get a kick out of those sorts of characters. People can empathise with them much more – sympathise with them. It's really nice when people say, 'I saw you in such and such and now I feel better about my life.'

Does that happen to you often?

Yes, I don't know what it is, but people seem to understand where I'm coming from. I've got a bit of a common voice, and from the feedback I've been getting, I seem to be a bit of a hero with little fat girls that have had quite a sad time of it. All the pretty girls have already got their role models, so it's nice for the little plain ones to be into somebody that they can relate to.

That takes me to your roots, and upbringing. You are of Irish descent and I read that your mother died when you were very young.

Yeah, Mum and Dad were both Irish and they came over to London in the 1950s. I was fostered by a woman called Joan Galvin. She looked after me Monday to Friday, and then I went home at the weekend. We lived in the flats across the road and that was between the age of two and five. Once I started school I was at home permanently. It was a very difficult situation because my brothers were eleven and eight when I was eighteen months, so there was talk of my being adopted, which Dad didn't want. I was always very aware that Joan was not my mum and she had four kids of her own. I had a great time, because Monday to Friday I had two big sisters and two big brothers, whilst at the weekend I had my proper brothers – so it was alright. The primary school, St John's up at the Angel, where we all went, had a close-knit Irish community, so everybody looked out for each other, keeping an eye on the flats. I was the lucky one really, because I didn't know any different. I never knew Mum, but it was extremely difficult for my brothers, and by all accounts Mum was a bit of a queen. She was quite an incredible woman. It all happened very quickly. She got stomach cramps, which were cancer, and six weeks later she was dead. It was a shock to the system. Now that we are all adults, I am completely amazed at how they coped, especially my eldest brother, John, who completely took over the role of mother. They both went to the London Oratory, a real top school, and had to travel to Chelsea every day from Islington, but still managed to come home, do tea, washing, as well as homework. It was amazing. My brothers played a very important part in my upbringing.

Are you from a theatrical background?

No, not at all. John's the artist because of his graphics; he went to St Martin's so he set the way artistically. I don't know anything about my mother's background at all, because she was adopted so I don't know her history. The older I get the more curious I get and I would like to know her history. I used to avoid it because we never spoke about Mum at home. I never really asked any questions. It's only now I've got older that I've started talking to older women who knew my mother.

You went to the Anna Scher School when you were about sixteen. When you think about the real roots of wanting to perform, how far back does it take you?

Quite far back actually, as according to my godmother, Aunty Nelly, I was always telling jokes and trying to be funny. My foster-mum, Aunt Joan, said to me recently that when she looks back on what I was like as a very small girl, she remembers me as always trying to let people know that I was alright. She said that I couldn't bear it if people felt sorry for me because I didn't have a mum, and that I would diffuse it immediately by being funny, by telling a joke or mimicking people. She said it carried on from there. That was my role, I was always telling jokes. In primary school whenever we did nativity plays I was never involved in the acting sense; I was always the reader because I was a very good reader and I used to get gold stars! That's down to my brothers, because they taught me. They also taught me right from wrong and manners. I was more frightened of them than Dad!

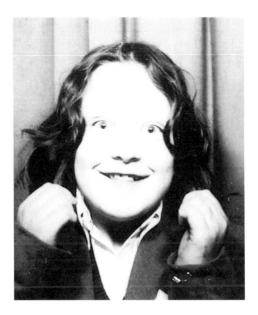

London, January 1976, aged eleven

Again, I read that your dad was unemployed and had a drinking problem.

Yes, though he wasn't unemployed all the time. Dad was a classic case of being suddenly left with three kids and not able to handle it. He died three years ago and before he died we had some amazing talks, and he said to me that he should not have married my mother; he was much too young. When we were kids it was rough at times. He had a bad drink problem and he could be very aggressive and violent. It was quite frightening because he would have binges, spend months pissed and we would not see him. We had to keep this to ourselves as kids, and not get anybody else involved in case we got split up, so nobody was really aware because we looked like we were coping. When he was around he was brilliant, because he was so guilt-ridden and trying to make up for the fact that he was not there for us. It was hard for him but we just got on with it, though there were times when we hated his guts. If he had not come back for a couple of days, we thought he might be dead, but then the worry of that was being split up. We all loved him.

It sounds an incredibly tough time for you. Could this experience be somehow linked to the desire to perform?

The minute I went to Anna Scher theatre, I thought this is just what I've been waiting for; it was just a way of getting things off my chest, in a subtle way.

Suddenly I could shout and scream at somebody and it would be okay. Also, I think when I was younger, my brother said that at seven, my outlook was about forty! As I've got older, I've gone back to being the kid I wasn't. I've got a childlike view of the world but I'm pleased about that. My upbringing helped with my acting, because I was able to empathise more with certain situations. I understood different sorts of people. It was a starting point.

Empathising with a part via your own real experience?

Yes, which is why I'm looking forward to doing *Tom Jones*. The character I'm playing is a real coward and she sits on the fence – a complete twat basically. What's good about it is that it's going to be a bit of a challenge, because even when I've played the lowest of the low, the most abused or ridiculed character, I've always made them winners. I just physically can't help but make them winners. But with this character she can't be, so that's great. I can play someone who people should not like – she's a pain in the arse. I don't want people to like her; I want people to laugh at her rather than with her so that's going to be a challenge just to try and make her like that.

What sort of performance challenge do you enjoy most?

I like it when I get a bit scared by a part. If it's a bit frightening it gives me a bit of extra energy, because I'm quite slothlike! It's good to have a bit of speediness; if you are crapping yourself it does keep you there!

Can you remember work you've done where you've felt very challenged and frightened by the part?

The role that stands out most is in *Mr Wroe's Virgins*,[4] which was a challenge mainly because that involved a lot of nudity and a lot of exposing myself. I was gippy doing that, but after I'd done it, I think it did me a lot of good in a weird way. It was very freeing. It did a lot for my confidence. That was a challenge, and again a character who had been brought up like an animal, and had been left to fend for herself. She had been badly abused so I wanted to get that right. It was based on the book, which is so fantastic, and I wanted the author, Mary Rogers, to be pleased with what I was doing. She was my main concern because it had come from her imagination. That was the most frightening thing that I've done.

You won a television 'Best Actress' award for that, didn't you?

Yeah, from the Royal Television Society. People often get confused and think I won a BAFTA which is embarrassing, but I got the RTS which is just as good, but BAFTA sounds so grand![5]

So you produced an excellent performance and won an award for the most challenging and frightening work.

Yes, I was just so aware of getting it right. It was important to me; writers are always my first concern. I'm a great respecter of the written word and that comes from being a kid. I've always loved books and it's hard work writing. If someone comes along and portrays one of your characters completely the way you did not see it, you'd want to kill them!

You've written and directed your own play – Mr Thomas[6] – is that why you feel so passionate about how work is interpreted and performed?

Oh yes, that's where it came from. I suddenly understood a little of what it's like to be a writer, and I've directed since then. I directed a play[7] at the Bush last year that somebody else wrote. I listened to him a great deal, how he saw the characters, making sure we both had the right vision on it, and also made sure that the writer really did want me to do it. It was the decision of the Bush theatre, but if Jonathan Harvey had thought I was not a good idea, then I would not have gone near it. A lot of the time writers are ignored – not so much in theatre, but on television their opinion does not come into it. In *Absolutely Fabulous*,[8] Jennifer Saunders will say, 'This is not Magda enough, what would Magda say?' I'll come out with things off the top of my head and she'll write it down. She really lets me just have a bit of a free way with it all, asking how would I change it. I'm very wary of doing it; I don't like to steam in there in case it comes across as a bit rude. I always think that what she's originally written is great anyway, but she just likes it to go a little bit darker and that's what I can come up with. I enjoyed playing Magda, because it was the nearest character I've ever played that's like me. Magda is what I'm really like when I'm in a hard mood, no bullshit, getting things done and just being abrupt – the nasty side basically. It's good fun working on that series with all those women.

Has it been important to be able to perform, write and direct?

It's all down to understanding people. I think that every actor at some point should try and direct something, so at the end of the day they can understand how hard it is to direct. Directors definitely get a bad press and I think it's all about empathy. You've got to understand the other person's point of view and a lot of the time you can't, unless you've been in their shoes. It has made me much more patient with directors. I can see why they get a bit stuck now and then, or when communication isn't going well. When I direct it's important that I'm only interested in ensemble, not main roles, but it being a team effort. Also I'm at my calmest when I'm directing; it's weird because when you are acting you are allowed to be a bit of a child, and you can muck around, sit around whispering in corners and be naughty! When you are directing you've got to be completely focused 100 per cent of the time. I like that; I like the discipline and it suits me. On the two occasions that I have directed, both different sets of actors really liked the way I did it. They said at one point that they were the most comfortable jobs they'd been on, where they felt they were included in everything, knew exactly what was going on and also felt part of a team. Nobody felt left out and that to me was so important. I always spend the first couple of days, not playing games, but sitting around and talking. I've just been fortunate that I've worked with so many good directors that you just take bits from each person. What you learn from them, that's the way I do it.

Do you think that being a woman contributes in any way to being an effective director?

I do actually, because I think it's a more gentle way of going about things. The directors that I've got on really well with are men who have been quite open about themselves. I see it as their feminine side; they are just able to talk about how they feel about things. I suppose the blokes like it because you are a bit of a mother figure with them, and you are being gentle and easing stuff out of them slowly. The girls like it because I don't think there is any male gaze going on there. I do think it helps. The first job I ever did was with an exceptional woman director – Mai Zetterling.

Was that the film Scrubbers?[9] *Did you enjoy that?*

Yes, I loved every minute of that. I'd only been out of Anna Scher's for a year; I had not expected to become an actress professionally. I knew I was getting on great at Anna's, but I did not have an Equity card. I started to go to college to study drama, but that was just so I didn't have to get a job. I didn't take it at all seriously and actually found it dull; I didn't like reading Shakespeare and texts. It was a further education college so the drama department was not exactly great and I was just plodding along when Mai Zetterling came along to watch some of the classes and I had an audition. That was my first audition and she got me my Equity card. When I told Dad I was working with Mai Zetterling he could not believe it! He told me she was his pin-up when he was younger, so when we finished filming, Mai Zetterling came round and had tea with him one day, which was fantastic! He gave up booze in the last fifteen years of his life and he was a sweet decent man. It was sad it took so long, but when he met Mai Zetterling, he was so shy. He was this little, shy, shaky Irish man and it was wonderful seeing them in the garden. Mai was so European, so extraordinary and always wore a little black karate suit, ready for anything! When I was seventeen, Mai said to me, 'Make sure you write, and don't just set yourself up to be the court jester.' She said that I could easily go down that route. By then there was a lot of interest in me and there was even talk of me at the age of eighteen doing my own comedy series. Mai said, 'No, you serve an apprenticeship otherwise you'll be here today, gone tomorrow. Do an apprenticeship then you can do things at your own pace.' I really listened to that advice. When I was twenty-one I got involved with the Red Lion Pub Theatre and just went there when I wasn't working, asking if I could assistant direct on things. So when I had big periods of unemployment, I wasn't really, because I was working in the theatre, just watching how other people directed, and tried to learn from it.

In 1997, is that still appropriate advice – to get an apprenticeship?

I think it's better in the long run. I think it's worse nowadays, because in the last ten years you've got to get rich quick, get there quick, everyone wants to be famous before they are twenty-five. I just find it's such a shame and sometimes when I meet young actors the ambition is quite disgusting. I think it's so unhealthy. I don't think there is anything wrong with being ambitious, but a lot of it is blind ambition.

Is there a need in you to perform? What drives you on, what motivates you to do this?

I definitely think there's a need, because there have been so many times when I've just wanted to not perform any more and just direct, but then a part will come along and I feel like I need to do this. I think if I just do this one then I can concentrate on my directing, but then parts keep coming along that are different and it's nice to have more of a choice. So it's got better as I've got older. I'm thirty-two now and I'm just coming out of that; the characters I play are really quite young in the head. Ideally, what I'd love to do in about a year is not do any acting at all – for about ten years – and just see if I can direct and maybe write. Then when I'm older, in my forties, I'd like to come back to acting. I'm not ready for a lot of the good classic roles until I'm in my mid-forties. I think it's fear that makes people do everything because this business is so … you can go in and out of favour, and I want to put a stop to my being fashionable before anybody else does! I want to walk away from it and then come back in and do those great theatre parts that are written for women of that age. I really want to do Kath in Joe Orton's *Entertaining Mr Sloane*. There are great older characters in Molière … I will go with the flow. Ideally, I would love to have a family and suddenly the acting thing may not appeal any more. At the end of the day, I'm a show-off and I don't want to miss out on something being good fun to do. That has been the most important thing to me over the last few years – having fun.

Has anyone inspired or influenced you as a performing woman in or out of the theatrical world?

Definitely Ken Loach; he is my hero. The realism and truth of everything he does; I just think he puts his soul out there. Even when I'm mucking about in a cartoon character in *Harry Enfield and Chums*,[10] I'll always try and make sure there's a line of truth going through it, which is what Harry's writing is like anyway. I think much of what Harry does is very similar to Mike Leigh; there are a lot of larger than life characters. I've always admired Mike Leigh. I worked with him a few years ago in a theatre job and that was a great experience. It was a really different way of working.

What did you particularly learn out of that experience with Leigh – about yourself or your work?

It was just the way he does it. It's improvised, quite secretive and only you know what you are doing, so I found the whole thing hysterical, such a giggle. You are wandering around thinking you know what's going on and you don't. It really taught me that I was not as clever as I thought I was! I was just as much open to manipulation as the next person, and I really prided myself on never being manipulated. I just remember laughing all the time. It was exciting not knowing where it would end and every day was different. You'd spend some days on your own for hours and hours, when you are meant to be thinking about this character! My sloth-like personality loved that. I felt like going to sleep all the time and he'd come in and say, 'What was Nelly doing?' I'd say, 'She was having a kip!' It was bliss; I loved it.

Was this the theatre piece It's a Great Big Shame?[11]

Yes, and it's a different kettle of fish when you are doing theatre, because there has got to be a time eventually when you know the whole story. Just for the sake of tech runs and stuff, so when you are doing a film with him you don't know what the whole film is about until you go and see it. It's very intense and Mike is quite a tricky man to deal with; he blows hot and cold all the time. You have to be very sensitive to his moods and very aware of that, because he is in character as well I think. He plays the character of God, because he'll control where you are going and what your fate is, so I think it must be difficult being God! It's fucking hard work, and it can do people's heads in. You often hear stories about people losing it a bit after working with him. It takes you a long time to get over it, and what was difficult for me was that it was at the same time that Dad first went to hospital for a check-up, so I was very much somewhere else anyway when I was working with him. Maybe that's why I didn't find the work so intense, because what was going on at home was much more intense, and actually going in and working with Mike Leigh was a way of escaping, so I didn't really find it tricky or hard on my brain or my heart. When it all ended I felt a great sense of loss. I was very shaky because I suddenly realised that I preferred my character, a homeless waif called Smelly Nelly, to myself. Nobody wanted to communicate with her and she was very much on her own. I loved being her, because ignorance was bliss. She was completely unaware that nobody liked her; she was very childlike, a simpleton basically. At that time, those two hours on stage every night, was when I was happy.

Have you become more self-questioning as a performer?

Yeah, just choices and that, I think things through a lot more. This year was quite weird, because I've always had an ambition to work with Theatre de Complicite, and they wanted me to do *The Caucasian Chalk Circle* at the National. It was amazing because I thought about it and decided not to do it, even though I'd been waiting to work with Theatre de Complicite. I think it was being aware that they are very much a big emotional troupe and I just was not ready as Kathy to get involved in all that. It's a shame, but now is not the time. If this had come up five years ago it would have been brilliant, but it just wasn't the right time for me, so that was really difficult. I was amazed at myself, but it's one thing I've learnt about myself, that I have to be in the right frame of mind for certain things. I felt a bit of a twit though, because Simon McBurney knew that I'd always wanted to work with them. I think that he was a bit confused by it. He phoned me quite a few times to persuade me, which was very flattering, so I sent him a card asking him to think of me in the future.

Could you identify key moments in your life as a performing woman in the widest possible sense?

Well I think writing the play and putting the play on. Well actually, it was when I did a rehearsed reading of the play. I did not expect to hear so much laughter and that was wonderful. From the minute that the first word was spoken, people were laughing, and I could not understand that, but then I realised it is my voice that's coming out of these five characters, so that was fantastic. Then I'm very proud of having done *Mr Wroe's Virgins*, because that was the ultimate challenge, so that was a key moment.

What's the most significant achievement in your performance work so far?

Probably the Mike Leigh play, doing Nelly. It's a great shame mainly because I'd done that sort of character before a couple of times, but working with Mike

Leigh was like I finally did that sort of character the way I'd always wanted to do it, the way I felt it should have been done. I just loved being Nelly because I knew that it wasn't because people loved her and I wanted to get all this love, but because I found her quite a pathetic character. When I was doing Nelly it was weird because I just felt so light on my feet. It just felt like I was floating around the stage and that I'd never felt so comfortable on stage. I think that's because of the Mike Leigh process, so you are prepared for anything. If anything goes wrong you'll handle it in character, and also because it was the last thing my dad saw me do, and also because he thought it was the best acting I've ever done.

Notes

1 *Nil by Mouth* was written and directed by Gary Oldman, starring Kathy Burke and Ray Winstone, Twentieth Century-Fox Film, 1997.
2 Honour in *Tom Jones*, directed by Metin Huseyin, BBC Television, 1997.
3 Sharon in *Common as Muck*, written by William Ivory, directed by Metin Huseyin, BBC Television, 1996.
4 Martha in *Mr Wroe's Virgins*, BBC Television, directed by Danny Boyle, 1993.
5 Burke received the 1993 Royal Television Society Award for 'Best Actress' for her portrayal of Martha in *Mr Wroe's Virgins*.
6 *Mr Thomas* was written and directed by Kathy Burke, The Old Red Lion Theatre, Islington, 1991.
7 *Boom Bang-A-Bang*, written by Jonathan Harvey, directed by Kathy Burke, 1995.
8 Magda in *Absolutely Fabulous*, BBC Television, directed by Bob Spiers, 12 November 1992 – 17 December 1997 (Three series).
9 Glenis in *Scrubbers*, directed by Mai Zetterling, Handmade, 1983.
10 *Harry Enfield and Chums*, BBC Television series, 1991–98.
11 Nelly in *It's a Great Big Shame*, directed by Mike Leigh, Theatre Royal, Stratford East, 1993.

Marianne Jean-Baptiste

'There was only one Oscar-nominated actor who wasn't
there, and that was me.'

Performance Context

Born: 1967, south-east London.

Prior/current commitments: Hortense in the Mike Leigh film, *Secrets and Lies*.

Post-interview (selected): Doreen Lawrence in *The Murder of Stephen Lawrence*, Granada Television.

Other: For her performance in *Secrets and Lies* Marianne received nominations for 'Best Supporting Actress' in the 1997 Academy Awards, the Golden Globe Awards, and the BAFTA Awards.
Co-composed the musical score for Mike Leigh's film *Career Girls* with Tony Remy.

Interview

Marianne Jean-Baptiste's responses to my questions on 4 June 1997 at the Royal National Theatre revealed the differences between her perceptions of herself as a performer, and her Oscar-nominated performance as Hortense in Mike Leigh's film Secrets and Lies.

Alison Oddey: *You're thirty, and were born in south-east London. Are you from a theatrical family at all?*

Marianne Jean-Baptiste: No.

What are your cultural roots?

My mother is Antiguan and my father is half St Lucian and half French. They must have been here in the 1950s. It was very hard for them, so it's not something that they talk about a lot. We do discuss certain things – not being accepted and having a really hard time.

Although you're British, are you often perceived as Caribbean?

I did spend some time there as a child, but it's really difficult to explain. What goes with you is your skin colour more than anything else. I'm British – that's what I am. You are treated in a completely different way because of the way you look, and so it seeps into everything. It's not as much you carrying the fact that you are West Indian or Caribbean, or African or Asian with you, it's more a fact of people saying, 'Where are you from?' You say, 'England', and people treat you in a way that is because of the colour of your skin. They ask a lot of questions and state 'black actress'. I say, 'Why do you write that? It's never a white actress. Who are you warning?' I often find that we don't have the luxury of just talking about the art form, it's always the colour thing, and my cultural background is always brought in. I was born here. It's very weird.

Do you feel your colour has stopped you getting certain parts?

Of course it has, but I refuse to allow it to be a problem. It is what it is. It happens all the time. There are a number of actors who just don't get the work they should be getting because of class, much less colour. With colour you are right at the back, somebody of a different class can get in first, but yes it's in everything.

So where did your first interest in performing come from? What's your first memory of wanting to perform?

My dad taught me to play the guitar when I was about five. I did drama classes after school when I was about seven, and I'd always done drama at school. The Inner London Education Authority (ILEA) was in existence then and it was always part of what we did at school – dance and drama. For example, we went to see the London Contemporary Dance Theatre and Polka Theatre. The interest was always there. I didn't grow up thinking I wanted to be an actor. I can't even remember deciding. One day, I just said, 'I'm not going to go to university, I'm going to see if I can get into drama school', and that was that. There was always music in the house and around me, whereas theatre and drama came from being at school and not quite enjoying it terribly, and wanting to do something to escape.

So performing enabled you to escape from the realities of school?

It was quite healing really because it turned a lot of things around; I was involved with various drama groups outside school. I'd be taken out of school sometimes to do performances and my class would be invited to come and see the production, which changed a lot of people's opinions about me in my year. I became this person who did drama, as opposed to this person who people didn't talk to particularly.

Why was that?

I don't know, it was weird, children are cruel. It's one of the things you dread, sending your children to school because you know what a misery it can be. I just think I was a bit different from people. I wasn't bullied, but I was if you know what I mean. It was not being accepted by the 'in' crowd and they would make your life hell if you weren't part of that. I developed a skill of being self-contained and able to get on quite nicely on my own, but it was in the fourth or fifth year when everything started changing and people started to talk to me. I still didn't make any friends, because I was used to being on my own. I made friends at college and drama school, but it was just a really weird time. It was very necessary, and I treat it positively.

So in a sense the origins of your interest in performing go back to being at school, which brought a shift in how you were viewed, and then you obviously applied to RADA.

Yes, but it wasn't a big deal or a life-changing revelation. I was doing drama in the summer holidays and at every opportunity, so I thought I might as well go to drama school.

You've been in the business for about eight or nine years, so why are you performing?

I enjoy it, it's a luxury, an indulgence. I'm not saving anyone's life but I enjoy performing in theatre, and doing music. With theatre, I enjoy the challenge of different characters, analysing and trying to portray them, trying to find their essence and conveying that truthfully. I enjoy all that breaking down and working out the character, but I'm seeking the particular things about someone.

Is it the challenge itself that is the particular thing about doing it?

Yes. I like performing live in theatre because of the electricity, the fact that nobody can shout, 'Cut, start again.' I enjoy the mistakes more than anything else, corpsing, things going wrong and getting out of it. I love that aspect of it. With film, I love the skill of being able to act on screen, somebody to say 'Cut, do that again', and doing it forty times trying to get the truth. You've got to be your own judge and jury really on camera, as well as trusting the director, which is very difficult. Sometimes they would do a cut that you didn't particularly like, but you have to do it. It's like music – if you sing a bum note on a record it is there forever; if you sing it live on stage, people forget it if you do something very nice after it – that is the difference between those two things.

So is that part of the challenge, being able to move from one medium to another?

Yes, totally. I'd like to concentrate on film at the present moment, because I'm just learning. I've done theatre for the last seven years and only a couple of television things. I'd like to explore the film medium and master it in some way, if you ever do.

Secrets and Lies[1] *was your first film, working with Mike Leigh. What struck you particularly about this director?*

I had worked with him before on stage in a play called *It's a Great Big Shame*.[2] It was his first play in fifteen years. I already knew his method of working and it was very easy to do it on film. It was made very simple because one didn't have to accommodate the camera ever – the camera always accommodated you. It was harder doing something like *Mr Jealousy*,[3] which was conventional film-making with a script and having to be in shot, which was a totally different experience. Leigh's way of working is brilliant in that the actor is really looked after in that way, being given the responsibility and opportunity to create a character from scratch without the boundaries that you usually have. You usually create characters when you are doing scripted things, but without any of these boundaries you are able to just dive into this person that you have programmed to behave, act and react in a particular way. So that in itself was a liberating experience for somebody to have. However, sometimes it was very hard and you didn't necessarily agree with what was happening with your character.

You mean in the sense of Leigh making the directorial decisions about what the character would do and what you instinctively felt like doing?

Yes, but you would have it out with him and say, 'I just don't think that character would do that because …' and if you had enough evidence to back it up you would get your way, basically.

Did the character of Hortense in Secrets and Lies *originate from a list of people you knew and develop from that starting point?*

Yes. What happens, which is really interesting, is that you will pick a person, basing her on two or three people, and because you've given them a whole different background, you take them and put them in a different score. You give them different parents, so that the character becomes a totally different person. However, she still has the essence of the person that is the source character you started with. Nobody else works like that.

What has it given you in terms of building your experience for dealing with the next piece of work?

It's very difficult because it is a unique way of working and it's very separate from anything else. I left doing that film to do a restoration drama, which was a big mistake for me. I shouldn't have done it. I should have had more time off and got over the experience. We worked for nine months and I was extremely tired by the time we finished. I went from one world where everything you did mattered to another world where it wasn't important who was standing where or who had what on, because it was already designed before we even walked into the rehearsal room. People had been given their parts and knew what they were going to say. It was a nightmare.

Was this The Way of the World[4] *here at the Royal National Theatre?*

Yes, I didn't know what had hit me. I was asleep for the first three weeks of rehearsal. Then I woke up and thought 'shit'. But once we started performing I was fine, because I was on stage and able to take control of the character and work with it. It really is a different discipline and you just change your head like Wurzel Gummidge. You put on your theatre head, put on your film head, put on your Mike Leigh head ... I think there is a lot to be said for that way of working, but I think there is a lot to be said about it because of the type of people that are used in it as well.

Actors who are keen observers of people and can relate to the subject of the film?

Yes, to a certain extent. I have seen people do things very unlike themselves, because they are such keen observers, and they are very perceptive about things, which they do well.

What was the hardest thing for you in terms of performing Hortense in Secrets and Lies?

The character was very self-contained.

Reminding me of the way that you described yourself at school.

She was – very independent. She is just calm and compassionate, with a lot of dignity. It was very hard to play this solid real character while everyone else around you is emoting all over the place and speaking in voices that are quite quirky. It was very difficult trying to do that and not telling them all to piss off, which is what I'd do! She was very different from me, sadly!

You wouldn't be so calm in that situation?

I wouldn't, I would have told them all to go to hell! I'd like to have the compassion and understanding that she had, but that barbecue scene was horrendous!

Do you have a need to perform?

Sometimes I have a need, other times I don't.

What would that need be exactly?

Just to get into another character, to explore a story and to see it come to life. Being part of that.

Do you enjoy the research aspects of the work?

Yes, I love that. The rehearsals I'm not too fond of, but it depends on what they are. I enjoyed rehearsing for *Mr Jealousy,* the film I did in New York, because there was a lot of improvisation. You do your research and then you go in and mess around with that information and use it. I enjoyed that, but sometimes rehearsing can be really tedious, depending on the director and the piece.

Do you think that you need specific skills to perform comedy?

I think some people are more talented than others. Some are very funny, but they can't act. They don't know anything about character, and just go in for laughs or pulling faces, as opposed to it being rooted in any kind of reality. Somebody like Brenda Blethyn is a brilliant actor and is also very funny. It's because of the truth element that she goes for, as opposed to using tricks in order to achieve what she is doing. Brenda takes her work very seriously (she's very professional), giving 100 per cent all the time. It was brilliant to work with somebody like that; it makes your job easier. I don't find comedy very difficult. The only thing I find difficult is not to laugh when I'm doing it, but I can imagine it to be difficult.

What makes the act of performing so satisfying?

Trying to get it right, the pursuit of excellence. That's satisfying, and enjoying it.

How often do you get it right?

God knows, but just keep chasing the dragon because if you did get it right, you wouldn't do it! It wouldn't be as appealing or satisfying. Just the joy you and others get from it. There must be nothing better for a stand-up comedian than a room full of people just belly laughing and then calming down and going again. Like Lily Savage, for example. I was going to say her as a woman comedian, but she is a man! They dominate everything, don't they, the bastards!

Has the image of the actress as 'strumpet' changed in any particular ways?

Actors take themselves terribly seriously now, and they no longer want to be glamorous or on every magazine cover. It's not about showing off and posturing but about serious work, so I think it's changed in that way. The [girl bands] are the slags now – they are the strumpets – and some of the super-models. So it has changed. But those good old strumpets were hard-working actresses, who just did a bit of prostitution on the side, but some of them weren't even prostitutes. They were told they were because they went on stage and enjoyed that! Good for them. Women need to get their sexuality back in the 1990s. It's almost become distorted in some way. It's like we have to reclaim that back again.

Is there a more positive sense of representation of women in the roles offered, or in new writing, which addresses these concerns of women in performance?

I live in hope really. A lot of the stuff that I've read is male dominated: the woman is there to be shagged, to be somebody's girlfriend, wife or lover, and there is no real substance or ability to control things and save her own life. Victims. It's quite frustrating. There is a need for writers to get down and do some good stuff for women.

Can you identify any key moments in your life as a performing woman in the widest sense?

Singing at Ronnie Scott's was a really big thing for me. I love jazz. I work in the jazz world, and to perform there at the age of twenty was 'wow' … Obviously, the Oscars was another. I think it was when I was completely dressed and ready to go, that was the moment. There is another moment when I was doing the Mike Leigh play in Stratford, where I started to laugh and I couldn't stop. That was a wonderful moment. I remember another moment when I was doing a play here at the National. The performance that night was terrible and I came off stage in a really bad mood, thinking, 'I hate this place, I hate this play, I hate this role, and this stupid wig doesn't fit properly.' I was being indulgently negative, which I hate, because it's really not that important. When I got to the stage door, Alan Rickman was in the foyer and he came over and said, 'Sorry to trouble you, I just wanted to say that I thought you were brilliant, that was so good'. I was amazed. Sometimes it's got to be about that, and not about you being precious about your performance to the extent where you're going back to your dressing room and being miserable about it. You've got to remember that you've got responsibilities to the people who pay to come and see you.

You're currently writing, and recently co-composed the musical score for Mike Leigh's new film Career Girls *with Tony Remy. What is your most significant achievement in the performance arena?*

That's hard. I think writing that musical score and performing *Secrets and Lies.*

Multi-talented achievements. Is that why you felt so strongly about being rejected by this country and not being sent to Cannes as one of the young British hopefuls and proof of British talent?[5]

Yes, regardless of the music or writing, the acting credentials speak for themselves. For that to be ignored, I found quite out of order. My whole point was the fact that there were no black or Asian actors there at all, not just that I wasn't there. To have two other actresses nominated for Oscars – 'Best Supporting Actress' and 'Best Actress' – to have them there and not me, I just thought was obvious.

All those who got nominations should have been invited, regardless of colour.

Exactly. There was only one Oscar-nominated actor who wasn't there, and that was me.[6] If you can't celebrate the Oscar nomination, then it goes to show that there are problems here, and that we are not looking at things in the right way. In a way I'm glad it did happen, because it just opened up a whole debate and the whole question of it in British film. We are so used to seeing women with long frocks or riding horses, representing a view of England – this quaint place with lovely buildings and loads of history. You don't see what's happening now. It has got to stop.

Notes

1 Hortense in *Secrets and Lies*, directed by Mike Leigh, co-starring Brenda Blethyn and Timothy Spall, 1996.
2 Faith in *It's a Great Big Shame*, directed by Mike Leigh, Theatre Royal, Stratford East, 1993.
3 Lucretia in *Mr Jealousy*, directed by Noah Baumbach, Mr Jealousy Productions, 1997.
4 Foible in Congreve's *The Way of the World*, directed by Phyllida Lloyd, Royal National Theatre, 1995.
5 British Screen organised a group of young British actors to visit Cannes to celebrate the 50th anniversary of the film festival.
6 Jean-Baptiste was nominated for an Oscar at the 1997 Academy Awards as 'Best Supporting Actress' for her performance of Hortense in *Secrets and Lies*. She also received the same nomination at the Golden Globe Awards and the BAFTA Awards in 1997.

Heather Ackroyd

In *Desert Grass*, Joshua Tree National Park,
California, 1991

'I haven't had the chance to be utterly dark, mad,
wicked or stupid, and performing provides that arena.'

Performance Context

Born: 1959, Huddersfield, Yorkshire.

Prior/current commitments: Exhibitions/Installations in collaboration with Dan Harvey – *Sci-Art*, Wellcome Trust, collaboration with scientists from Institute of Grasslands and Environmental Research (IGER).

Post-interview (selected): Exhibitions/Installations in collaboration with Dan Harvey – *Mother and Child*, Out of Sight, Santa Barbara Museum of Art, California.
Floating Field, Akerby Sculpture Park, Sweden.
Slate Circle Line, Hanley Cultural Quarter, with Levitt Bernstein Architects.
Photosynthesis, The Icehouse, Hull, Photo 98 and HTBA.

Other: 1998 – RSA Award Art for Architecture in collaboration with Dan Harvey and Llewelyn Davis Architects for the Edward Penn Abraham building, William Dunn School of Pathology, Oxford University.

Interview

I wondered at Heather Ackroyd's abilities and desire to be both actress, for example, as Kristina in the RSC's production of Strindberg's Easter, *and performance artist, drawn to the world of sculptural installation and visual art exhibitions with Dan Harvey. I interviewed Heather at the University of Kent in Canterbury on 18 March 1997.*

Alison Oddey: *How would you describe yourself?*

Heather Ackroyd: I would say as both artist and performer, although to a certain extent it is dependent on the situation. When Dan[1] and I are involved in doing the exhibition work, then we are discussing our work in terms of being installation artists, or visual artists or sculptors. When I work with other companies or other people, then I regard myself more as a performer than an actress, because the majority of my work has stemmed from the collaborative process of devising, rather than working with existing scripts, plays and characters.

Having said that, you acted at the Barbican for the Royal Shakespeare Company in Strindberg's play Easter, *which hadn't been performed for about eight years, directed by Katie Mitchell in 1995.[2]*

I really wanted to work with Katie, because I like the precision of her work. She had seen earlier work of Impact Theatre,[3] as well as *The Desire Paths* with Graeme Miller.[4] I was delighted when she asked me to work on the play, and the timing of it was very good. We didn't have anything in place for four or five months. It was a short contract, which for the RSC was quite unusual. I felt real affinity with what Katie was doing with Strindberg's writing, and I found myself coupled with Adrian Rawlins, who I was at college with, and with whom I set up the very first theatre company.[5] It was a strange twist of time or fate, which was shocking at first but very liberating.

Was this at Crewe and Alsager college?

Yes, that's where I studied a degree in combined arts, where I particularly pursued sculpture, the visual arts and performance; but very early on my passion and interest was in devised work. I liked the chemistry of collaboration, that imaginative forum, and even at college we were starting to present work in non-theatre situations. I could have taken certain opportunities, looked for representation with an agent, gone for television and theatre, but it never sat easily with me. It's always been a kind of tension. I've never regarded myself as an actress, who would work with a script and interpret character. I'm much more interested in something that exists in a tangible form within a pool of collaborators.

That is evident in your work with people like Graeme Miller, The People Show, Lumiere and Son, and other companies.

Yes, working with a company, with a director, who has conceived the ideas and who has a strong pre-conception about where the work goes. You *are* involved in an interpretation, but at the same time the unifying factor has always been improvising to find material. It's actually about trying to find something that is essential and has a very strong connection to the performers that you are working with and to the world that you are establishing, but equally it is inevitably rooted within your experiences. It's to do with finding and exploring, and I like the freedom of that. It's just like a process of sculpting, of making, actively bringing something from an embryonic stage through a metamorphosis to a piece that people see. I don't think it's ever finished. I could never say that I have done a finished piece of devised theatre. There are always things which are inevitably changing and permutating.

Are you from a theatrical family?

No, not at all, although my parents were in an amateur dramatics society for a short while. My parents have always been into growing and gardening as were my grandparents.

Aged ten

What attracted you to the notion of performing, to the theatre, and to being creative?

Theatre was always a strong fantasy world, and adventure. I was always off in the woods exploring, fascinated by derelict houses, but I can never remember saying that I really wanted to be an actress. I had a secure, steady upbringing with my parents, but there was something in me, which made me want to get out and explore. I remember having a yearning to leave the familial nest as soon as I came of age, and having a huge need to go and travel.

Being an itinerant appears to come easily to you, making installations abroad, such as The Divide,[6] *which had a budget of about £75,000.*

Part of the reason that Dan and I have worked abroad a lot is because the offers of work have been there, and we both take to travelling very well. I really enjoy getting completely away, being in a different environment, because you don't have any domestic preoccupations and can focus 100 per cent on the work. In some ways, there is an even greater intensity to instal-lation work than putting together a performance piece. It's like an ongoing performance in a way, particularly if you're doing a piece on the street. You're completely open to the public eye, which I like, and it is one of the pleasures of doing public work.

That is evident in a lot of your growing pieces, for example, Grass House[7] *in Hull (1991), where people would walk by the house at different times of the day, seeing the house at varied stages of grass growing completion.*

When we first arrived there, it was completely overgrown and strewn with rubbish. We had to clear that out of the way just so people could see the front of the house, and so that we could get our scaffolding rigged up. People thought that we were re-rendering the house, doing some pebble dashing. At one point, when we had the first growth of grass, which is light green and quite patchy at first, this woman stopped and commented on it being a mildewed house. She came back a few days later and was so embar-rassed. She didn't realise what we were doing! She said, 'Now I realise that it's grass!'

What does performing give you?

I think that it has always been a very changing scenario: what I get from it now is very different to how it was. To be honest, performing used to really scare me. I can remember a number of performances, where I nearly threw up in the toilets, because I didn't think I could physically do it. A chronic shyness would come over me, and I thought that I must be perverse to be doing this. It was more than stage fright.

What did it feel like?

It felt like I was physically putting myself through something, and sometimes on stage, it felt like a living nightmare. I'm certainly not a 'natural' performer, whereas some people are. I've really had to work at it, it's been the ultimate challenge to do it, and yet, I've been driven to do it. At its worst, it has felt quite profound to be doing it, but the other side to that is reaching moments of physical electricity with a group of people on stage and the audience have it too. Nothing is easily gained through any of these processes; it's always a challenge, a confrontation and an exhibition of some kind or another. It has to involve some kind of revealing and transformation. It has to go some way beyond the self, touching something, which is more universal.

Is performing a kind of heightening of the self?

It's a channeller because you are putting yourself through a process, where you are squeezing something out, which is a performance with others. I think that you definitely get a heightened sense of awareness through that focusing of energy and commitment, and all the other things that go with performing.

Is there a need to perform?

The need to perform for me may be different from others, because it's not so constant in my life. I haven't performed for eighteen months, but at the same time, I know that I will have to in another eighteen months. I haven't had the chance to be utterly dark, mad, wicked or stupid, and performing provides that arena.

I'm reminded of your performance in Impact's The Carrier Frequency,[8] *which I saw in Leeds in 1984.*

The early performance work, particularly in the 1980s, was really physically demanding. There were lots of thrashes when I was working with Impact when we used to do physical damage to ourselves. There was a wanton darkness or madness, which was in response to the darkness and madness of the world. *The Carrier Frequency* was a very angry, disturbed piece of work. It was a difficult working process, and I struggled to understand the vocabulary of post-modern language. In some ways, the Impact work was anarchic, which was quite frightening but very addictive as well. It was very much generated by the chemistry of the company. People exist with multi-faceted abilities, being performers, writers, composers or directors, and it's quite hard to hold a group together, particularly as commitments change as life develops. If I wasn't having a child at the moment, I'm not quite sure where I would be going in terms of performance work.

Do you find that the identities of artist, performer and mother-to-be compete and conflict with each other?

The forthcoming motherhood remains to be seen, but I'm sure that there are going to be conflicts. One of the things that I loved about working with Katie Mitchell was the 100 per cent commitment. How do you have that with a baby? In some ways, I'm relieved that there are different strands to my work, for example Dan and I have been invited to work at the Exploratorium Science Museum in San Francisco, so it will be us and the baby. I have a feeling that the child is going to be there with us, wherever we are, and part of our process.

If not, we'll have to adapt our work and not be able to do such ambitious things.

So it will be a process of negotiating all that?

It has been a constant negotiation, negotiating the identity of being an artist and of being an actress. I find it completely acceptable that some people may know me as a performer and not as a visual artist, and the other way round. In terms of multiple identities, perhaps it's the ability to keep all the plates spinning.

Can you identify any key moments in your life as a performing woman in the widest possible sense?

One was when I worked on *Short Sighted*,[9] which was the third performance piece with Optik theatre after college. I remember that I had watched a documentary about the Masai people, and seeing this extraordinary jumping, leaping and physical abandon. I had been quite seized up over a number of things, but I remember going into rehearsal and we were improvising some stuff, and something just came out that was very inspired by that physical dynamism. Something gave, something opened up at that point and there was a release. That was a key moment. Another key moment was when as a child, aged three, I went missing. I was abducted. I was missing for eight hours. It was a key childhood experience. I remember nothing before that. I remember that so vividly because of the extraordinariness of the situation, but I survived it. I survived it, because at three and a half, your consciousness is quite different. It had a bearing on the rest of my upbringing. I was probably never the wild teenager I wanted to be. At eighteen, I wanted to go out and make different marks in the world. Performing has been a key to that – doing performance work, initiating ideas, taking on responsibilities of being a director and bringing a performance of my own imagining into being – *Uses of Enchantment*.[10] It was that experience which paved the way to take on the scale of work we've been doing. Meeting Dan was a very key moment, and I think the scale of the work we've done together has been a significant achievement.

Notes

1 Dan Harvey.
2 Kristina in Strindberg's *Easter*, directed by Katie Mitchell, RSC Barbican (The Pit), 1995.
3 Impact Theatre Co-operative and Russell Hoban, *The Carrier Frequency*, Institute of Contemporary Arts (ICA), London, 1984.
4 *The Desire Paths*, directed by Graeme Miller, devised with Heather Ackroyd, Emma Bernard, Tyrone Huggins, Liz Kettle, Michael Sherin. Warwick Arts Centre, 1993.

5   Optik Theatre, company members Heather Ackroyd, Adrian Rawlins, Paul Bown, Barry Edwards, Clive Bell (music), Margery Edwards (voice). Crewe and Alsager College, and UK touring 1980–83.

6   *The Divide*, collaboration with Dan Harvey, New Zealand International Festival of Arts, 1996. A large-scale site-specific piece involving carving a huge slice through the condemned Circa Theatre, in the centre of Wellington.

7   *Grass House*, Heather Ackroyd and Dan Harvey, music by Graeme Miller, commissioned by Hull Time Based Arts (HTBA), 1991. 'The idea was to take a derelict house in its simplest form and bring it back to life' (Harvey). The façade of a Victorian house is clad with seed and clay; with the passage of time, light and growth, the area is soon a verdant expanse of grass and life. Grass curtains were grown to complement the domestic setting and two living sculptures (cast from the body) were positioned in ground floor windows. Public viewing through the ground floor windows into the two rooms.

8   *The Carrier Frequency*, Leeds, 1984. Text by Russell Hoban. Music by Graeme Miller and Steve Shill. Company: Heather Ackroyd, Pete Brookes, Richard Hawley, Nicky Johnson, Claire MacDonald, Graeme Miller, Steve Shill.

9   *Short Sighted*, Optik Theatre Company, 1983.

10   *Uses of Enchantment*, directed and designed by Heather Ackroyd, The Place Theatre, 1988, and the ICA in 1989. Devised with Emma Bernard, David Coulter, Graeme Miller, Cindy Oswin, Jan Pearson and Richard Strange.

Jo Brand

'I like making people laugh ...'

'A lot of people assume that I am the person that they
see on the stage – that I go around breaking men's
bollocks and hating men, but I'm not like that at all.'

Performance Context

Born: 1957, London.

Prior/current commitments: National Tour.

Post-interview (selected): *Through the Cakehole*, produced by Channel X for Channel 4 Television.

Like it or Lump it, Vera Productions.

Jo Brand Burns Rubber, a one-off documentary about the RAC Rally, Vera Productions, Channel 4 Television.

Other: Nominated for the Perrier Award at the Edinburgh Fringe Festival in 1992; won the Time Out Award for 'Best Stand Up' in 1990 and the Comedy Awards for the 'Best Club Act' in 1994 and 'Best Stand Up' in 1995.

Books: *A Load of Old Balls – Men in History*, Simon & Schuster, 1995; *A Load of Old Ball Crunchers – Women in History*, Simon & Schuster, 1996.

Interview

Jo Brand's blunt sense of humour and thought-provoking hilarity was apparent both in her London home on 29 October 1996 and in a second interview on 20 March 1997 at the University of Kent, where, dressed in black and wearing sunglasses, she arrived hung over from the night before.

Alison Oddey: *How long have you been performing stand-up?*

Jo Brand: About ten years now.

Does being a woman stand-up require any kind of training at all?

No, I think it's a bad idea to have training. I think being able to do stand-up is a very natural thing, helped along by age or experience. With me, I didn't start until I was nearly thirty. I'd been a senior Sister for a couple of years, which meant that I was used to having a bit of authority really. I think that made all the difference. I was also fairly used to speaking in public.

Is this as a psychiatric nurse?

Yes. Having been to workshops for stand-up comics, I personally don't think they're a good idea. I think they tend to bland everyone out a bit by making stand-ups uniform in the way that they approach the job. All the best stand-ups I've seen have developed on their own.

Presumably, training is useful in terms of microphone technique.

Exactly. I didn't do anything like that, and I did some terrible fuck-ups when I started, such as not being able to get the microphone off the stand or pulling it apart. So that very practical stuff would help because it makes you feel more confident.

Do you still get anxious before a gig?

Yes. When I first started I was nervous about a week before, and now I've got it down to about an hour really. I went to see Victoria Wood last night, and we're both doing this benefit together in a couple of weeks time at the London Lighthouse. They've invited ninety people for some food and they want us to mingle with them an hour before the show, and they just don't understand that you can't think about anything except going on. You can't really talk to people, you can stand there and nod like a moron, but it's a real effort to concentrate on anything else an hour or so before you go on.

What made you decide to leave psychiatric nursing in the end?

Well, I did them both for a couple of years. I think the final push was being offered *Friday Night Live*.[1] Working in a psychiatric emergency clinic, I felt that I'd be in an awkward position if people, arriving in some sort of crisis, saw me on television doing my quite rude stand-up. So many people's delusions centre around the television, that I thought it would be totally weird. That was the stopping point. I left so that I would not have to come back after *Friday Night Live*.

When you are performing, what kind of audience are you looking at?

Well, very varied really. The age range is very wide. Mothers will bring their fourteen-year-old sons and daughters, but quite old couples in their sixties will also come too. The majority of them are in their thirties, and it's either groups of women or couples. Not many groups of lads, thank God.

Why do you say that?

Because I don't like lads in any shape or form. I think once you get more than three blokes together – if they're those sort of blokes – it introduces a sort of animal element into the proceedings whereby they're competing with each other to behave badly and showing off.

When you look at them, do you see a sexed audience?

In terms of being able to distinguish between them? No, not at all, it just seems like a big lump of people. Durkheim said that the sum of society is more than its individual parts, and audiences are as well. They almost have a character to them, so you can find out in the first two minutes what their character is – either a grumpy, tired or a drunk person – and you approach them in that way really.

So what motivates you to keep performing stand-up?

Well I'm a fairly sort of pragmatic, down to earth person and I'm motivated by mainly a protestant work ethic on the one hand, but also a desire to continue doing this job because I like it. I like making people laugh, but I don't really think about it in any more concrete terms than that. I don't think about the future and I don't have a career plan. I just wait for things to come along and if I like the sound of them I do them.

Have you always liked making people laugh?

Yes, I have. I've always liked laughing myself as well. I think the world is a very grim place and I think being able to laugh, even at the most horrible aspects of it, lightens things a bit really.

When you were a child, growing up in Kent, did you play the comic person in your family, or at school?

No, not really. Everyone in my family was quite comical. My mum's got a great sense of humour.

Is there a family theatrical background?

Not in the slightest. My great-grandfather was a sort of music hall performer. He was a singer, but I don't know very much about him. That's quite a long way back, isn't it? I don't remember him.

How would you describe yourself?

I would say that I was easy-going, sympathetic to people, slightly depressive, angry about certain things and friendly.

Aged six

Is performing a way of expressing your anger?

Very much so. I think that it's a very definite outlet for saying that there are lots of things that piss me off, and I know that piss other women off. Women are not taught to be articulate in that way. I'm aware of the enormous amount of misogyny there is about, which is not just directed at me, but at every woman. I'm angry that a lot of women choose to ignore the fact that it exists or to minimise it. A lot of people assume that I am the person that they see on the stage – that I go around breaking men's bollocks and hating men, but I'm not like that at all. I think it's a bit naïve of people to assume that you are that person that they see there, which in a lot of ways is very superficial. It is an element of myself, which doesn't come out very often in real life, because I like getting on with people and am naturally conciliatory in my life. I tend to keep my trap shut much more.

Watching you in performance, you seem to be quite hard on yourself sometimes, and the anger almost turns on yourself in a way.

Absolutely, I think that's the sort of person I am though. I always use that sort of humour – self-deprecating humour – even before I went into comedy. That was tied in with thinking that I might as well get it all out, say it before someone else says it and say it worse than someone else would say it, so that gets it all out of the way. What point is there in someone abusing you when you have already abused yourself? If someone heckles me with, 'Fuck off you fat cow', I just say, 'I think we've covered that already, have you not been listening?' I just find that a good way of dealing with it really. If we all stopped being so obsessed with people's appearances, feeling that we had to judge them and comment on them, that would suit me. I'm not looking for Dawn French-type glamour shots in silk because I'm not into that whole side of things. I've never regretted looking the way I do and I've never wanted to be beautiful. I think it's a burden really rather than anything else. So I would be quite happy if people respected each other a bit more on all levels: appearances, colour, gender, disabilities and illness.

Does being a fat woman contribute to why you appeal to some audiences?

I think there is more to it than that because if there wasn't I would just get fat women coming to see me. Lovely as that would be, it's not like that! A lot of men come to see me. For the vast majority of people that do come, it's not about man-hating or fat, but to do with things about unfairness, hypocrisy, lack of respect and ignorance. If I did really hate men, my life would be a nightmare and it's not, because I don't. There is this constant argument that I am a female Bernard Manning and that if men said things that I say about women, they'd get in a lot of trouble, but that's such a spurious argument because of the sort of social constructions in our society. It's to do with one group that is powerless being dominated by a group that has a lot of power. That's why I personally think it's alright for me to abuse men, but it's not alright for them to abuse me and other women because of the power gap between us. If I do jokes about the way to a man's heart is through his hanky pocket with a bread knife, I am doing that from a standpoint of fantasy, because it's not an accepted norm that women do that. Whereas if a man does jokes about beating up his wife, that's unacceptable to me because that happens. It's a very common phenomenon so you can't really do jokes about things like that. I see it as a rather more complex argument than just I'm wrong because I'm slagging off blokes.

So your political ideology motivates you to stand up and perform?

Yes, but having said that, it's very important that you never forget that your job's actually making people laugh. I think it's quite easy to be swayed into just preaching or trying to push a particular political viewpoint, which simply won't work if it's not funny. So if I write a joke and it's funny, but it's not got what I really want to say in it, I'll still do it because it's a funny joke and it gets a laugh. I don't write stuff that fits in perfectly to my kind of political ideology because I think that's wrong if you are a comic. If you've got particular political arguments you want to push, you should be a politician, not a comedian. If the two work in conjunction, fine, but it's important to be funny really.

Is it easy to locate the roots of your desire to perform?

No, I don't think so. It wasn't a desire to perform really, it was a desire to make people laugh. I never wanted to be an actress or a singer, or anything like that. It probably came early on when I watched comedy on television, watching people like Beryl Reid, Joyce Grenfell or Morecambe and Wise. It just seemed to me to be a great thing to do, but in a very kind of airy-fairy way, not in any sort of sense that I thought about it very hard. It's also got something to do with the fact that I was a bit frustrated that in social situations women don't get listened to, because there is more attention focused on men.

How much of your performance work reflects the self?

It's only an element of what you're all about. There's a bit of me that really likes shocking people. If I have a choice between the very horrible joke and the not so horrible, I'll always go for the very horrible one just because I enjoy that really. I like swearing as well. I'm always getting letters from people who are small-town Tories, who would walk over a dead beggar in the street, but would worry about having the wrong tablecloth on for guests. I really hate that sort of attitude, so anything I can do to get up their noses I try and do.

So that's a conscious plan?

Yes. There's an element of consciousness about it.

Have you always liked shocking people?

Yes, from when I was about twelve probably. I had a very happy childhood and then a fairly horrendous adolescence. I had a very bad relationship with my dad when I was an adolescent, winding him up tremendously, because he was so pompous and a bit like the people that I've been describing – placing the emphasis on all the wrong things. I quite enjoyed behaving very badly. I think the sort of comedy came out of the second bit really.

How do your parents feel when they watch you perform?

Well, my mum has a really good laugh, because my mum's quite like me. She's a psychiatric social worker, so she's no stranger to the horrible side of life. Whereas my dad is a bit old-fashioned. He doesn't like it. He doesn't like women swearing or women talking about periods and vaginas publicly. So there's a big gap between them, which is obviously why they separated twenty-five years ago. My mum was at one with my father until I was about ten, and then they started to grow apart. She changed a lot, and became what she really wanted to be, which she wasn't when I was that young. It was very valuable having her learn those lessons before I did in a way, because it gave me a leg up so that I bypassed all the crap that she had to go through.

Is performing stand-up a way of escaping the self, as well as enabling the construction of self?

I'm not sure that I really think of it as an escape. Knowing a lot of comedy performers, I think it's a bit of an outlet for emotional disturbance. I think most performers are emotionally disturbed in one way or another – some a lot more seriously than others, but I don't think you'd get round to performing if you weren't. There's something about it that pushes certain sorts of people into it. If you talk to other comics you find that they have very similar emotional crises and backgrounds. It's a push from the inside of you that makes you almost want to tell people about what a shit time you've had.

Do you envisage a time in your performing career when you'll be able to stop telling people what a rotten time you've had?

I don't think anyone gets rid of it unless they have analysis for fifteen years, but even then it's pretty risky. Comedy is ageless, so there's no reason why you can't go on forever.

Are there particular women you admire or respect both in and out of the world of women stand-ups?

Well I tend to admire women who have strong opinions and don't appear to give a toss about what anyone thinks of them. I like women like Clare Short, Glenys Kinnock, or Janet Street-Porter, who somehow don't seem to fit into the expected image that most of us still have of how women should behave really. I think Jenny Eclair is great. She sort of explodes onto the stage and just lets out this huge roar at people. People can't quite take it in. I like to watch audiences when Jenny is on because they almost don't want to let themselves laugh at it. They can stand back from it, and see that it's very rude, very over the top, and it's hitting them straight between the eyes. That's what I like about Jenny – the way that she goes for it big time and doesn't seem to hold back at all. I'm very fond of French and Saunders, as well as Victoria Wood for different reasons. I admire Victoria Wood because I think she crafts her stuff very carefully. She's sort of interested in language and I think you can see that by the way that she does her stuff. We're very different obviously, because she's sort of settled on the minutiae of everyday life of middle England, which I do nothing about at all. French and Saunders are kind of natural sort of slapstick women performers really. It's much more visual with them, and it's the relationship between the two of them. I think they're great.

You've been described as a jobbing comic within the league of French and Saunders and Victoria Wood. Where would you place yourself?

Victoria Wood and French and Saunders are slightly more starry in the sense that they've been around longer, they're more established, they don't really mix with the proles any more, they don't do small gigs. They have great big expensive houses and they're more glamorous really, I suppose. Whereas with me, I still do small clubs and I'm not particularly interested in show-biz parties or any of that old crap. They do adverts; they're in a different league altogether I would say from me. They're mainstream, they're on BBC1 and I never have been. I wouldn't really want to either because you can't say fuck, wank and bollocks on BBC1.

It's a short list: Victoria Wood, French and Saunders, Jo Brand, Donna McPhail, Hattie Hayridge and one or two others. That seems quite alarming to me in a way.

Well it does to me as well. One would have thought that by now the number would have grown considerably, but it's stayed pretty much the same. I think there are a lot of elements to that. I still think that the male domination element of it bears down on a lot of women and discourages them from even trying it, but I also think that women are a lot more sensitive than men. They suffer the knocks of the job a lot more badly, so they give up much more easily. If the woman has a bad gig she thinks it's her fault, whereas the man has a bad gig and thinks it's the audience's fault. I think that's how it works generally.

If I think of the equivalent male stand-up league, including Jack Dee, Lee Evans and Harry Hill, then it strikes me how much less the men use personal material and how much more surreal the content appears.

Yes. Well I think that's men and women all over. I think women are very talented at knowing what they need and expressing their emotions, whereas men are absolutely hopeless at it. So, therefore, that's reflected in the way that they do comedy. It's almost a direct line from the male behaviour and personality onto the stage really. I think just because there are more male comics you do get more variety of comedy, but none of it is particularly emotionally expressive. It tends to be played sort of far away from the person really.

Can you imagine a new wave of women stand-ups in the twenty-first century, who have developed a kind of distanced, deadpan, slightly impersonal style?

No. I can't imagine that ever happening until women truly have equality with men, and that's not going to happen in the next hundred years. I don't think it will ever happen.

Having said that, you'd still want to encourage younger women stand-ups in the future.

Absolutely, definitely. What I'd encourage them most about is to stick at it. We all have to change ourselves a bit for the stage. There are times when I'd like to do five minutes on quantum mechanics theory, but I'm very aware of audience expectations, so I keep it a lot simpler than that sometimes. I do find that frustrating, but it's part of the job. You can't make your name on a certain ticket and then decide that you want to be a poet. That will really wind people up, so you stick to what people like you for. That's the rule, I think. I would say to any woman who was starting out to just try and keep it fairly simple for starters, and to expect that the first fifty of those are going to be fairly appalling. Not have two bad ones and then give up. People say things about comedy, such as, 'I don't know how you can do it' or 'It's the most scary thing in the world.' That's rubbish. The scariest thing in the world is getting killed, being in a nuclear war, getting punched, or getting raped. All that's bound to happen is that you get humiliated and that's been happening to women for so long, it's only more of the same that you get off a building site. I mean what's the big deal about men being horrible to you? I don't get it really, I just think, 'So what?' It's strange.

I suppose it could seem like a long time to stand there on your own.

Yes, but you don't do that at the beginning. You never get the chance to do that until you're fairly experienced, in which case you should be able to handle it by then. You're doing five or ten minutes at the beginning, and that's just about right really. I think it's sad when someone is really talented but they can't see it, and they don't use it to bolster their self-esteem.

Has feminism helped the role of the female stand-up comic in any way?

I think it has, in the sense that at least some women have gone into it and had a go at it. For a while, on the cabaret circuit in the 1980s, audiences were far more open to the idea of women performers. However, since comedy has become more populist and people from every class have come in to see it, it has regressed a bit to women being assessed purely on their appearance. I think it has gone backwards in that way.

Is there a particular problem for the female stand-up entering the twenty-first century?

Yes – having the confidence to move into more general areas of comedy rather than sticking to exclusively female concerns. Confidence to do politics, to do engineering or whatever. It's very difficult to do anything at the moment to be honest, because I think as far as attitudes towards women are concerned, we are in a bit of a two steps forward, one step backward situation. I think that's going to last for ages – hundreds of years. I think it's a question of not becoming so bland that you're not saying anything. I would like to think that in comedy, particularly with women, there are enough women around who don't just drop aspects of things that they feel strongly about for the sake of getting their own careers a bit further. I think that's what has happened with a lot of men, and what will happen with a lot of women as well. I think that the problem for what you would call alternative comedy is commercialism. People are so quick to sell their souls, and that's what I would really like to tackle.

Does being an itinerant come easily to you?

Yes. I've never really wanted to be in one place for very long and I'm quite happy living out of a bag; in fact, I prefer it. I love staying away and wandering about. When I trained as a nurse, we had to move every six months, which lasted for four years. A lot of people didn't like that, but I loved it. I loved the fact that I didn't have to get loads of stuff out of boxes. I'd just leave it because I knew that I'd be moving again in a few months. I have this picture in my head that I'm settled somewhere, but it's not really me. I like to keep moving on.

Why is that?

I don't know really. I left home when I was sixteen, and I've always moved about a lot. I just got into the habit of doing it. I suppose that I had a cynical view of settled happy relationships because of my parents splitting up in my early teens, so it's tied in with that I think. It's strange, because I don't actually like travelling abroad a lot. I like travelling around England, but if I go on holiday I just want to come home!

What does home represent?

Home is people really. It's also feeling comfortable in a particular environment, as well as getting back to people who know what you are really like, as opposed to people who have only seen your exaggerated persona on stage. It's being able to relax.

Can you identify any key moments as a performing woman in the widest possible sense?

Well it's positive and negative. I can remember getting really slagged off in Edinburgh for the first time, which was like being kicked in the stomach. It was a very weird feeling and I didn't respond very appropriately, because I went to sort out the bloke and had a go at him. I thought it was very unfair and that there was some hidden agenda, because he was a friend of someone that I knew did not like me. What he'd written didn't correspond with what happened the night he was reviewing it. Basically it was a great night, but he said it was shit. What was important to me was the fact that what he said did not reflect how the evening had gone. My favourite moment is when I was sitting in a cafe off St Martin's Lane with a friend of mine, just having a coffee before we went to the theatre. A woman, who must have been late seventies, if not early eighties, came up to me and said, 'Jo Brand?' I said, 'Yes.' She said, 'You've changed my life' and just walked off. I just thought that was fucking amazing, someone of that age to come and say that. I loved that.

What do you see as your most significant achievement?

I suppose doing my first hour-long show, because you piss about for years doing twenty minutes and there is this feeling around that the true test of a truly talented comic is that they can hold an audience for an hour. Also, I feel it's a very significant achievement because I'm very lazy. Just going up to Edinburgh and doing an hour made me think that I'd really cracked it, and I got nominated for a Perrier award that year as well.[2] Steve Coogan won it. Six months later I had loads of people saying well done on winning the Perrier award and I'd just say, 'Thanks a lot!' I couldn't be bothered to tell them that I hadn't.

Notes

1 *Friday Night Live*, London Weekend Television, February and July 1988.
2 Nominated for the Perrier Award at the Edinburgh Festival in 1992.

Imelda Staunton

'I don't know what sort of actor I am, but I do know that
while I'm doing a scene, I'm playing the audience.'

'I think this job allows one to extend one's childhood,
dressing up, being told you are good, that's what we all
want in the end.'

Performance Context

Born: 1956, London.

Prior/current commitments: Adelaide in *Guys and Dolls*, Royal National Theatre.

Post-interview (selected): Stella in *Is it Legal?*, written by Simon Nye, Hatswood Films for Channel 4 Television.
The Nurse in the film *Shakespeare in Love*, Miramax Films.

Other: Olivier Awards 1985 – 'Best Supporting Actress' as Bessie in *The Corn is Green*, Old Vic. Olivier Awards 1991 – 'Best Actress in a Musical' as Baker's Wife in *Into the Woods*, Phoenix Theatre.

Interview

At the Royal National Theatre on 18 July 1997, I sat on Imelda Staunton's dressing-room sofa, and enjoyed her sense of fun and ability to make me laugh. Imelda is highly skilled at her craft, and her stunning performance of Adelaide in Guys and Dolls *is testimony to that.*

Alison Oddey: *You're currently playing Adelaide in* Guys and Dolls *at the Royal National Theatre,[1] and having recently seen the show, it's absolutely evident that you adore performing the role.*

Imelda Staunton: I've seldom felt as comfortable playing a part as I have done with this, but then I think that this is my third time in fifteen years playing this role, so I should feel comfortable or get out of it! What makes it so comfortable is my history with the show. I know it so well and every bit of the show is just like being at home. Also, to be able to give the amount of pleasure and enjoyment that the show gives to people is an extraordinary gift. I've done it three times, and I think that's enough now!

So is this the most satisfying role you've ever played?

It's becoming more that way. I did Sonya in *Uncle Vanya*,[2] which was satisfying and horrible at the same time. This isn't horrible; this is satisfying. I'm having a lovely time and I have no emotional luggage to take home with me. With Chekhov you are much more drained and depressed, and that is something

I wouldn't want to take on board at the moment. This gives me enormous energy. Physically it is tiring, but when the overture starts, you are just up within two minutes. It's a magical piece of theatre and I think this particular production is pure magic. It would break my heart to see this show done badly because it's just too good a piece, faultless in its structure, and therefore utterly satisfying to play. You never think, 'Oh God, it's this scene again.' The work was done in 1940 when they took it all over America before bringing it to New York. They did all the work so that we can just sit in the cream, which is very nice.

Can you describe when you are performing Adelaide, what it feels like?

Extremely powerful, and that's a very attractive sensation. I think I feel more powerful doing that than I do in my daily life. I've learnt that power, it's a technique and it seems to work best with good material. I don't know what sort of actor I am, but I do know that while I'm doing a scene, I'm playing the audience. I think something went wrong last night and I've been thinking this morning that I need to try and listen harder to how they're going to react, although you can't tell how they're going to react, and that's why you've got to be as quick as that. You think of a bit of timing, but of course there're about fifteen hundred people out there, who could change your timing. You're on the ball, but I'm always trying to plan it. I do really enjoy that feeling of absolutely having them there. That's why I get so frustrated if I feel them slipping away, and know it's absolutely my fault. It isn't always, but you feel it is, or I do, because you want to have that power over them – in the kindest possible way without being a member of the Gestapo; also people like to have power over them. An audience likes someone to go 'sit there and just let me move you around in your head'. I think an audience senses if somebody's a nervous performer, that is, someone who hasn't got the power yet. People want to have someone in power. As an actor, I think you can have the really delicious power.

You're not a control freak then?

No, not in my life. I like it in my work. I think I'm fairly controlled in my work. I think a lot of actors are freer than I am, and therefore sometimes I feel my one criticism about myself is that people say, 'I've never seen you give a bad performance.' I think only really brilliant actors give bad performances, because I feel a very safe performer. I envy people who can actually be a fantastic actor but really appalling in something, because I think they push their barriers and I don't ever do that. I think that would be a criticism I would have of myself.

Does performing make you feel safe? Is it a safe space for so many hours a night?

Totally, absolutely. I am trying to think of a theatre show where I haven't felt that comfortable. I am sure there is one, but not in recent years, because I think it's my duty to myself to make it safer than safe. You think safe is dull and I'm aware of that, and it does slightly worry me.

I don't think you are dull for one minute. The fact that you're thinking in response to last night's audience – how you might re-work that bit tonight – suggests risk rather than safety. That seems to me to be part of the appeal or attraction of what performing is about.

There are two schools of thought. It would be just as good to me to not even think about it because I can't alter it; the audience will dictate how that goes. So there are different ways to approach what you think may be a slight problem, and I think this piece is more difficult. It's written in such a rhythm, which is to do with the music. Vocally, it has such rhythm and comedy, that it is quite obvious how it should be played. I can change things slightly but I think I stay within my own limits. Partly because I never want to do anything that I don't feel completely truthful with, and partly because I never want to do anything for the sake of a change. Maybe in years to come I will start doing that, but I just feel honest in my work. I don't feel exciting, I feel honest.

How would you describe yourself?

That's hard because you see yourself as something very different. I always think that's a hard one because one is not the same person all the time. I'm aware that I perform for people and I can be very funny. I enjoy being funny. I enjoy people finding me funny, as well as an attractive person to be with. On the other side of that coin, as with all of us, is the person who is lacking in confidence and as paranoid as the next person. It's just which percentage is higher on each day. But I suppose I am fairly level inasmuch as one can be. I think this job allows one to extend one's childhood, dressing up, being told you are good, that's what we all want I think in the end.

So are the roots of your desire to perform located in childhood?

I have written evidence from when I was fourteen. School plays, drama after school, but how does that begin? My mother was a musician; she played the fiddle and Irish accordion. She and her brother performed in a band in Ireland, so there was a slight performing scenario there. We didn't have any books in the house, so I hadn't read fantastic stories, but I wanted to do that. I watched a lot of television, more than was allowed. We had a lot of big Irish parties, but I would be mortified if someone asked me to sing. So it wasn't like it was easy and I felt comfortable – I couldn't bear that at all. So it's interesting that I then wanted to perform! I suppose that's to do with performing in front of strangers, which is easier than standing in front of three friends and saying a poem. But I did do *Beggar's Opera* when I was fourteen. I started a diary then, thinking, 'I want to be an actress.' I wrote that I knew that Mum and Dad wouldn't want me to be, but I wanted to do what would make them happy. I thought they wanted me to be a teacher. My drama teacher said I should audition for drama schools, so I did, and I went to RADA.

Were you an only child?

Yes. My mum was twenty-one but she also worked all the time, so I went and stayed with a childminder. I also had my grandmother and aunts, who were very young. My grandmother was in her forties so I was involved in a young family, which is a very different life to the one my daughter, Bess, has now. There's much more one to one attention, and much more angst-ridden older parents worrying about everything instead of just having a kid and getting on with it. There's no such thing as a perfect parent. You can only be the person you are with your child – that is all you can do. I'm not the woman who gets up and bakes every morning and provides teas morning, noon and night – I can't do it! However, I can sing to her, and I can have mad times with her. I think one gives oneself a very hard time being a parent, and I don't think one takes one's own virtue seriously enough. You are so busy thinking you should be doing this or that – it's absolute crap. You must just be what you are, bringing up your own child. You must be yourself, and that's hard.

How do you deal with the competing identities of Imelda the performer and Imelda the mother?

It's getting easier because one feeds the other. They all should be the one person and it's just that at different times one has the upper hand. One needs to be called out more than the other. When I was doing the show last time, Bess was ill and had to go to hospital for the night. I came and did the show but I stayed in hospital with her that night, and that's when you want to be the mother. You have to push that down for a minute and sing a couple of bloody songs. I remember really having to hold on to that because my mind was full of that. I was thinking, 'Just concentrate!' Jim was with her, she was absolutely fine and it was just a virus, which had gone the next morning. That's where you have this computer in your head, which is fantastic because it allows you to be very different things.

What motivates you to perform?

I really enjoy it. I enjoy rehearsals, getting it wrong in order to get it right and performing well. When I perform well it feeds my confidence. It's like you are only as good as the last job you did. I won't go away from home to do theatre, so I've limited myself slightly but I do need to do it. It's like the job I've done for twenty-one years which is very fulfilling whether it's good or bad. Doing the odd bit of telly isn't fulfilling. Theatre is the most fulfilling because I don't have a career that does very interesting films, so I get my nourishment from the theatre and usually money from the other! My work is a lot of my life and easing a child into it has been a difficult thing to do. It's become much easier and enjoyable now that she understands more about what I do, and that I'm not going away for some strange reason. She's got two actors for parents and she sees us enjoying what we do. There's no leaving the house at the same time every day, saying, 'Oh, bloody office'. I paint my nails, sing my songs each night, and I can't think of anything nicer. I think women have had a very hard time just doing what they want to do in the last one hundred years or longer.

In terms of the profession, do you think that the image of the actress as strumpet has moved on?

Yes I do. And yet, women doing what they want to do, must be a bloody strumpet. If they're not in that kitchen or hospital, if they're not being pushed down and told what to do, then they must be some sort of strange being. Strumpet becomes a sexual thing, and has the sexual energy of actually saying, 'Fuck off, I'm going to do that.' It's interesting that a woman with power is very attractive. Power, confidence and getting what you want is sexually attractive. Even to use that parody of the 1980s, women in power suits being very attractive women, and strumpet for a woman who wants to do what she wants: being free. I think it's moved on for some, but not for all.

Are there more roles and opportunities for performing women?

Yes – mind you, it still goes on, the next young beautiful thing. That's always been, that will never change, because men run the business. Quality is still recognised, which I think is important. There's Emma Thompson with two Oscars, the only woman ever to get an Oscar for acting and writing, who still gets paid less than John Travolta for the American film they're doing together at the moment. It's outrageous. It's not the money, it's the complete principle. I think in acting it's getting better, but I've always felt fairly equal in a rehearsal room situation. It's not like, 'Let the men speak first darling!' It is equal. I've never felt like the little woman as it were, and that's very freeing. I've only known this workplace; it's been very comfortable and fairly caring. I think the women directors, designers and female stage management are not too badly off. I have mixed feelings about it, but with this job I am at home in the day, so I feel like I'm putting in my time. I think I'm fairly lucky in that our timetables change and we are at home an awful lot.

Have you worked with many women directors?

Jane Howell,[3] Sue Dunderdale,[4] Antonia Bird[5] – I could count them on one hand. I wonder if it is a thing to do with control, wanting control, and women being very good at taking second place. Men like to be leaders. Unfortunately, we have only had Margaret Thatcher to think about, but there aren't that many female leaders. Whether it's because they have just been having children, or just been the carers as opposed to hunters or protectors.

Is it also that the role of the director is not compatible with a woman's role in society?

I think you've got to be a leader as a director, and I think that a lot of women aren't just by their natures. Or they lead in a gentler way; they are not prepared to be dictators. Back to the kinder sex, the gentler sex. The business is run by men, and a lot of good men. However, there are some extraordinary women directors, for example, Deborah Warner.

Has anybody inspired or influenced you particularly in your career work?

I get inspired by my contemporaries, and I find that so encouraging. I can't believe that I'm part of a generation of actors, who are appearing in leading roles at the National Theatre, and that now I'm among them. Many were at RADA at the same time – for example Tim Spall, Juliet Stevenson and Alan Rickman. I get a great buzz out of being part of that group. I think it's important to respect the people who you are with now, and it isn't always people who are older actors. You can greatly admire Peggy Ashcroft or Judi Dench, but I think it's important to aspire to someone in your own age range and in your life now. It's now we are doing it, and now we should appreciate it, for example, Janet McTeer's Nora in *A Doll's House* was stunning! Then she went on to Broadway, got Tony awards, was taken out by Al Pacino showing her New York. Bitch! Bitch! So she's having a wonderful time and quite rightly, it's fantastic. No one has offered to take me around London – no one!

Has Janet McTeer got children?

No. Well spotted! I love seeing other people's work and I get a great sense of joy out of someone like Janet – she's a great mate of mine – just being extraordinary. If it's her turn now, then it will be your turn another time, and if you don't get a turn, you don't get a turn. That's it.

'When she was small', London

Is that something you learnt as a child?

No, it isn't. I wasn't really spoilt particularly as a child; it's why I like this show – everyone gets a turn. I don't particularly like shows where there's one performance that really stands out, because I think that (a) it unbalances the play, and (b) it's very selfish and indulgent. That's one thing I'm not as a performer. I'm fairly hard on myself, but I think I'm not a 'Look at me.' I love passing the ball.

Well, I think that was blatantly clear in your performance, the way you wanted everybody to be part of that. It's also evident that you enjoy performing comedy, but is there something particularly attractive about a woman who can be humorous?

Yes, extremely. I think anyone who doesn't take herself completely seriously is always attractive. Humour is a great diffuser, and a great weapon. What is it? What is attractive? It's just to do with not taking yourself seriously. It lets people in a bit more somehow, gives access, but it's absolutely within your control. Humour can pull you in and it can push you off without that person really knowing it. I think it enables you to move around very well, coping with very different and difficult situations. Humour is warm. When someone cries, they're very vulnerable, and I think laughing is only the other end of that. There's melancholy and there's humour. To be able to use your humour to ward off the melancholy, as a self-healing device, is very useful. It's a great deflector. I think you can cover up a lot with it. I think used well it can protect you and help you win over situations.

Have you ever been a stand-up or performed a one-woman show?

My bottom's going in and out at the very thought of it. I think one-woman shows can be very precious. I think they've got to be so cleverly done not to be wanky. It's got to be so interesting, otherwise it's just boring to watch one person doing their favourite bits. I'd rather just do it at a party. If you've got somebody like Alan Bennett writing for you then I can't imagine anything nicer, but to compile a one-woman show or do stand-up like Emma Thompson does, I take all the hats I've ever worn off to her. I just think it's brave in the context of this luxurious job we are all doing.

Is there any reason why you might perform alone?

It would have to be because I like doing good writing. Not performing a couple of bloody poems, or even good poems – are there bad poems? I find those things a bit suspect. I am trying to think of an amazing one-person show that I've seen … I think stand-up is fantastic. What I'd like to do is for someone to write it within a play for me – to be a stand-up performer. Another aspect of acting is having the confidence to be someone else, but also to be yourself. It's more comfortable dressing up and being someone else. You are yourself all day long, so I don't want to be myself up on a stage, but I'm sure stand-ups become that person at that time.

Stand-up plays with the self, rather than performing a character or a part. Is performing a heightening of the self in some sort of way?

Well, it's a heightening of certain aspects of yourself. When I did *Uncle Vanya*, it was a heightening of being very, very sad and so you just turn that bit up. I think you just turn on the things that you need, when you need them.

Are there aspects of yourself that are invisible in a daily context, but would appear in a performance?

Yes. I find it terribly hard to have any confrontation in my personal life. That's to do with my parents. I witnessed a lot of verbal arguments. As a child I must have thought, 'I'm never going to argue with anyone, it's too painful.' It's also very unhealthy, but I can do very good anger on stage, which I love doing because it's out. I can't get really angry about something without just flooding into tears, feeling very guilty and not being able to handle it. I love playing parts that can either break down and not control it, or be very strong in my anger because I have it in me, but I don't know how to do it in a positive way. Doing *Uncle Vanya* for six months nearly killed me, but that was because she was a very unhappy woman, which made me unhappy.

Is being an itinerant part of the appeal of performing?

A little bit; the best moving around is within a script. Each job is a different script and that is the best movement. For six years I worked in repertory, going all over the country, and that was great. What was greater was the work. I would have been perfectly happy to stay in the same place for six years, doing all the different parts. It's no good travelling around if you are not doing what you want to do.

You played some marvellous roles in those six years, and yet you were young and inexperienced. Did these opportunities stand you in good stead?

Absolutely, I don't think you get good by standing at the back watching other people. I think you get good by going on and doing it, being rubbish and then trying again. That's why I never wanted to be at the Royal Shakespeare Company, or come here to be at the back. Carrying a spear isn't work, and I never wanted to do that. I'm glad I didn't. When I came here *Guys and Dolls* was my first job. I was watching Julia McKenzie, Bob Hoskins, Julie Covington and Ian Charleson work. I had never seen actors like that. I then knew that if I wanted to be like that I had to get better. If I had gone to the RSC and watched those people maybe I would have got better but only by doing it, not for two years saying, 'Oh yes, my lady'. I would have been so pissed off, but it was a different calibre of acting when I was watching those people and I wanted to be as good as that. Again, when Julia McKenzie left, I did play Adelaide in 1983. I dread to think what I was like, but I thought, 'I've got to do this, I've just got to.' I'm a great one for – 'just do it' – you are not going to kill anyone by doing it.

Is that also true when you are rehearsing?

You have to make an idiot of yourself, go for it. I always want a director to tell me how to do it, help me, just help me. I've got all this technique and ability but you've got to channel it for me, because I can't see what I'm doing. I think as you get older probably you are more aware; you think, 'Oh trust me, this will work, I know.' I get very frustrated with directors, who don't do anything. They just say, 'Lovely, lovely, do that again then.' 'Well, are you going to say anything, are you going to help?' I'm quite outspoken when it comes to that. I want them to work as hard as we're working, and all the good ones do, but they're not all good.

Can you identify some key moments in your life as a performing woman in the widest sense – a memorable moment?

I remember on the last night of playing *Piaf*[6] at Nottingham, thinking that I'd never get a part like that again. You know those actor stories of the greatest parts you've played, or the greatest experiences you've had playing a part. I just remember, because I can sing and yet I don't like musicals. *Piaf* is a fantastic acting piece, and has fantastically emotionally charged songs, and I loved that combination. I don't like girly girly musicals and *Piaf* was what I can do best. I can do good emotion, I can sing and I can get cross and it had all of that in it. With Sonya, I did go to depths, which I didn't know I had, so that was a turning point for me recognising this talent in myself. I loved performing *Piaf*; I loved every second of it. I love performing this. With Sonya, I loved every minute of it, but couldn't wait to finish it, so it wasn't, 'Oh, I would love to play Sonya tonight.' This show, *Guys and Dolls*, is a one-off that has happened to me three times. You don't visit parts again, and I will never do another production of *Guys and Dolls*. I have been asked but I just wouldn't do it, and I actually feel now that I've sort of got it right and it's very satisfying. I think that's a rarity, to be able to say that. But even now, even this time around I've changed things that I thought I was completely happy with three months ago. I thought, 'Bloody hell, I think I ought to do this show for the rest of my life!' So Piaf and Sonya have been the most important things for me. It's interesting that they are both people with great tragedy. There's been no television I've done that has equalled anything.

Other key moments in your personal life?

Having Bess – the biggest journey, which will continue for the rest of my life. All these parts come and go, and as an actor you're used to that. Every day a little death, the show's dead, it's gone. Move on. There's sadness, but there's excitement at the next possibility. When you've a child, it gives you something that you can't let go of, you don't want to let go of, which is different with a relationship. That's obviously been the biggest change and has made me slightly better as an actor. I care less. I don't care less insofar as I will worry if a scene is wrong … I'm really grateful for that, because if it all goes pear-shaped I've still got her. I don't want to overload that, and I won't because I recognize it. I don't want to put all my energies into her because I think that's as unhealthy as putting no energy into her. It's just having another focus apart from yourself, and acting is very self-focused. That can become indulgent in a lot of cases, and I'm not really interested in that. I think the best actors are people who have other things in their lives. Michael Gambon makes guns, does silverware, metalwork, things like that, and he has other things in his life. A few nights ago, there was the twenty-first anniversary of the National Theatre, a big gala performance and a big dinner upstairs. I was invited, and sitting there thinking, 'Well I'm only here because I'm the new girl in a musical at the Olivier, and then a woman came up to me and said, "Can I just say you are the best Sonya I have ever seen."' Here I am saying, 'I'm only playing Adelaide', but I happen to think it's the best musical in the world, at the National Theatre, directed by Richard Eyre. What more do I want? I've given up a whole year to do this role and there's nothing I wanted more. I'm loving it, and yet, next year I want to do something that's a bit weightier. Although this is a role that I think is the weightiest you can do, but I want to do something more serious, just to ring the changes.

Notes

1 Adelaide in *Guys and Dolls* (based on a story and characters of Damon Runyon, music and lyrics by Frank Loesser, book by Jo Swerling and Abe Burrows), directed by Richard Eyre, Royal National Theatre, 1996–97.
2 Sonya in Chekhov's *Uncle Vanya*, directed by Michael Blakemore, Vaudeville Theatre, 1988.
3 Keefe's *It's a Mad World My Masters*, directed by Jane Howell, Theatre Royal, Stratford East, 1984.
4 *Us Good Girls*, directed by Sue Dunderdale, Soho Poly, 1988.
5 Bridget Bennet in *A Masculine Ending*, directed by Antonia Bird, BBC Television/First Choice, 1992 and 1993.
6 Piaf in Gems' *Piaf*, directed by Crispin Thomas, Nottingham Playhouse, 1981.

Juliet Stevenson

'Primarily, I suppose, I love telling people's stories – being
on a stage inhabiting someone else's story but drawing on
my own, using my own life experience, recycling it to
interpret and give shape to other people's realities.'

'Being on stage can be a very potent form of living –
life with the boring bits taken out.'

Performance Context

Born: 1956, Kelvedon, Essex.

Prior/current commitments: Jean in *Stone, Scissors, Paper* written by Richard Cameron, BBC Television Screen 2.
Grusha in Brecht's *The Caucasian Chalk Circle*, Theatre de Complicite, Royal National Theatre and tour.

Post-interview (selected): Annie Lee in Lee's *Cider With Rosie*, Carlton Television.
Beckett Shorts, Royal Shakespeare Company, Stratford and Europe.

Other: Olivier Award for 'Best Actress' for Paulina in Dorfman's *Death and The Maiden*, Royal Court/Duke of York's, 1992. Time Out Award for 'Best Actress'.

Interview

A continuum of answerphone messages, faxes and emails surrounds the experience of interviewing Juliet Stevenson, who conveys her passion for performing through two interviews conducted with her on 22 January 1997 and 10 June 1997 in Highgate, London, offering an intelligent, articulate view of the subject. Her performance of Grusha in Theatre de Complicite's Royal National Theatre production of Brecht's The Caucasian Chalk Circle *reflected no less than that.*

Alison Oddey: *How do you decide what to perform?*

Juliet Stevenson: I find job decisions difficult to make, for the most part. Having children now – one daughter and two stepsons – both complicate and simplify the process of making job choices. The well-being of your family life actually refines your reasons for why you want to work at all, what it's about, and who for. If you are going to leave your child to go to work, you really have to have a strong sense of what you are doing, and why you are doing it. There's nothing like the cost and effort involved in organising childcare to focus the concentration in rehearsal, or on a film set, or whatever. Having gone through all that trouble and heart-searching to create time in which to work, you don't want to squander it when you get there!

As a working full-time mother with a young child, it's never easy to resolve the conflict of both identities. There's also the question of 'Me' time disappearing completely, which means that the self receives no nurturing at all.

Well, I do know working mothers who manage to hold on to the concept of 'me' time – in that they clear time from their children not just to work but also for their own pleasure, leisure, or whatever. I'm not one of them! Perhaps I'm particularly subject to guilt or preoccupation with my family but I can't justify it. Actually, it's not really about justification, it's about desire. I don't really want to. In a way these categories are questionable, in any case. Work time *is* 'me' time, surely, because apart from the routine bread-winning stuff, I work to engage my mind, imagination and creativity. In this way, the self is nurtured. But it's also nurtured by many aspects of family life, and profoundly so by being with children. Not all the time, by any means! Politically, there are things that could be done to make it a lot easier for working women, but speaking as one, I don't think that you can ever be happy in an uncomplicated way. There is no solution, and all you ever achieve – at best – is some kind of balance to keep yourself sane.

What were your perceptions of theatre when you first started?

When I came into the theatre, at twenty years old, there was a much more highly developed sense of company – of ensemble. The most inspiring stuff that I had seen up to then was largely the product of strong ensemble work, whether it was Brook's company, or the RSC, or foreign companies visiting, or politically-motivated fringe companies. I was very thrilled by the notion of the collaborative ideal, while at the same time nurturing the same individualistic ambitions as any other young actor. I knew I wanted to be part of something that is bigger than all of us. The RSC had an amazing ensemble of actors when I joined it – Jonathan Pryce, Jane Lapotaire, David Suchet, Alan Howard, Glenda Jackson, Alan Rickman, Paola Dionisotti, Zoe Wanamaker, Patrick Stewart, Ruby Wax and many more. That company was very feisty; it had a sense of what the RSC could and should be, and periodically challenged the management and directors about such things. It was politically conscious in terms of the company's internal working conditions for actors, but also – more significantly – in terms of making connections between the work and the outside world. This was shared by some of the directors too, and real creativity was forged in the making of those connections. Also, for a young and very inexperienced actress straight from RADA, as I was, the company's commitment to training and nurturing actors was fantastically exciting and liberating. I remember sonnet classes with John Barton in lunch hours, early morning voice and text sessions with Cicely Berry, workshops on Saturday mornings that David Suchet ran voluntarily, amongst a lot else. So, while carrying my spear and sporting my wench wigs, I also learned an enormous amount in a short space of time. I was hungry for it all and I was lucky – and it reinforced my instinct that talent, status, ego notwithstanding, theatre is a collaborative event. No matter what you are playing, you have a right to be concerned with issues of design, music, light and all the component parts of a production. This was the very late seventies and early eighties, and I guess we had not yet felt the cold blast of individualism, of the me-ism that was shortly to take over, and which is in many ways anathema to the idea of ensemble, even to real collaboration.

Where do the roots of your desire to perform originate?

That's difficult to pinpoint. I don't think I know the answer really. I certainly don't know where the *need* to perform comes from, or why it's there. But it's a significant question because I really do think there is a strong connection between why a person comes to acting in the first place and what they do when they're up there on a stage, or in front of a camera. There's a profound difference between the performance given by an actor who acts to conceal who he/she is, and the one given by an actor who acts to reveal it. I'm pretty sure I'm in the latter category, but I don't know why. I do remember vividly an incident that happened at school, which was like a kind of light being switched on. I was nine, newly arrived at a boarding school, uncertain about pretty well everything, as I remember. One day, some sort of concert for speech day was being prepared for, in the form of various readings of poetry and prose. I was very junior so the expectation was that I would recite something appropriately simple. I happened to pick up a sheet of paper with a poem by W.H. Auden on it – some kind of adult love poem – probably to another man, quite elusive in its meaning to me even now. I read it then, and knew immediately that I could communicate it. I remember the sensation – I was shot through with a desire to serve the poet, to be the conduit through which this poem with its shapes and sounds and rhythms was to be heard by the audience to come. I had no real understanding of the poem's sense, and was far too young to have had comparable experience to that expressed in the piece. It was the rhythm that caught me – the poem's pulse, its repetitions, the musicality of its thought. The rhythm of it meant something to me, quite deeply but without being articulated. In the decades since that time I've come to understand much more about the ways in which rhythm is meaning, and how the rhythms of spoken language communicate meaning to the hearer that resonates far beyond the level of literal sense. Anyway, that incident at school was one of those quantum leap moments for me, I guess, and from that point on I became increasingly hungry for acting opportunities, though for a long time I had to live off scraps. I sometimes remind myself of it, of the moment when I first looked at those words and longed to be the vessel through which they were communicated. That remains a very clear definition of what acting is about, of what we're for.

So what is the thrill of being 'up there' or on stage performing?

I think the thrill is manifold – there are many different things that I love about performing live, and on a good night they come together and the fusion of them creates the thrill. Primarily, I suppose, I love telling people's stories – being on a stage inhabiting someone else's story but drawing on my own, using my own life experience, recycling it to interpret and give shape to other people's realities. Exploring the dimensions of those realities is part of the thrill. Then, to sense that people are witnessing it all, understanding it, identifying with it or rejecting it possibly, and feeling how the audience's responses subtly alter how the story is told and heard. That's the greatest source of the thrill, and it's what no other medium can match – the sense that what you do up there can go in many directions at any moment. It all happens in the instant, and then the next, and the next, which incorporates mistake, fallibility, inspiration and mood. The known – which you've rehearsed and prepared – meets the unknown. There are never two identical audiences – people may rock with laughter one night and be silent the next. The performer/audience relationship is, to some extent, an anarchic beast. You never quite know what's going to happen, and that's how I like things to be. Being on stage can be a very potent form of living – life with the boring bits taken out.

Do you come from a theatrical background?

No, not at all. My parents were both interested in theatre. Music, I think, was their greatest interest, but they both love theatre and both of them had amateur experience. I think my mother was very keen to act at one time in her early adulthood, but probably wouldn't have dared even to voice such an ambition, let alone pursue it. Hers was the generation growing up during the war for whom there were very few choices. I didn't go to the cinema or the theatre very much as a young child because we were living in army bases abroad. Very few films came to those places, and we had no television. So I didn't have those influences in my life until we came back to England when I was about ten. We saw more theatre then, mainly at the local rep, which I always loved going to. The first theatre experience I had that completely blew me away was when I went to Stratford and first saw the RSC, when I was fifteen. It was John Barton's production of *Richard II*. I'd never seen anything like it. It impacted on me like falling in love for the first time – I was reeling from it for long afterwards, couldn't think about anything else much, couldn't sleep or eat for excitement about what I had seen, heard and felt. I saw that production six times that summer, hitching up to Stratford, queuing for the standby tickets and standing at the back of the stalls, even following some of the actors home after the show just to touch the bricks of the houses they lived in! On the family holiday that summer, I remember shutting myself away in my room and learning great chunks of the play by heart, which I can still recite to this day. I don't know whether I wanted to be Richard II or the actor playing him – for me, they had fused into the same thing, I think. Anyway, I was in love with all of it, but after the infatuation with the actors and the show died away, the love of the words remained. During the following year a group of actors came to our school and performed scenes from *King Lear*, then workshopped it with us afterwards. I had no desire to play Cordelia; I wanted to play King Lear – so I did for an hour or two that afternoon, and experienced saying those words out loud like a drug entering the system. I guess that time was when the dream was really born.

In Paderborn, Westphalia, 1958, aged two

What is the satisfaction of performing, and has it changed in twenty years?

In certain ways it has changed. I think it's harder now to achieve a sense of satisfaction from performing. I used to get an enormous thrill simply by stepping out onto the stage, into that lighted space. I still get a sense of thrill, quite often, but it's seasoned in some way. When you're very young, just starting, everything is there to be learnt, so whatever I was asked to do was a learning experience. After twenty years of work, that learning curve levels out gradually – that's why these days my criteria for saying yes or no to a job offer are primarily to do with whether or not the job will take me to new territory, offer challenges. If it feels as though it will be easy or comfortable, don't do it. If the prospect of it alarms you, if you're not sure if or how you will realise it, say yes. That is principally where the greatest satisfaction lies these days, in feeling that you are in the process of achieving something that is difficult for you, that you are still pushing at the boundaries of what you know, and moving on. It's like being more than alive, everything is heightened. I think this has a lot to do with why I'm drawn to it, and why it pulled me even as a young child. Being brought to the edges of human experience, and to the edges of yourself. I don't know anything else like it.

It's June and you are currently in The Caucasian Chalk Circle *at the Royal National Theatre with Theatre de Complicite,*[1] *which I saw last Wednesday evening. What prompted you to take on Grusha and to play this part? What motivated you to make that choice?*

I had seen Complicite's work and admired it very, very much, and also recognised it as being quite different from the work going on around. I loved its European-ness, its physicality, theatricality, wit, sensuality – the way it acknowledges its influences but has found real originality. It's so great when you watch something in the theatre and long to be a part of it. But I didn't imagine I ever would, coming from a tradition of more text-based work for the most part. So I was incredibly excited when Simon McBurney rang me up one night and asked me if I'd be interested in doing 'Chalk Circle' – delirious, in fact. I was nervous as hell that he'd decide against it, changing his mind or something. I had not a second's hesitation in saying yes to the job when the offer came in, partly because I love the play, but also because I have always wanted to explore Brecht. I felt instinctively when I read it that 'Chalk Circle' would be a very good play for Complicite to work on – its structure and its themes seemed to lend themselves to this company's ways of working. I also loved the thought of playing Grusha. I knew she'd be difficult for me. So, many things came together in one pretty irresistible package, and all of them challenging. I have long wanted to work much more physically than is possible in most rehearsal rooms, and this play in some ways demands a physical approach – Grusha's story centres around her journey, a physical journey over mountains and bridges, across rivers and ravines, carrying an increasingly heavy child. She's literally on the run for two-thirds of the play.

The piece also has a huge cast of characters and a wide variety of landscapes, so it requires a very fluid way of working – the actors have to change character often and fast, as well as creating the physical terrains. I felt sure that Simon would be able to devise processes in rehearsal that would solve the great staging challenges that this play presents to a director, and that the exploration of those processes, as a company, would be fantastically interesting. And it has been – Simon has the capacity to achieve these things simply and creatively, with real theatrical inventiveness, and without recourse to technology. It's a joy to work this way, having worked such a lot in theatres where the design decisions have been made long before the actors start rehearsal, and where so much relies on the technology available to designers. Whereas with Complicite, you start with a group of people in a room and you make everything out of that group of people. It's the sort of theatre I love to watch, so I'm very happy to be a part of it.

A challenging process, which enabled you to explore the text in different ways to how you might normally approach a play.

Yes, very different ways. More or less diametrically opposite, in fact, to the way I am accustomed to approaching a part, a play. I don't have a single or even consistent way of working, because each job will require its own approach according to the nature of the piece, but I do always start with the text, the words. They've always been the springboard. But this time, we didn't go near the text for weeks. We had eight weeks to rehearse, and for the first four we concentrated almost exclusively on physical work, and games, improvisation, rhythm stuff, singing. We might occasionally look at a few lines of text as the basis for an improvisation, or to explore different ways of telling the narrative of a scene, but we never sat and read the play or analysed it, nor did we rehearse individual scenes or discuss character. In about week five we began work on the play solely in terms of finding its physical shape, staging it. I had relished every moment of rehearsal up till then – was completely exhilarated by the process – but I did begin to feel a little bit apprehensive at this point, because questions of staging are inextricably linked in my mind to an understanding of the text. (My character moves from A to B at this point because she's feeling or thinking X, and so on.) How could we then be staging scenes whose inner life we had not yet begun to examine? But I went with it, because that's the way Simon was working and I'd decided to trust him. It became a little scary as time went on, because hitherto I've always worked from the inside out with a character, raking through the language she speaks for clues as to the 'whos' and 'whys', before committing to decisions about staging. Now I had to continue to put all that on hold while we gradually developed the play's choreography. By week six I still had very little idea about who Grusha was, certainly who *my* Grusha was or what she felt like. It was an exercise in holding my nerve, to some extent! At times, and more so the nearer we got to the first preview, it was difficult to hold faith entirely with the process, because I felt I hadn't really begun my own journey into who I was playing and why she said or did anything. The word 'why?' was not being asked in the rehearsal room, or not in relation to character psychology anyway. I wasn't sure when or even *if* I'd have a chance to let my instincts loose on the business of finding Grusha – and how would I ever get at her if we were never going to work on the text, and ask questions of it? Simon had talked about the image for Grusha, the image that had inspired Brecht to create her in the first place – Brueghel's painting of *Dulle Griet* striding through Hell with her loot – but we hadn't done more than look at the portrait occasionally. How to get inside it though? Then one day, perilously late on, he came into the room with a tub of hair grease, smarmed my hair flat to the scalp with it, wrapped a rag around my head and ripped a couple of holes in it through which he extracted my ears ('shame they're not bigger, Juliet'), and then bound my legs and arms tightly with an assortment of rags and bandages. Then he suggested a pair of large, jutting false teeth, and since these were not immediately available he made do with stuffing my gums with wads of toilet paper. That was basically it, and I realised I had better get on with it. Looking back, I think I was partly in shock. Though also partly relieved that a start of some sort, *any* sort, was being made on getting my character together. Not having a lot of time or choices left available, I just decided to go with it, as best I could, (though privately deciding that I would, for now, indulge Simon in the question of the sticky-out goofy teeth, but bin them well before going anywhere near the public). I began to try to move inside this image. Very crudely at first, feeling bewildered as to how I could find the inner person to inhabit so idiosyncratic an external shape. I had no experience of working this way, no tried or familiar formula for making this transition. So it was time for the deep end. I jumped, made a fool of myself, jumped again, and kept jumping really, and surprisingly quickly began to feel somebody filling up inside, somebody squeezing into the shapes and contours of this imposed mould. Her walk emerged, her elbows sprang into life, her neck and jaw began to have a life of their own. What began as terrifying became increasingly exhilarating – because I could feel this Grusha developing while still not having really examined a line of her text. I'd never worked in such a way before. But this quite soon became very liberating – I had not been able to arrive at her by use of my brain, which made it much easier, in the end, to earth her, to believe in myself as an illiterate peasant who is guided by instinct and survival skills. Besides, it's such a relief, a thrill even, to break with all your familiar ways of working, to abandon the safety net of what you know. It's a measure of the faith I had in Simon McBurney that I went on with what felt so risky – I think with another director I might have held more tenaciously on to my own reins, under duress! I am fantastically grateful to him for what

I've learned. I feel freer than I have felt in a long time – freed from myself, or certain aspects of myself – while able to use myself fully, if that doesn't sound paradoxical. (In fact, when the appalling false teeth arrived I so enjoyed the transformation they helped to create that when he suggested chucking them out as being no longer necessary, I wouldn't hear of it.) So yes, being in this production has involved a pretty extensive reversal of the way I am used to working. I think I feel part of a genuine ensemble for the first time in my life – and that's an extraordinarily powerful sensation. When, at the end, you see teenagers amongst the audience standing and cheering, it's invigorating to think that this is Brecht – that this is 1997 – and they have loved it. We're told quite often that this sort of play is irrelevant now – as being a political dinosaur – but the response from audiences has knocked that judgement for six. The play's poeticism, tenderness, wit, thought, theatricality, toughness seem to emerge in Simon's production and people are very grabbed by it.

Has it been rewarding to work with Simon McBurney?

Yes, very. He has very deep and sure instincts about what the theatre is, and can be, and has studied and trained and read a lot about these things too. So he has a wide directorial vocabulary at his fingertips, and an extensive knowledge of craft. He has a huge amount to offer, in the room – a limitless number of games and exercises through which to explore both the play and the means by which its narrative is told. He is very hardworking, quite tough – can be quite a task-master. He doesn't hand out praise lightly – it requires a good measure of self-confidence to work with him, I think. I like all that. Above all, I guess, he has real vision. He works on the rehearsal floor very instinctively – I don't think he ever comes in at the start of the day with a grand plan in his head. He sort of sculpts the thing with the clay of the company as it goes along. Experiment and trial are a big part of the process, which is one of the things I've most loved about it. (I've always thought that was how a rehearsal process should be, ideally.) I've talked a bit about it being an ensemble, but at the same time Simon is pretty autocratic in the room; he does not invite a lot of shared discourse about how we are going to work. He's authorial as a director, very much the boss, but does rely on a lot of input from the company in terms of energy, commitment, courage or skill, and will explore other people's ideas if he smells the interesting possibility in them. You do feel you are contributing to the shaping of the thing to some extent, largely through the frequent use of improvisation. Quite a lot of ideas that have now gone into the show came from those improvisations, so there is a sense in which the production has pooled contributions from the company. But the style of the production comes from Simon; it evolved very much through his vision. I think most of the company would say that they did their individual character work on their own. He leaves a lot of that up to the actor, and indeed I've never had less dialogue with a director about character choices and psychology. After that rough outline of Grusha's external image and dynamic, he pretty much left me to get on with it, which is fine by me – that I *am* used to! To some extent the company worked with each other on that stuff – since everybody is present in the room all day and every day (there's no such thing as a private or individual rehearsal call) either working or watching others work. A climate is created whereby it's possible to help each other out if necessary. It's unusual, in my experience – normally, actors are fairly proprietorial and even defensive about their individual choices, and exchanging thoughts about a scene requires careful and very tactful handling! There's something very robust about the kind of rehearsal room Simon creates. Again, I've loved this, and found it really refreshing. He demands that everyone takes responsibility for the whole – and it leaves you with a sense that this baby has been born to eighteen parents.

What has this experience given you in terms of where you are now as a performing woman?

It has restored my faith a lot. I had been through a couple of years of feeling a lack of direction, even depressed at times about how and where to work, and who with. I had felt quite stuck, uninterested in many of the things I was being asked to do, and uneasy about quite a lot of what I saw going on around me. Questions like, 'Who is theatre for?' and 'Why do it?' were coming into my head far too often for peace of mind, and I didn't know how to move myself on, where to look for the kind of challenge I talked to you about earlier. So this opportunity came at a time when I felt great need of it. I know I'm working in new territory in this show, and I know the show works. I shall be very sad when it finishes – I think I may wonder where to go next. I hope we will work together again some day.

Can you identify key moments in your life as a performing woman in the widest possible sense?

Well, there are two big moments in relation to acting that spring to mind, as being times when a large and significant penny dropped. One was when I was nine years old – the poem, which I told you about before. That was one of those quantum leaps that happen in a second, and change your life in some lasting way. The second one happened when I was at drama school, sometime towards the end of my second term there. I had arrived at RADA with very little confidence about acting. Whatever confidence I enjoyed at school earlier on seemed to disappear in the face of the seriousness of an academy which trained actors to be professionals, and where the walls were lined with lists of the glittering alumni who'd passed through it before me. I was struggling with aspects of it – when it came to the productions we had to do twice a term, I didn't know how to get up and play another person, how to move from being me to being someone else. They didn't really help you much with that. I was okay in the classes, working on voice, body and movement, but in rehearsals for the plays I was really struggling. During the second term, we were doing Shakespeare's *Antony and Cleopatra*. It's a huge play, so they divide the main roles up between two or three students per role. I was doing the middle chunk of Cleopatra. I'd just turned nineteen and had no experience to play an erotic, exotic middle-aged creature, and it seemed beyond my furthest reaches. I was disastrous in rehearsal. One day, the director (who was of a rather old-fashioned, do-it-like-this school) completely lost his temper with me. He stood up and berated me – 'Juliet, this is pathetic, it's virginal, Home Counties, middle-class, repressed ... '. He went on like that for a while, an entirely personal attack which I suppose erupted out of his frustration. The rest of the class were standing around listening to all this, so it was completely mortifying in just about every respect. I stood there, agonised and shaking, and two options came into my head – to burst into tears and collapse into the disaster of it all, or to walk out of the room and the Academy and go to university instead. But then suddenly I was filled with anger – I was outraged that he should talk to anyone like that. He was attacking the most private areas of my adolescent self, exposing me in that way. I remember, palpably, the feeling of fear turning into rage. So I did not burst into tears, I didn't leave the room, and we started the scene again. It was the scene in which Cleopatra is visited by a servant, who tells her that Antony has married somebody else, so she goes crazy with this servant – beats him up, screams at him, threatens to kill him, and then collapses into her grief. We started the scene again, and suddenly I felt the rage in my system pouring itself into the text, into Cleopatra's words. The very lines I had been struggling with all those weeks began to come out of my mouth completely differently – suddenly they were all I wanted to say, as though nothing less than Cleopatra's cosmic invocations and passionate outrage could express my own. I remember the whole room going quiet. I could feel what was happening, as though I had jumped out of a window and was now flying, and thinking, 'This is it! This is what acting is, it's right down in the gut, that's where you connect with it and with who you are playing, and the rest takes care of itself.' We got to the end of the scene, there was a silence, and then the director said, 'Right, thank you, now we are getting somewhere.' After that, everything changed – I had felt what it was to inhabit somebody else, to use my own thinking and feeling to fill out their shape and size, to speak their words as being the very words necessary to say at that moment. From that day, my confidence grew – I knew what it was to act.

And your most significant performing achievements so far ... ?

That question is almost impossible to answer – I mean, significant for whom? Audiences, critics, me? Depending on whom, the answer might vary. There are things I've done which may have a particular significance for me, but have not had a huge fuss made of them, and of course vice versa. Perhaps those times when your own feeling about a show coincides with its public reception become the ones which feel most significant – *Death and the Maiden*,[2] for example, which was a play I loved doing and which also had great acclaim. I was extremely happy, of course, that it went down so well, but I think the reason that it stands out for me as perhaps one of the more significant ones was because it seemed to speak for people in certain ways that I could recognise clearly. It resonated strongly for people in need of a voice. I had many letters which spoke of this, so I was able to go into the theatre every night to perform it with the feeling that it served a significant purpose. That sense of certainty is rare, in my experience. There are moments in different things where I do feel a sense of achievement. There are bits of *Truly, Madly, Deeply*[3] which I'm able to feel quite proud of, because they are very free and happened in the moment. But if that film ranks as one of the more significant pieces of work, it's more to do with the nature of its appeal to people – I do love the fact that its appeal cut right across boundaries of class, race and gender. It was genuinely populist, but never strained to be so. Perhaps what I'm trying to say overall is that universality is what counts most – if a piece of work achieves universality in its audience's response, then it has more significance for me than other jobs, in retrospect. I'm proud of this production, at the moment. I'm even proud of aspects of Grusha, if that doesn't sound arrogant, because I feel I have managed to transform.

Can you give me a moment where you feel really proud as Grusha?

That is difficult, because it might change night by night – but sometimes I look down and I don't recognise my own hands – they are behaving differently.

Notes

1   Grusha in Brecht's *The Caucasian Chalk Circle*, directed by Simon McBurney with Theatre de Complicite, Royal National Theatre, 1997.
2   Paulina in Dorfman's *Death and the Maiden*, directed by Lindsay Posner, Royal Court/Duke of York's, 1991.
3   Nina in the film *Truly, Madly, Deeply*, directed by Anthony Minghella, co-starring Alan Rickman, BBC Television/Samuel, 1992.

Kathryn Hunter

As King Lear in Shakespeare's *King Lear*, the Young Vic,
1997

'This is what I'm here for – to interpret.'

'I went through huge recriminations as to whether I had
the right to play King Lear.'

Performance Context

Born: 1957, New York.

Prior/current commitments: King Lear in Shakespeare's *King Lear*, Young Vic. Co-director with Marcello Magni, *Everyman*, Royal Shakespeare Company, tour.

Post-interview (selected): Mother in Lorca's *Dona Rosita, the Spinster*, Almeida Theatre. Brecht's *Mr Puntila and his Man Matti*, directed by Kathryn Hunter, Almeida Theatre and UK tour.
Rebecca Gilman's *The Glory of Living*, directed by Kathryn Hunter, Royal Court Theatre.

Other: Olivier Award 1991 – 'Best Actress' for Clara in *The Visit*, Theatre de Complicite, Royal National Theatre.

Interview

I admired Kathryn Hunter's fervent search for continued exploration and discovery in the role of King Lear, as she reflected seriously on the work in the kitchen of her London home on 27 September 1997.

Alison Oddey: *Would you describe yourself as a performer or an actor?*

Kathryn Hunter: Maybe as an interpreter. Originally I wanted to be an interpreter of languages and I suppose I've ended up being one, but not of the United Nations, which is probably more traumatic than going on stage.

You're Greek, were born in New York, but brought up in England?

Yes. I came here when I was two, but my parentage is Greek. We had a double culture at home and went to Greece for holidays, and now I go as often as I can. My father is from Khios and my mother from Piraeus in Athens. We spoke Greek at home and went to Greek Orthodox church for weddings, christenings and funerals. In the Greek community you have to attend all these things. When I went to university at eighteen, I absconded. My mother became the black sheep of the family, because she was quite anarchic and did things women aren't supposed to do. It is a culture of arranged marriages. We were let off the hook. I have a twin sister, who trained as a social worker and now is a social policy worker working for organisations like the National

Council of One-Parent Families. She now works for Accord, which is an organisation that focuses on women's groups mostly in Africa and south-east Asia. We are very close.

Have you got any other siblings?

Two older brothers.

So you are the youngest. You went to university and then RADA?

I went to Bristol first and did French and drama, but I didn't finish because I got into RADA. I should have finished. I did two years and I loved it, but that's the impatience of eighteen-year-olds! Off you go.

So what actually attracted you to wanting to perform and to the theatre?

I don't know. It doesn't go in the family except I've noticed my uncles on my father's side are hilarious storytellers, so there is a sort of streak there. There were school plays. Being Greek Orthodox, we went to a Spanish Catholic primary. When we were doing *Snow White and the Seven Dwarves*, I had to play the wicked witch. When I had to say, 'Apples for sale', Mother Angela said 'Louder, louder, nobody in the hall will hear you', and I remember thinking, 'Why should I speak louder, if there is nobody there? When they are there I will speak louder.' So I remember that quite vividly. There was an Oscar Wilde play and somebody fell out and I stood in and apparently was quite funny, but I didn't feel even then that this was what I wanted to do. At secondary school, there was Michelle Wade, who runs a cafe in Soho and does theatre there. Michelle persuaded the drama teacher at this all-girls school to do *Joan of Arc*. She was a wonderful Joan and all of us played monks, and again, I don't remember thinking, 'This is what I want to do.' Michelle would do me her audition pieces, which were fascinating because they'd be about prostitutes, but again my directing maybe came out then because I enjoyed watching her and commenting on the work. At university, I auditioned for a production of Brecht's *In the Jungle of the Cities* and it was at the 'tech' that I got hooked. I didn't know what a 'tech' was – I was greener than green – but it was the experience of this whole team of people engaged in a final event. That was what really hooked me and I remember that day vividly. I thought, 'This is what I want to do', to be involved in making something together. Then on a more personal level, I did *Ring Round the Moon* at the drama department. I didn't realise I was playing a funny part, but I remember on the first night I said something and everyone collapsed into huge laughter. The physical sensation was intoxicating. I was thrilled. So those were the two turning points where I felt this was what I wanted to do – that laugh and that 'tech'.

Is performing still to do with the thrills of making people laugh or being part of a team?

I'm sure the team has a lot to do with it, to be engaged and have a focus of one's work and life working in a team. Then I do love to make people laugh. I just did a little part in Lorca recently after doing *King Lear*[1] at Leicester, and that was wonderful. I thought then that I'd love to do a roaring comedy. I think comedy is considered second rate, not really culture. Yet people like Chaplin and Buster Keaton are the highest artists, as well as the great clowns. They are every bit as extraordinary artists as Olivier or Maggie Smith. I have a huge respect for the great comedians and clowns, because I think they touch the essence of the human condition, which is simultaneously comic and tragic. I remember when I was doing *The Skriker*[2] by Caryl Churchill, that it struck nerves that I could very much relate to. It's a play of our times about our world – very much a city play, although a green play on another level – and how we are destroying it. I played an underworld creature who comes out of the earth and steals a human being as revenge for humans destroying and polluting the world. It's about basic drives more than psychological characterisations. The Skriker assumed about thirteen different characters. I do love that sort of transformation or going into other people's skins; not just a woman of my age and background, the further away the better. I just find it more exciting as an imaginative exercise. So I remember cycling back after the show and thinking, 'This is what I'm here for – to interpret.'

To interpret what exactly?

I suppose to interpret human experience if possible. You know something about human experience that may be common to most of us, and without Caryl's play, I wouldn't have been able to do that. Caryl was actually talking about our fragmented world and this schizophrenia that we all have (that we are all a part of in this fragmented world), and those huge drives that exist in people, often subsumed because we've learnt to be cultured and civilised. I suppose it was interpreting something that Caryl had intuited, quite dark, but Caryl is also very funny so that's good.

Why perform then – to be an interpreter of human experience?

Playing is an innate part of us. That's why theatre doesn't die (and hopefully won't die), because we do crave to understand human experience.

So are all actors just children wanting to play?

I think we are all children, aren't we? I don't mean it in a derogatory sense. I think we forget our sense of play as adults, and that's when we become boring!

Do you have a need to perform?

I think at one time I did. I do feel more recently that I am stricter with myself. If I feel that I'm not giving something, then that's not good enough, and therefore, I shouldn't perform, because I'm not up to standard. It's a need to live in the world of the imagination. I live quite happily there. Maybe several years ago I lived more exclusively in that world rather than the real world, but now I think that the so-called real world is a university as well.

So you have to offer something worthwhile in performance. You strike me as someone who takes her work very seriously – giving your all.

My partner says that I take things too seriously, but I just don't think it's worthwhile if you don't. I went through huge recriminations as to whether I had the right to play King Lear. I thought about it again last night watching Judi Dench in *Amy's View*,[3] thinking that I don't have the life experience that she has, so how could I dare to play it. However, I know it was an honest endeavour, rather than, 'I fancy playing a big part now.' I've been obsessed with Lear since I was an adolescent. I fantasized about playing Lear and then Helena Kaut-Howson asked me, and I couldn't say no. I jumped in at the deep end. I do think it's tempered with this sense of, 'You'd better have something to offer', to try and sound it to its death, which of course with Lear was a huge task. I would wake up suddenly every day as if there was this hook in my heart saying, 'Dig deeper.' How do you go deeper? Even when I went on holiday for two weeks, my body still didn't realise that I wasn't playing Lear. I got three letters from this gentleman, who loved the performance and production. The play meant so much to him. He had served in the Second World War and perhaps because Helena brought out the whole warring aspect a lot, the play spoke to him passionately and vehemently about the human condition. You know what happens with friends when you talk and you come to understand a certain aspect of your experience, and there is the bond of having shared. The other person trying to get into your skin and often the listener is as much in pain as the one speaking. That connectedness of a friendship is the same in the theatre.

You've recently finished performing King Lear *at the Young Vic[4] – what was your greatest challenge?*

On a very simple level to chart his journey on a practical level and then to live it. It was a very spiritual journey, and of course, it's the physical things that prompt the spiritual psyche to go on its journey. If they had thrown him out and he had gone into the Hilton International, he may not have found his soul as it were. He has nowhere to go, it's cold and there is a storm. There is something about those physical conditions that one has to really take on board. I have found in a storm that you have to constantly revive those senses. I know it's a storm of the mind as well, but I think that the physical proposition that Shakespeare gives is very important. Shakespeare's exploration of the rationality of madness is extraordinary, but there's a logic there. He talks to the elements because there is no one else to talk to; there's the fool but the fool is always telling him off. So he tells them what to do; he orders them to destroy humanity. It's one thing to do those famous speeches and another to understand the inner chart rather than just shout, so it was immensely challenging. I'm very grateful to have another opportunity in Tokyo, and then perhaps I would like to have another go in ten or twenty years' time. I'm sure not being a parent makes me less well equipped. One can intuit some things, but I found myself very much trying to imagine being my parents and being rejected. The other thing that I felt was a sort of taboo subject in the play was about the hatred. When the love doesn't function properly and isn't allowed a proper channel. Shakespeare is very courageous. He dares to talk about that, from child to parent and from parent to child.

There is the idea that love is somehow implicit within the parent/child relationship. Also, a notion of duty somehow.

Yes. I think when it's not expressed in simple ways, like time being spent together or an exchange of not necessarily momentous things, then Lear is saying, 'Which of you shall say doth love us most, that we our largest bounty may extend, where nature doth with merit challenge'. So it's as if he is saying, 'You've got to deserve what I give you', but I think that kind of demand can only come from feeling unloved or needing to hear that he is loved. Of course, he can't admit it himself, so he says, 'I'll give you a reward in material kind, that is my love.' However, he hasn't given the simple love. It was great to work with Helena, who had a very personal connection to the play. However, it goes from those family bonds – the microcosm, macrocosm. We started very specifically on those relationships. What was completely useless was to think that this was a great tragic classic. What helps is to go into those relationships and the huge passions in that family unit. I think it is an everyman journey, which is why I agreed to do it. I read it again after Helena asked me and I questioned my right to play this, and why I identified with Lear when I was fourteen.

What was the answer to that?

I think that maybe the experience of being eighty has some connection with being fourteen in the proximity to death in a character like Lear, who is very passionate and needy. There is this myth that people grow older and contented, wanting less and needing less, but I'm sure that's not so in passionate people where the need for reassurance and a sense of meaning is huge, and akin to the adolescent period. The thing in adolescence where everything is huge – the world is terrible or wonderful – where you throw yourself into idealism or a horror of the greed, corruption and degradation of humanity. There are big absolutes and in a character like Lear, I think there are certain connections to that adolescent state. Adolescence is like a storm. Old age in certain people can be a storm, where you give up your role or projects. He surrenders what he has and then he says, 'Well who am I, if I'm not the King or your father – who can tell me who I am?' It's extraordinary.

You directed Everyman[5] *for the Royal Shakespeare Company last year – how important is directing to you?*

I love directing. I love co-directing with Marcello. When I first worked with Theatre de Complicite, the company always encouraged devising, because a lot of their work is devised. Being an 'outside eye' meant watching improvisations and making suggestions. Then Helena Kaut-Howson, who used to be Artistic Director of Theatr Clwyd, asked me to direct and I accepted. I wanted to accumulate lots of experience, so I thought I'd take the opportunity. I loved being concerned with the overall vision and I found it very exciting. The closest thing to motherhood, thinking, 'Who needs what?'

In the sense of taking on lots of people in different capacities and providing them with something?

That's right. Actors are very like children who have needs, so you can't be condescending. Most of all it has to be a nurturing relationship. As a director, you have to enable always. Directing is about prompting the creativity in the actor himself, who will then take it on and surprise you. It's not a question of the actor executing your commands because that ends up deadly. You can see an actor who is being directed and is following the director's notes. Of course, a director will give notes but they are just like acupuncture, waking things up.

So the needle starts the flow of energy … As a performer, you've worked with a number of impressive women directors – Complicite's Annabel Arden,[6] Katie Mitchell at the Royal Shakespeare Company,[7] Helena Kaut-Howson,[8] Phyllida Lloyd,[9] Nancy Meckler,[10] Annie Castledine[11] and Liane Aukin[12] in radio. Does a woman director bring something particular as a performer?

With a woman director, there are more common things to talk about in terms of sounding the experience of the person you are playing. Whereas with a man, you get on with it yourself because you assume that the man doesn't know much about a woman's way of operating. With a woman director, you can go and say, 'At fifty, what are the concerns of this woman?'

Does this also relate to the function of directing as nurturing and enabling, although there must be male directors who are very good at that.

I hadn't thought about it before, but Max Stafford-Clark[13] and Simon McBurney[14] are two very strong men with particular methods. I would say that they have so-called male ways of operating which is to construct. Simon is a hugely talented man with a truly great sense for theatre-making. He will construct, whether it's a devised piece or a play, a piece like a house, building its foundations and then the large structure in great solid blocks, and only very much later go into detail. I love Simon's way of working, because I think that if the director can lay foundations and build the scaffolding, then there is something for the actor to breathe into. Max has a very different method, which is to do with working with actions. You find a transitive verb to describe what you are actively doing to another person. I persuade, I seduce, I reject. I ... , whatever. In the end what it's about is ensuring that there is always a relationship going on, because you have discussed these transitive verbs with him. He is orchestrating, laying down the musical score to be adhered to. It's quite dictatorial in one sense, but what he does ensure is that there is never vague acting going on. It's very clever and effective, but it's like construction work. The women I've worked with, for example Helena Kaut-Howson, who goes through tiny details, employ a different method of work. I have worked with Les Waters,[15] who had a much more feminine approach and was more into detail. Somehow detail is seen as a more feminine thing. It's also true of Simon McBurney's work, that he's fantastically precise about details.

Can you identify any key moments in your performing life up to this point that have been particularly significant to you for whatever reason?

I remember once in *The Visit*[16] being appalled because the whole bent of this woman's life was to plan a revenge for fifty years. So you are playing this, imagining it and substantiating the whole experience with the history of it as well. I remember one evening being appalled at this hatred that had come up because of this betrayal, which is completely fictional. It was one instance where your imagination just makes things so vivid that fiction and reality get confused. I was quite shocked that I could imagine this level of hatred. You know these theories that people have about healing that you imagine killing off your cancer cells.

The power of the mind?

Yes, to put it nicely. Another key moment: I remember playing Juliet when I was very young with a bad limp. I remember very clearly the sense of the verse being like an extraordinary exhilarating engine; it was emotive, more to do with the earth, a huge natural engine that carried you. In Acts 4 and 5, she is there continuously, living in the present time, and I remember the power of the verse, almost taking me. I don't know if it was the power of the verse or the situation, but I was operating on very many levels at the same time. In the London run of *King Lear* I came closer in the last scene. There is preparation and then there is surrendering to the moment – the imagining of that loss. You come on and the noise of your grief comes out, and you ask other people to grieve with you. Then, it was almost a scary moment, because I remember something took over. You are not speaking the text; it's almost as if you have to allow that to happen, otherwise a little part of you wants to come back and be in control saying the lines. If you dare, you can just go on to that other level.

So that was a key moment when that happened?

Yes. It's not just being – the task is always to be – but it's something about the writing, and the size of that grief. It's not just Lear and Cordelia, an old deposed king and his daughter, but it's also about loss itself. It's almost terrifying to understand that, so you almost hold back from it, but somewhere I would wake up, hooked. There were certain things that you know and certain things I don't know about the storm still, but the last scene is about human loss itself and it's absolutely huge. You approach it and you draw back, because it's terrifying. I don't know if they are key moments or things I just remember. *The Skriker* was another one. I felt that being all those people (in the sense that we are all many) was very vivid. Again they are very practical things; you have to work practically on the difference of each character, their body shape, the curvature of their spine and the quality of their voice. It's not airy-fairy stuff, but it was beyond just thinking it. I did feel (after that thought of, 'Oh, that's what I'm here for – to interpret'), that it was to express that we are many as well.

What would you like to achieve in the future?

I'd like to be a great clown. That would be a wonderful dream.

Notes

1 King Lear in Shakespeare's *King Lear*, directed by Helena Kaut-Howson, Leicester Haymarket, 25 February–15 March 1997.
2 The Skriker in Churchill's *The Skriker*, directed by Les Waters, Royal National Theatre (Cottesloe), 24 January–21 May 1994.
3 Dame Judi Dench in Hare's *Amy's View*, directed by Richard Eyre, Royal National Theatre (Lyttelton), 1997.
4 Young Vic production of *King Lear*, 25 June–2 August 1997.

5 *Everyman,* co-directed with Marcello Magni, RSC (The Other Place), and tour, including Brooklyn Academy of Music, New York and Kennedy Center, Washington, 1996–98.

6 Clara in Dürrenmatt's *The Visit* (adapted by Valency), directed by Annabel Arden and Simon McBurney, Royal National Theatre (Lyttelton), Theatre de Complicite visiting production, 13 February–25 April, 1991. Paulina in Shakespeare's *Winter's Tale,* directed by Annabel Arden, Theatre de Complicite, 1992.

7 Big Rachel in Arden's *Live Like Pigs,* directed by Katie Mitchell, Royal Court, 18 October–13 November 1993. Cassandra in Euripides' *The Women of Troy,* directed by Katie Mitchell, Gate Theatre, 19 July–17 August 1991.

8 Serafina in Tennessee Williams' *The Rose Tattoo,* directed by Helena Kaut-Howson, Theatr Clwyd, 5–20 May 1995. Sister Jeanne in Whiting's *The Devils,* directed by Helena Kaut-Howson, Theatr Clwyd, 20 November–19 December 1992. King Lear in Shakespeare's *King Lear,* Leicester Haymarket, Young Vic and Tokyo. See note 1.

9 Antiochus, The Bawd and Cerimon in Shakespeare's *Pericles,* directed by Phyllida Lloyd, Royal National Theatre (Olivier), 19 May–20 August 1994.

10 Angelica and Louisa in Molière's *The Hypochondriac,* directed by Nancy Meckler, Lyric and Leicester Haymarket, 1987. Electra in Sophocles' *Electra,* directed by Nancy Meckler, Leicester Haymarket, 1987.

11 Susan Barton in Coetzee's *Foe,* adapted and written by Mark Wheatley, directed by Marcello Magni and Annie Castledine, Theatre de Complicite, UK and International tour, 1996.

12 Molly in *Nicola Johnson,* directed by Liane Aukin, Capital Radio, 1984.

13 Melinda in Farquhar's *The Recruiting Officer,* directed by Max Stafford-Clark, Royal Court, Australia and Canada, 1989. Liz Morden in Wertenbaker's *Our Country's Good,* directed by Max Stafford-Clark, Royal Court, Australia and Canada, 1989.

14 See note 6. Actor in *Out of the House Walked a Man* (musical scenes from the writings of Daniil Kharms), devised by Theatre de Complicite and directed by Simon McBurney, Royal National Theatre (Lyttelton), co-production with Theatre de Complicite, 1 December 1994–6 April 1995.

15 See note 2.

16 See note 6.

Fiona Shaw

'Being a performer is not a job, it's a philosophy, and it
is an alternative life in a way to the structured life of
ordinary people.'

'… acting is about trying to be a satellite for something
bigger than yourself.'

Performance Context

Born: 1958, Cork, Ireland.

Prior/current commitments: Performing T.S. Eliot's *The Waste Land*, New York.

Post-interview (selected): Miss Brodie in *The Prime of Miss Jean Brodie*, Royal National Theatre.

The Last September, Thunder Pictures.

The Last Machine, BBC Television.

Other: Olivier Award 1990 – 'Best Actress' for Rosalind in Shakespeare's *As You Like It*, Old Vic; 'Best Actress' for Electra in Sophocles' *Electra*, RSC Barbican; 'Best Actress' for She Te/Shen Ta in Brecht's *The Good Person of Sechuan*, Royal National Theatre.

Olivier Award 1993 – 'Best Actress' for Young Woman in Treadwell's *Machinal*, Royal National Theatre.

1997: Awarded a doctorate at the National University of Ireland.

Made Professor of Drama at the University of Cork, Ireland.

Interview

Fiona Shaw warmly welcomed me into her London home on 6 March 1997, and talked about performing T.S. Eliot's The Waste Land, *only interrupted once by a phone call from Deborah Warner in France.*

Alison Oddey: *What did performing T. S. Eliot's* The Waste Land[1] *give you?*

Fiona Shaw: I discovered by performing this short text that it is a sort of fax of the twenty-first century. I found that performance ceased to be about necessarily playing characters in a play, and that it is about engaging totally with the imaginative and emotional reality of the poetry, allowing oneself to be a conduit for what may be a more lively visual truth than the poet even intended. By that I mean that I'm not sure if I'm in any way true to the style of T. S. Eliot, but that if I can stay open as one does with Shakespeare, something of the essence of what he's trying to do will be revealed. So my conception of theatre has moved on. My big concern is not about parts but about what the nature of theatre and performance is, because unlike many other things, the point about theatre is that it has to redefine itself every time you perform. You can't do a performance like the one you did before, and you can't do the aesthetic changes second by second, and in fact, as soon as it's achieved then it's over. We live in an incredibly banal time in England, where people put on productions that are like other productions. That is why theatre hasn't much meaning in the city any more. Most of the theatre, even the stuff that is praised in the press, is in fact, old. It's been newly rehearsed, but it's old. A lot of the actors have to deal with the fact of just getting it on, or most of the designers are caught by commercialism or whatever, but very few people are really moving the theatre as an experimental force forward. I suppose in a way *Richard II*[2] was an experiment right in the heart of the institution, and I'm very grateful to the National for allowing that. Not many theatres would have allowed a woman to play *Richard II*. It was absolutely right that they did, because it makes the National connect to experiment. *The Waste Land* is its own thing. I started it off as a festival piece and it has just grown and grown. It was directed by Deborah Warner and lit by Jean Kalman, so I had two great theatre practitioners on this thirty-seven minute poem, giving it the right size. In New York, we played in a desolate old porn cinema on 42nd street. The audience went into this desperate theatre, covered with plastic sheeting except over the 200 seats we were allowed, and their eyes were opened by the choice of architecture and their mild disorientation. It was very beautiful inside and lit fantastically – just little licks and hints of things that people could see, very honest, just light bulbs on this empty stage. I performed the poem aided by the punctuation of these light bulbs – quite straightforward.

How easy was it to find the right choice of building or theatrical space for the performance?

Deborah took a year to find a building. She went three or four times to find it. We were going to do it on the twin towers, in the Rockefeller Centre, in a modern urban building, and then at the last minute, when they decided to give up, this cinema revealed itself. It's been such an overwhelming experience of simplicity, having come from *Richard II*, where there were twenty actors and elaborate lights. It has been refreshing.

Has it shifted you somewhere else now?

I hope not, because having done that shift, one has to shift on. I can only fantasize about all the poems I'd love to do, but they are really less interesting than the one I've done. One could do a marvellous theatrical interlude event based on Coleridge's *The Ancient Mariner*. What I've enjoyed discovering about *The Waste Land* is that there is a possibility of creating theatre out of pieces not necessarily written for the theatre. Many playwrights are trapped

in the notion of what the theatre is, and the notion of theatre is not necessarily the same thing as the notion of a play. It is becoming deconstructed
like everything else. For example, you couldn't really write what Robert Lepage
is saying, and what he does in the theatre. It's invented, rather than written.
When I see Act 3, Scene 2 on a play, I faint, because I think maybe the writer
shouldn't declare that, maybe we should find out where Act 3, Scene 2 lies in
the play. That's not to say that I don't have immense respect for craftsmen
like Ibsen, where the construction is so fantastic that it's a sort of rubric – it
turns itself. You are trying to find pieces of writing that would make good
theatrical evenings, or come up with a radical aesthetic brushstroke that
forces the audience to see an old play in a new way, like changing gender. If
you play a king, you can't play every king just because you are a woman, but
sometimes it might work and that's what is interesting – why doesn't it work?
So this area of turning things on their heads interests me, but you have to
find the right things to turn on their heads.

Did playing Richard II *leave you with any desire to play more kings, for example,*
King Lear?

I don't deal with things in that way. *Richard II* was a theatrical experiment –
not even an acting one – because the experience of playing *Richard II* for me
was very hard. I wasn't able to use my full capacities; it's quite a handicap not
to play your gender in a production, which is full of people who are playing
theirs.

In what sense is it a handicap?

In the sense of not having the history of a man who could play *Richard II* – I
know it's only pretending – but you often play much more from the history
of who you are than you think. So I kept on feeling I was slightly translating,
I was slightly trying to speak fluent French is what it felt like. I felt that I was
serving the idea as well as I could, but the relief of doing *The Waste Land*
afterwards – of just going back on to the horse that I knew how to ride, which
was full of different voices and full of men and women, but not dependent
on *my* history. In that way I'm very glad I did *Richard II*, because Tiresias sits
at the centre of the Waste Land and Tiresias is a man and a woman. Of course,
I felt that I had a lot of experience in the year of playing a male character and
playing Millamant,[3] who was the woman of a century. So I had had a very
Tiresias year, and I very much enjoyed the idea that people could change and
switch for a moment. However, the switching for a moment is different from
actually embodying the entire person, so I only played an idea which is hard
because you can only play a person really.

That's what you discovered through that experience?

I probably knew it in advance, but it interested me at the time because I'll do anything that's dangerous. I have a mortal terror of boredom. I feel boredom is absolutely the grave, boredom is the grey silence that maybe lies ahead. I am amazed at how many people put up with boredom. I love going into unknown territory.

Where does that come from?

I have no idea. It is remarkable how one pursues this cycle of acting in a non-religious way and this heightened silence of performance is very near the heightened silence of the hermit or the monastic. When you ask me why I do this, all I know is that it's something to do with rendering. The only way you can render yourself is to render everything you know, and the only way you can get to that hopefully is on the terrible challenge of courting failure. Agony; you have to abandon all you know to even hope to get it. I'd say that's very near to performing – that it is a pursuit of heaven, an absolutely false pursuit, which probably can't ever be fulfilled, but sometimes you get a glimpse of it when you don't expect it.

So in that last year, with everything you described, did you get a glimpse of it then?

I suppose I did get a glimpse of it in New York. I loved playing *The Waste Land* in Paris, but to be honest, I did feel moments in New York of that heightened sense that I would not wish for anything more than what I had at that moment. I was very lucky to have Deborah turn up every few weeks from London to re-look at it, to have her come and rework it so much, buffing it up and making it even more accurate. It would change slightly over the time, and she would take all the developments in it and buff them up, so that I did feel we were getting deeper and deeper into this poem. I was enjoying the doing of it in a way that used every ounce of one's skill and openness, releasing you from your skill and mastering your skill at the same time. It didn't murder me like *Electra*[4] nearly killed me to do, but it was as hard as *Electra* – only thirty-seven minutes long. I did feel it then – a very heightened feeling, wonderful and very rare. You don't get it often. I didn't in the rest of the year.

You've been performing for thirteen years, giving and going on dangerous voyages – how important is that danger and challenge of the role?

My father recently said to me, 'Have you not thought of doing a normal play?' I'd love to do a normal play, although it's not the job of theatre to be dealing with the normal in this extreme world that we all live in. At the moment tragedy is more important than comedy, much as I adore comedy, and of course, comedy is a great relief to play. People adore playing comedy and it makes the audience feel good, but actually tragedy is the great healing force if it's well done, because tragedy allows the viewer to see the depths of the human spirit. I suppose that I did want that when I was little. I wanted to be an actress – I didn't know what it meant – but I've got more respect for that now, for wanting something and you don't know what it means. I love rehearsals, where I don't talk much – I just do it. I do it wrong, then do a double thing and do different 'paintings' – like sketches. It's a fantastic thing in a group, there are a few of you inventing the world and discovering things, like *Alice in Wonderland*, as you go along inventing what you see and then performing it, so ideally you get to work on it more. It's a heavenly task really, but the downside is that it is so exposing that you really have to *want* to do it.

You obviously really do want to do it though?

I go through bouts. There was a lot of wanting in that period with the RSC,[5] which took some of the best years of our lives. I was there aged twenty-six to thirty, performing pretty well nightly and you get a lot of it done in that time. It's an enormous amount of your life and I don't want that. Having said that, the heavenly period in New York could have just gone on and on, because I adored it. I was completely content.

It gave you complete satisfaction?

It did. More than anything in the world, I had as an adolescent wanted to go to RADA. It was a quantum leap for me to come from Ireland and go there. When I got to RADA, of course, I had completed my only desire in the world. It was the first time I experienced control of my life, and I could make something I wanted to happen. I adored every day of it, and was privileged to be there. It's a fantastically indulgent thing in one way, but it was very good; it shaped things that had been a jumble in my life. It was only then that I discovered why I wanted to go to RADA. The danger thing didn't hit me for a long while. I just wanted to be asked to do jobs (asked to act), and that was a natural, reasonable desire in a young actress. I just wanted to be allowed to have a go at this or that, and I left RADA on a high and was taken on by the National immediately. I made a film, and then went to the RSC, where I played leading roles within two or three years of leaving RADA. I got very into the nature of language, so I had a very fulfilling education by doing that. I had a marvellous time at the RSC with Juliet Stevenson and with Alan Rickman, who were both my seniors and really helpful to me. They were really welcoming to me as a new sprog, and they taught me a lot. By the time I was thirty, I had a whole classical career done. I had this mad year in 1989, at the end of which

I finally did this tragedy *Electra*, and it changed my complete view about what the possibilities of the theatre were. What I didn't know then was that once you go into that realm of discovering its possibilities, you are also excluded from the ease of just enjoying the performance. So in a way I lost my innocence then – I can no longer do the things that I'm asked to do next. I've tried to only do what I want to do, and I've tried to make those choices in earnest, rather than with one eye to the future.

You've lost your innocence, so in order to be true to yourself, you've got to go with what you feel.

I have ridiculous desires. I'm always hoping someone is going to come up with a fantastic idea better than the one I have come up with and, of course, people aren't necessarily thinking like that, why should they? I'm not saying everything has to be earth shattering, but for the kind of energy and time you put into a theatrical project, they have to be of some use, otherwise you are wasting the audience's time. I have maybe lost that cavalier, boulevard relationship with the theatre that so many people have kept, and maybe it's because I've had the experience of something other, so I'm always trying to reach for this other experience.

An extraordinary experience?

Yes, I have had that experience in *Electra* and *Hedda Gabler*,[6] which was just a tremendous voyage really. In a way, the benefits of that went into *Machinal*,[7] because I discovered for myself this very difficult area of acting that used more than one's mind and body, and used one's weakness. That's what I've discovered, that people are not really interested in your strength, it's your weakness that releases the truth, so you have to be very vulnerable when you are acting.

Can you elaborate further?

You have to play against your strengths really. I found *Machinal* very good training for that, playing somebody who couldn't articulate. It's a complicated thing to play, because you come with everything you know and all the privilege of your life. It's very hard to play the underprivileged, because you have to undo all that you have and not come as yourself, but come almost as your other self – as the un-self. Acting can be very selfish, but it can be anything you want it to be – it's a fantastically amorous and generous activity. You have to be in love with the desire to perform, and somehow be in love with the audience. You have to be giving them a present, something they didn't know before, and you have to offer yourself. You have to somehow love your fellow performers, because you share this game with them, so it's full of love and big heart ideally.

How do you see that audience when you are playing?

My overall feeling is that you judge the evening on a series of dialogues with the activity itself, thinking that it either went well, badly or needed to push forward, so you are steering a very fast car, which is what acting feels like a lot of the time. I feel very well disposed to the audience, and of course, particularly if they feel very well disposed towards me. Press nights are notoriously difficult, because the loved child will behave lovably and the unloved child will behave terribly. Charm, the open-hearted warmth, is often very hard to conjure on a press night, because you feel waves of hostility, not neutrality even. There might be one's own fear, but one feels these waves of negative energy, whereas on a good night, you feel this wave of good feeling in the first ten seconds. I don't believe that it's not coming from them. So press nights are very hard!

Is that also to do with a sense of knowing that you are going to be criticised?

I don't take criticism well. I've never liked it. I was very strictly brought up, and I hated it then. I don't get great joy from praise, which is very classic. It makes me feel more neutral, which maybe is a more pleasant feeling than feeling horrible.

Were your parents hard on you as a child?

I remember my upbringing as strict, but in many ways it was most indulgent.

Strict as in rules?

Rules, and a sort of discipline, so I am not particularly disciplined now. I am disciplined about work, because it consumes me, but that's not discipline at all, it's just that I get obsessed with it.

What tempts that obsession?

Excitement is very important. I am consumed by it, because it's a way of life. Being a performer is not a job, it's a philosophy, and it's an alternative life in a way to the structured life of ordinary people. There are things that you can't control; for instance, a whole generation of us has been done out of film careers, because there was no film industry of any value. Our films have not come anywhere near the standard of our theatre. You are a hired hand in film

As a senior infant (right) at the Mercy Convent, aged four

– the crudest colour cast for your shape or your size, or some very overt quality in you. We all wear these envelopes of bodies, but we are quite other beings inside. I suppose the joy of the theatre is that you can explore those other aspects of the nature of being, but film just takes the external qualities. When I was in New York, I had a big talk with Meryl Streep, who said that she would have loved to perform *The Waste Land*. She realised that she couldn't, because her face is so publicly the size that it is that she can't now flick it to develop the muscle to do something like a solo poem. I began to see the other man's grass – there she is locked in a world – they give them a film career but absolutely stop them having an experimental theatrical career, which is where they all started out. Whereas those of us here, who have experimental theatrical careers, don't really have the film careers we would like, so it's quite healing to be privileged to meet people on the other side.

I presume it's also a privilege to have experienced a unique performer/director relationship with Deborah Warner?

I haven't done that much with Deborah, but everything I have done has been of significance to both of us. She's very different from me; she's quicker, quiet, inarticulate, very dogged, disciplined and thorough, but she has taught me patience and I'm very glad I learnt that. She's tested my patience and I test hers, and I think I'm always relieved when we do a new piece. I'm relieved we did *The Waste Land,* because I thought *Richard II* would be the end of it. There's Hildegard[8] as well, so that's three of us have worked together for six or seven years, only on and off. It has been blessed. I'm sure it will end some time and I'll be very sad when it does.

Do you view performing and acting as different things?

Performing is delivering, and some people are very good at delivering. Acting is about discovery. Performing can also be tricks, but acting is about trying to be a satellite for something bigger than yourself. To be a good stage actor one has to try and investigate the language, to allow the language to affect you. The language transforms you by its nature. In classical acting that's possible because the language is fantastic and much more difficult than modern plays, where you have to invest ordinary language with poetic significance. I suppose acting is the capturing of poetic reality at any one moment. A talented actor is someone who can do that.

Who do you think are the really great actors?

The great actors are those who manage to make the time that they are living in completely relevant to the play, whilst being true to every other aspect of the play.

Where did the roots of your desire to perform come from?

They are inherited; my mother adores performing and she never did. I think that generation had a tough time. She had a couple of degrees in physics and ended up in ICI. I think that's quite hard. I made that leap that she might have made, if she had a bit more ... people hadn't a clue how to go about things, wanting to be an opera singer and actually getting to be one was out of her ken. She sang every day of her life and she loves it. So that's part of it, but there wasn't a great tradition particularly. There was no line between the family dramas and theatre. The root desire may be a fear of an ordinary job, it could have been a terror of academia or a terror of place – getting caught in Cork – there's no doubt it got me out of the only world I knew. I loved it because I knew everything about it. I anticipated a whole life there, but somewhere I knew I wanted to be away.

Does the terror of academia come from your mother?

She has an M.Sc. in Physics, but she wasn't particularly academic. My father is a surgeon not particularly academic, but there was a great respect for the university and it was the great saviour of that post-war generation. People who before the war would have had no education and suddenly are given an education, so there was a whole new class of people invented I suppose. It became a great symbol of freedom, and of course now it has come to its great power, which is that the Irish are incredibly well-educated and ready for Europe, and not trapped by any hat-doffing to England.

You seemed to suggest that you didn't want to get into academia.

It's where I would have gone. There weren't that many alternatives. If you weren't going to be a nurse, or a doctor, or an engineer, you would probably go into academia. It's a very pleasant, medieval way of living really. I probably would have gone into that, but I got out.

Why are you still performing today?

I perform now, because it's what I know how to do and it continues to excite me. I'm performing now, because I'm rooted in it. I'm much more interested in acting than being an actress. Maybe the reality is retrospective. There's no doubt you've been doing it all the time, it's what you are. People are often very surprised that I'm an actress.

Why is that?

I suppose it's associated with a sort of lifestyle of fur coats or glamour. I'm very glamorous in my own way and vain. I have disguised vanity. I pretend not to be, but in fact I am very vain. We are all vain.

You seem very focused in terms of your work and how you are progressing – is that true of all aspects of your life?

Not at all, I'm very unfocused. I have a great desire to write films. Plays for the theatre are so impossible; I couldn't write for theatre. Films are easier. You just have to deal with the landscape, and you don't have to make a metaphor of the landscape. So I'm trying to write. I get a scene written, then don't do anything for weeks. I have no method at all, so I struggle with myself on that. I go through bouts of being terribly disciplined. I've often been described as intense and it's not at all how I experience myself, because I am happy to change course at any time. I'm like my mother. I have elements of an artistic temperament that aren't particularly good. I often forget to reply to calls, so I have to really struggle and come here in the mornings and go through a list. Time. I have a very bad problem with time. I often find that I must reply to something, which is already two or three days on, but I think it's only the next day – is that the time?

Notes

1   *The Waste Land,* directed by Deborah Warner, Paris, Toronto Festival, Montreal and Liberty Theatre on Broadway, 1996–97.
2   Richard II in Shakespeare's *Richard II,* directed by Deborah Warner, Royal National Theatre (Cottesloe), 1995.
3   Millamant in Congreve's *The Way of the World,* directed by Phyllida Lloyd, Royal National Theatre (Lyttelton), 1995.
4   Electra in Sophocles' *Electra,* directed by Deborah Warner, Royal Shakespeare Company, Barbican (The Pit), 1989. Olivier Award for 'Best Actress', 1990 and London Critic Award, 1990.
5   Performed at the RSC during 1985–89: Celia in *As You Like It;* Tatiana in *Philistines;* Madame de Volanges in *Les Liaisons Dangereuses;* Erica Mann in *Mephisto;* Beatrice in *Much Ado About Nothing;* Portia in *The Merchant of Venice;* Mistress Carol in *Hyde Park;* Kate in *Taming of the Shrew;* Lady Frampul in *New Inn;* Electra in *Electra.*
6   Hedda Gabler in Ibsen's *Hedda Gabler,* directed by Deborah Warner, Abbey Theatre, Dublin and West End productions, 1991. Shaw received the London Critics Award for this role in 1992.
7   Young Woman in Sophie Treadwell's *Machinal,* directed by Stephen Daldry, Royal National Theatre, 1993. Olivier Award for 'Best Actress' 1993; Evening Standard Drama Award for 'Best Actress' 1993.
8   Hildegard Bechtler, designer.

Dawn French

'… – only driven by chocolate!'

'If you're a comedian in this country, the industry wants
you in the comedy bubble, finding it rather odd,
ambitious and cocky of you to think that you might
want to cross over into drama.'

Performance Context

Born: 1957, Wales.

Prior/current commitments: Clara Soppitt in J.B. Priestley's *When We Are Married*, Savoy Theatre.
Bev Bodger in *Sex and Chocolate*, written by Tony Grounds, BBC Television Screen One.

Post-interview (selected): *Then Again*, Comedy Revue, Lyric Theatre, Hammersmith.
The Vicar of Dibley, written by Richard Curtis, BBC Television.
Murder Most Horrid, BBC Television.
French and Saunders Christmas Special, BBC Television.

Interview

*I sat at the top of the Groucho Club in Soho on 4 June 1997, absorbed in deep con-
versation with Dawn French, which was so much easier for interviewing than being
in the restaurant – 'The restaurant isn't open yet Dawn, but we can open it for you!'*

Alison Oddey: *I really admired your recent stage performance in J.B. Priestley's play
When We Are Married[1] at the Savoy Theatre, having only seen you in television or
film comedy.*

Dawn French: I'm glad that you liked it. It was tough to pull off, because there
were moments when you tend to hide away any instinctive comedy skills
you've got, thinking that I'm not allowed to bring out my funniness here, when
confronted with a legitimate director and actors. I had a lot of decisions to
make with that play. You have to prove yourself to colleagues, which is quite
complicated. It wasn't until the end of the Chichester run that we were all as
one in that play.

Are you from a theatrical family?

No, absolutely not! My dad was in the Royal Air Force and came out to be a
newsagent, and my mum has had all sorts of careers, mainly trying to make
ends meet for the family. She's a remarkable woman – Amazonian in strength.
My dad died when I was about nineteen, so Mum found a whole new life at

quite a young age. She's only sixty-three now and she had to build a new life for herself over twenty years ago. She is now a counsellor for drug and alcohol abuse, having set up a centre in Plymouth where I'm from, which is for single women with serious drug or alcohol problems and their children. It's the first centre of its kind in the country, costing her a lot of money and a lot of her life. She's a very compassionate woman with a lot of time and very generous-spirited. Her life has completely changed, because she wasn't like that at all, or wasn't able to explore it. If I ever have half her strength, I would be very glad.

If your father was in the RAF, then presumably you were a child itinerant?

Yes, absolutely, like a lot of 'crab kids', as air force kids are called. Sometimes you would move every three months, but usually you'd move every eighteen months to a new camp.

A physical upheaval followed by meeting and making new friends?

Yes, but I don't remember that as a bad thing. I quite enjoyed that. I'm quite gregarious. Mum has reminded me of times when I used to sleepwalk, so maybe the disarray of moving, meeting new friends and going to new schools all the time subconsciously had an effect, but I consciously remember it as a very happy time. We spent four years in Cyprus when I was a kid, aged six to ten, and I only remember it being totally halcyon days – going to school for three hours in the morning, then swimming all afternoon on your own at the beach with your brother, and being picked up at six in the evening. My memories of that are fantastic.

You mentioned a brother …

Yes, I've got a brother, who is three years older than me. He's a radical left-wing housing manager, who would probably disagree with that description. He works for the Probation Office in Cornwall, rehousing people on probation and he oversees various big housing projects down there.

You went to the Central School of Speech and Drama to train as a drama teacher rather than an actress, and I read on the Internet that you wanted to be like your drama teacher at school, whom you idolised.

Yes, I did idolise her, partly because I was at boarding school because my parents travelled around so much. I was at a small friendly school, which I loved, and I did drama twice a week after school with Christine Abbot. I just loved her. The school was an old Gothic abbey and she was in a tower. I had to go up the steps to this secret room in the tower with her, and this was part of the reason for having a real crush on her. Not a mother replacement crush, but I just thought that she was fantastically eloquent and clever. She was quite strict and we did LAMDA exams, where we had to prepare and do speeches. It was that arena that I've found in rehearsals for anything ever since, which is the part I enjoy more than the performance. In rehearsals, you are exploring what something is and just focusing it a bit. That's what we would do, we would just talk about anything we were working on at the time, and I think I just enjoyed her wit and intelligence. I just wanted to be around her on my own, and I didn't want to share her with other girls. I just wanted to be her. She had trained at Central, recommended it, and that was why I applied to Central. I had no desire to be an actress whatsoever.

Is that where you met Jennifer Saunders?

Yes, I wanted to be a teacher and Jennifer could not have had a more different attitude to the whole thing. She didn't want to be in London or a drama school of any sort. Somehow she got a place on that course by not even wanting to be there. She was there completely by accident, taking it all very lightly, but a complete breath of fresh air when we were being a bit over-serious about it all. In fact, I was so serious about teaching that I was a bit of a swot really. We were there together for three years, and shared a flat together. Then I got my first job at Parliament Hill School, a big girls' comprehensive, which I loved. The girls were very high-spirited and good fun. I was also moonlighting, doing *The Comic Strip*[2] in the evening. Jennifer hadn't got a teaching job and was basically spending her dole on champagne and doing *The Times* crossword. She had an extraordinary lifestyle. She didn't have that Protestant work ethic that I had, where you absolutely had to fill your day full of work – even if you enjoyed it, you had to be working hard. She didn't have that at all, and she was the one who found out about *The Comic Strip*, and suggested we do it. I enjoyed it very much, but did it secretly at night-time and went to work during the day. Then we had the chance to go on tour as *The Comic Strip* group to Australia for three months, so I knew that I would have to dump my job, which was a very big decision for me. I talked to the headmistress of the school, asking her for advice. She told me that I would regret it if I didn't go, and that there would be a job for me at the school if it didn't work out. That was great – I had everything covered and I could go. In 1980, we could earn £200 a week, which was a lot of money then, much more than teaching, so I knew that it was a viable option.

What attracted you to performing?

I couldn't believe that I'd get away with it and I still can't quite believe it. It feels like when your mum tells you off for showing off in front of your friends, but you are not going to stop showing off because it's good fun and your friends like it. I get paid for doing that now, so I feel a bit guilty for making such a good living out of something that I enjoy so much. Paid to dress up, pretend to be somebody, have all my friends around me, being part of a big gang, shouting and misbehaving, which is extraordinary! I can't wait for somebody to rumble me really! From time to time they do; that's what critics are there for. As time has gone by, I have become more serious about it, making sure that I do it properly. I do know how hard it is to write anything good, and I know how much crap is around.

Is there a specific reason why you perform?

No – I know some people are set on their particular course, but my course was very different. In a way, it was an accident and then once I had fallen into it – legitimised in my mind as something I could earn and be quite good at – I then felt validated by taking this course. However, every single job that I've done, I am completely surprised that I am still doing it! I'm perfectly aware that in our business you can lose it very quickly for all sorts of reasons, and especially for women aged around forty. It's quite difficult to get people to regard you as a central character in a drama, even in a comedy, unless you've created it yourself, which is what we've done for 98 per cent of the time. I don't feel driven to perform at all. I feel driven to work, but I don't feel driven to perform.

What does performing give you?

Performing is good fun, but I get as much pleasure from being around the crew, casting or the development of the script. Whatever performance I give is going to be there forever, so whatever mistakes I make are going to be public and irretrievable, so that's slightly scary, but there's no point being scared, you just have to get on with it.

Why perform then?

I'm not really qualified to do anything else. I could probably retrain and teach again, which I have considered, but somehow my time's not up yet for that. I still feel that I haven't done some of the things that I would like to do. I would like to direct a bit, and I'd like to write something that I can follow through with. Also, I'm in the fortunate position of doing another series of *The Vicar of Dibley*,[3] working with Richard Curtis and that cast, who are like my new gang to socialise and have fun with. Why wouldn't I want to do that job again? I don't have to write it, and I'm allowed a few little rucks during the rehearsal time, but it's a completely enjoyable job and there's no reason to stop doing it yet.

Is it difficult being both comedian and actress?

If you're a comedian in this country, the industry wants to keep you in the comedy bubble, finding it rather odd, ambitious and cocky of you to think that you might want to cross over into drama. However, if people from drama want to cross over into comedy, that's okay, and they are bound to be very good at it, probably better than comedians! To think that anybody has woken up and decided to be a comedian in the first place is so alien to me. Certainly in the 1980s, it was something you did in the evening as a hobby. The opportunities that present themselves to you are the moulding of how your career goes – the fact that Jennifer and I might have always considered that we could write what we did – it never occurred to us not to do that. It happened that we had to write a new sketch every night at *The Comic Strip*, which was a hardship, but I think it's what everybody should be doing. The same goes for every single sketch in *French and Saunders*;[4] we only did it because we thought it was funny. I don't think we've ever thought, 'What are we trying to say here?'

How do you perceive the current state of comedy to be?

Comedy is so diverse and I'm constantly surprised by what's happening and how it's changing. What I've noticed a lot lately, and I really like it, is how surreal things are. Things are going away from the political, and that's possibly because we don't have Thatcher any more. When we had Thatcher, we had a thing that was so evil, big and obvious, that there was something political to rail against. Jennifer and I never did actually, but Alexi Sayle and quite a lot of the people that we worked with did, and we were called alternative comedians. We were regarded as performing in a slightly different way – without those specific political references – as if we had made a choice to perform in a particular way. I never knew quite where that title 'alternative comedian' came from. If you had to describe somebody that was alternative, it would be Victoria Wood, who has escaped the whole pit of PC-ness throughout her entire career, but she's never been referred to under that banner; she's kept herself completely separate from it all. Again, as with us, it wasn't a conscious thing, it just happened. Now it's much more surreal – for example Vic Reeves and Bob Mortimer in the BBC Television series *Shooting Stars* is a weird, wonderful comedy that hasn't got any political meat at all, but is exceptionally funny and I like that. It's a sort of surreal movement happening inside comedy, which is great. I don't know where it comes from, and I bet Vic and Bob wouldn't know how they write their stuff – they just do it. It comes out of the relationship that happens organically between the two of them when they are together, and they are a bit like that when they are off-stage.

What do you find attractive about a woman who is humorous?

Everything. I find the same about a man who is too. All the men I've been attracted to, other than Steve McQueen and David Cassidy, who are just gorgeous boys, and any possible relationship I've ever considered, has always been with a funny man. I couldn't imagine it being any other way. I think the same about women. I think it's very sexy to be funny and I absolutely love it. It's odd that you get a cocktail of emotions about women who are funny. Firstly, it's jealousy, but very soon after, you are so glad to be a punter and to be enjoying it. I can go and watch Victoria doing her show, two masterful hours, well-written and thought through. I know she goes through a lot to get to it, but the first emotion I have is fury that I'm not as funny as that person, or that I'm not doing it at that moment. It only lasts for about a minute and then you are just so glad.

Would you like to do stand-up?

I'm not driven to do it, but I wouldn't turn it down either. It must be very scary. In fact, Tony Grounds and I would quite like to write a stage show. He asked me if I'd like to do a monologue, and the idea attracts me, but I won't cry if I don't.

In the course of talking to you, it has become apparent that you clearly state terms and conditions for every job you do.

I do, but I am aware that I couldn't have done that ten years ago. You only earn that with time, and I push it as far as I can to make everything enjoyable. It doesn't hurt, as long as nobody else is affected, or it doesn't take money from where it is supposed to be on screen. I don't think there is anything wrong with having enjoyable working conditions. It's in my contract now that for every show there is chocolate on the set, which is very sad – only driven by chocolate! It's good news for the crew, who likes it too!

Has becoming a working mother made you re-examine what is important to you?

It has, because the fact is that, morally, nothing else should be as important as that. That is the dilemma, because you've made a huge commitment, and you know that when push comes to shove, that is going to be your first choice. However, there is another whole person inside you that is the person you were until that moment, which you can't just put aside, unless you are dishonest. So the juggling of both things is what you then spend your life doing. I don't think there is any room for guilt about any of it; I just don't hold with that. So many women do and that is the problem; they think they are failing. I have never felt any of that. I gave the first year up entirely to her, because we adopted her. I felt that she'd already had one rejection, and that she needed to feel totally safe coming to our home. I was quite proud of myself for doing that, because I'd never stopped working before and I found it quite hard to do. I was ready to go back to work and to being creative at the end of that year, although it took about two years afterwards to start being sharp in any way. I couldn't think fast, I had lost confidence, I couldn't read books – which is why Jennifer and I started a book club.

Are you ever able to give yourself time to do nothing, to think and be quiet, or do you like most women deny this time for yourself?

I don't think that I've ever given myself time for just nothing. I don't give myself time to read a book, to sit in the garden, or any sort of healing time. It sounds terribly hippy, but totally isolated time. It's why people turn to meditation or alternative therapies, because what they are allowing themselves is that bit of time.

For me, it's an aromatherapy massage, booked on a regular basis.

We feel by having a job and having a child, we are already having everything, so who are we to assume that on top of that we deserve some aromatherapy! It's absolutely essential to have something every now and again, and I don't do it! Stress will show up in people in different ways. For me, it shows up in my voice, which means that I can't do my job if it's bad.

How do you deal with these contradictory identities of performer, working mother and wife?

I do escape occasionally. I used to do it a lot before Billie arrived, but it was never very noticeable because it was just part of my everyday life. I felt the need in that second year to escape being anyone's mum or wife at all. I went to a friend's house in France just for two days, taking lots of bottles of St Emilion, cheese and bread with me. Everybody was fine about my having a break, but all I wanted to do was weep for two days. It was as if I had a big reservoir ready to weep. No particular big pain; it was just tiredness, worry and all the bad things. It was as though I'd put them in a drawer and got on with everything quite well, but I knew that I needed to open this drawer for a little while. I wept until my eyes were puffed out – I think I was enjoying it a bit too much. I was imagining how good it would look on film, and I think

I was watching myself doing it in a rather self-indulgent way. I did it for two solid days, came home and felt great. I needed to escape those roles of partner, because I work in partnerships a lot in my life – as wife, comedy partner, business partner, and I often work in twosomes. I'm very comfortable with that, but occasionally just need to cut loose a bit so that I can return refreshed. I think that's quite healthy.

Does the word 'strumpet' hold any resonance for you?

I suppose there is a bit of strumpet in all of us – unless you've got a bit of earth, mud and sex in you, there's no heart really. Certainly people still think that if you are loud and a bit of a show-off, it's very unfeminine. I remember in my teens being the girl who was never afraid of telling rude jokes, but knowing that it isn't a role that gets you a boyfriend easily in the long run. It's a rare thing to find a guy who will relate to that slightly strumpetty person in you. Far too many of us fell for 'girliness' too early on, knowing that was an easier route. The common choice was to fall in line and be feminine, which I've always had a bit of a problem with.

In what way?

I regard myself as completely female and I've never doubted my ability to be sexual or anything like that. The whole issue of the clothes raised a lot of things about weight and self-image, which I've thought about a lot, but I cannot place the time when I was confident about my size or sexual prowess. I was aware that my role in a group of girls was to be slightly badly behaved – not enough to get caught – but to use language in a different way, challenging or being a bit cheeky. I'm not all-out brazen, but I see the need to get in touch with the slightly bad girl in me.

Do you think that the 1997 image of the performing woman still has that quality of strumpet as you describe it?

I think Jo Brand would be regarded as somebody who was a bit of a strumpet – a bit full of herself – and Jenny Eclair would be regarded as that by a lot of men. They are absolute champions to a lot of women, who would give their eye teeth to be like them, but they are not so palatable for a lot of men and the older generation. However, there have always been those loud, brash, honest women to give us the edges of where we belong, which is great. When it comes to Juliet Stevenson, however, or the lovely Judi Dench, who I want to play my mum in a situation comedy so badly, they are not regarded as strumpets in any way. They are fine, elegant, graceful women, who are bright and clever, bestowing us with their charms and talent. Men think that about them too, so that chorus girl feeling about all actresses being a bit tarty is gone. In the area of stand-up comedy, there are still girls that are a bit challenging – fighting for their right to be there – and I thank God for them.

Perhaps the image of strumpet is now more applicable to the new models and fashion culture?

It's certainly fashionable to be slightly strumpetty, to pout, to be angry, not care and be slightly tarty. The imagery is so strong now of girls on motorbikes with angry looks and short skirts, which part of me applauds and part of me worries for them. I find that image of the druggy, angry girl very phoney. It's a very curious message, in the same way that being incredibly thin is a curious message to give any woman. We are supposed to want to look like that and behave like Courtney Love. Something in me does want to do that, and something in me wants Billie to do that. To have a defiance, but at the same time, I wouldn't want her to be rude in any way, which isn't very helpful to anybody.

Can you identify a key moment in your life in the widest sense of being a performing woman?

If I thought about this for a week I'd probably say something different, but my first trawl of thought is my dad. I do remember very clearly something that he said to me. I think I was about fourteen and I was going to some kind of dance, disco or party maybe, and I had asked if I could stay out very late because I knew that there would be boys there, and snogging potential. I knew that other girls were going to be there late and possibly, not sex on the cards, but major petting! I was very excited about the whole thing and I was probably going to go further than I had gone before, and I'd built up to it for weeks. Anyway, my dad was going to drive me to this party and he was going to collect me at two o'clock in the morning. Before we left, I knew that my parents were worried about it. I had probably given all the indications and signals, although I thought I was covering them up, but actually telegraphing the fact that this was going to be quite an important night. My father asked me to come and sit down in the front room and I thought, 'Here we go, I'm going to get the lecture', which I'd had a few times before about not smoking, and not doing this or that. He did something, which was probably just a trick, but it really worked. He took my hands and looked me in the face, and basically told me how completely gorgeous I was. He said that I was the apple of their eyes and how much they had wanted a little girl, what a prize I was, how proud they were of me, and how if anything ever happened to me it would destroy them. That was it; that's all he did. I wouldn't let anyone get near me at this fucking party. I think that it was a clever thing to do, because he knew that was the effect it would have on me. That I would go out eight times as big and confident, never needing to feel gratitude for the attention of boys. I was grateful for that, because I was fat and a bit of a joker. Everyone wants to be fancied and loved a bit, and you will actually take the dregs if that's what is left to you! He was telling me not to do that, and not to assume that I didn't deserve absolutely the best and that I wasn't completely gorgeous – physically and spiritually a fantastic person. I've never forgotten it, because not only did it work that night, but also it's worked ever since. I never assumed that I deserved anything less than something very good. I don't think it would have been the same if my mum had said that, because I would have regarded it as a bit sentimental. She was always telling me that she loved me, but for my dad to do that ... I think he knew I was right on the edge and I would have shagged somebody that night given half the chance. He knew he had to get me back from that sexual edge there, and make me feel that there wasn't anything I had to do to prove anything, that I wasn't being clever by doing it, and that I shouldn't feel blessed by some boy shagging me basically. It should be my decision and it should be something good later on. All those things were wound up in it and he did it in a very clever way. The only reason that I've remembered it is because people have said, 'Why are you so confident?' I couldn't think why I was and that was the only thing I could trace it to, probably along with day-to-day good parenting and a confident, happy childhood. I just remember that night with him saying that stuff, and it was very important to hear. Even my brother says the same, and we've all had our sorrows. To lose your dad when you are young is very difficult, and there has been lots of pain, as in any family, with all sorts of dysfunctional stuff going on, but we've actually been a tightly linked group of mum, dad, son and daughter.

Notes

1 Clara Soppitt in J.B. Priestley's *When We Are Married*, directed by Jude Kelly, Savoy Theatre, 1996.
2 French was an original member of *The Comic Strip*. Her *Comic Strip* work includes: *Five Go Mad in Dorset; Five Go Mad on Mescalin; Slags; Summer School; Private Enterprise; Consuela; Mr Jolly Lives Next Door; Bad News Tour; South Atlantic Raiders; G.L.C; Oxford; Spaghetti Hoops; Le Kiss; Wedding; Calvi; Strike* (the film which won the Golden Globe Award in Montreux, 1988); *Four Men in a Car*, Channel 4 Television.
3 The Vicar in *The Vicar of Dibley*, situation comedy written by Richard Curtis, BBC Television, 1994–
4 French is the 'French' half of the comedy duo 'French and Saunders'. *French and Saunders*, BBC Television (five series), 1987–98.

Miranda Richardson

'I feel that I have got to be serious about my craft, and yet, should also be light about it. A lot of the time, I don't manage to be light about it.'

Performance Context

Born: 1958, Lancashire.

Prior/current commitments: Pamela Flitton in *A Dance to the Music of Time*, Channel 4 Television.

Post-interview (selected): Queen Mab in *Merlin*, Hallmark Entertainment. Dinah in the film *The Big Brass Ring*, Brass Ring Productions. Miss Fowl in the film *Jacob Two Two and The Hooded Fang*, Shaftesbury Films.

Other: 1992 BAFTA Award – 'Best Actress in a Supporting Role' in the film *Damage*; 1993 Academy Awards – Nominated for an Oscar for 'Best Actress in a Supporting Role' for *Damage*; 1994 Royal Variety Club of Great Britain – 'Best Film Actress in a Supporting Role' for *Damage*.
1995 Academy Awards – Nominated for an Oscar for 'Best Actress' in the film *Tom and Viv*.
1998 BAFTA Television Awards – Nominated for 'Best Actress' for *A Dance to the Music of Time*, Channel 4 Television.

Interview

Insights from the analytical mind of Miranda Richardson were plentiful as I stroked her sleek, immaculately groomed Siamese cat on 23 January 1997. We talked in an atmosphere of apparent calm in her London home – the opposite from her Oscar nominated performance as Viv in the film Tom and Viv.

Alison Oddey: *Can you describe the satisfaction you get from performing. What does it give you?*

Miranda Richardson: It's difficult. Film acting is much more to do with moments – whether you've got the moments right – than a whole chunk of something. It's the feeling of being in character and that you are prepared for whatever work you have to do that day, but you are not so prepared that something else cannot happen. It sounds like a contradiction, but you are not so technically bound that you don't allow other thoughts to come in, and it is what I call 'chasing a moment'. The same is also true on the stage, because you don't know when something like that is going to happen. Sometimes it's just a feeling of – 'I could live here on stage, I feel very comfortable. There happen to be quite a lot of people out there, but oh, it's a nice space.' Time expands when you are there.

So it's a kind of distillation of love in a moment, with all the trivia of life distilled and only the important bits remaining?

Yes, I think that's true. That distillation is almost like a sort of poetry, that kind of unexpected moment, where you just go 'I get it.' But it's not only you that's getting it, it feels like all of them out there are getting it, and that you are all part of that. It all happens at the same moment suddenly, and every audience is different. It's an extraordinary unit out there, which is prepared to absorb what is going on onstage, and there is all this energy being generated, flowing back and forth. I do find some of it quite mystical. I have quite often said that I would love to see a chart somehow of performers' energy when they are on stage in performance. I'd love to see what people describe as auras and what the energy field is doing at any given moment in a play. I think that would be rather amusing if somebody is supposed to be giving their all, and in fact, their energy is quite dim and they are just very technically and wonderfully producing the goods, and most of us are taken in by that. What is it that makes you want to watch something? What is it that makes one person believable and another person not?

Equally, what drives you and motivates you to continue performing?

It sounds very trite, but sometimes it's as simple as it's something I can do. It is my work – it is just different to a lot of people's. It's not a nine to five, it doesn't have the same sort of rules, as well as being kind of random. The other part of it is if you are lucky enough to be engaged on the right project, then it is a sort of need to tell that story, and probably not just you. It's the team, or whoever is making this film, play or television series. You want to do it to the best of your ability, because you understand and want to convey something about human nature, and it's trying to be truthful. Those moments are to do with the truth … almost holy, and it's embarrassing to say that. It's inspiration, it's what people in other media have to sit and wait for; for example, a writer may be writing, but not necessarily getting what they want out of it, until a connection is made.

What attracted you to performing?

Well, it was something I could do. When I was quite young I could make people laugh, which was nice and I enjoyed that. It was something that had an effect and I didn't know what I'd do, some sort of academe probably. It was a bit thoughtless really. I happen to have had quite a good education and so that next step was university, not necessarily thinking about what would happen after that. I had a very good English teacher and I began to enjoy language. It's a feeling that something worked through you, and that you have a facility for.

So you weren't preoccupied with thoughts of wanting to be an actress?

No, I wanted to go and do English, and it was a really gradual turning around. I thought I'd do English, and then I thought I'd do English and drama, and then just drama. I was gradually whittling it down, and then in the end I went to Bristol Old Vic Drama School instead.

What do you think that drama school training gave you?

I've no idea. What you want when you come out of drama school is to be utilised. The idea is that you are some finely honed tool and somebody is going to see exactly what you can achieve, using you in all these great productions, and of course, it's not like that. It's very dissatisfying most of the time. You sometimes get that tiny little role and see people bursting with energy and enthusiasm, whilst a lot of the time you feel like you are throwing back on yourself. There are some terrific directors out there, and everybody needs to be directed. Even the really big wigs want to be directed, including the ones with the reputation for being somewhat tartar. It's exactly what they want, someone to stand up to them, saying, 'that's not right … do it this way … let's try this.' That's the big nightmare: that somebody, not out of laziness, but out of perverted respect, thinks that they don't know how to direct you.

Would you ever turn work down if you thought the director wasn't going to challenge you, or provide you with some kind of learning experience?

I might. It absolutely depends. If it's a piece I didn't know (if it's new, wonderful writing with experienced actors attached), then you might be able to do it between you. However, if it's a film, then it's also got to be a director who has a visual appreciation and knows what they want to do. It's very hard to know a lot of the time, and it's a question of trust.

How important is the working process to you?

The process is what you remember, and if the film is good then that's great as well. If the process is bad, it doesn't really matter if the film is a deep success, because it's like that was a sweat, and unfriendly.

It sounds like it's very important to have a team of people, and a sense of working together.

Yes, I don't go as far as to call it family, I am not unrealistic like that. I wish I could in a way – I might get more out of it. For a lot of people, particularly on films, they see it as a sort of surrogate family for seven or eight weeks, chatting to everyone in the trailers all the time, but I've never really achieved that. I might achieve it with one or two people on location …

Where would you say your performance actually comes from?

I'm humbly grateful to the collective unconscious. I absolutely believe in it, and it's a kind of a fusion of text study and the imagination that is sparked off hopefully by the writing. It can actually be sparked off by anything. I think for that to happen the writing does have to be good, because that is what engages you and then sparks you off so that anything can fire. Sometimes, you just get a mental image of what somebody might look like in one particular shot, and the shot might not be built up like that, but it just gives you a feeling of that person in your head, and you build on that. It feels like a very truthful image of what that person is, and somehow suggests a whole person.

When you're performing, how do you see the audience?

I like not to see them if I can possibly avoid it, not clearly anyway. I don't mind being aware of bulbs, but I don't really want to see them clearly. I feel them as a unit, unless I'm shocked out of that by a particular section of the audience being very noisy, or getting up and moving. It's like breaking a web when that happens. It feels as if it's a kind of two-way hypnosis. When I first start rehearsing something, I feel that I am in some sort of physical net, which I have to expand, if not break through. It's not a net in the sense of something negative, just a very slight fold that you can cushion. I certainly feel in film as if I'm being drawn into the camera. On stage, I assume that the audience is willing to be entertained. With my first job in Manchester, I felt very negative towards the audience, I don't know why. I don't think that it was that I felt superior. I can remember shouting at them in the wings before I went on.

You were angry with them – for being there?

Yes, probably.

That implies that you didn't really want to go on and do it then.

It does. It seems like that, but I don't know why that was – maybe I wasn't happy with the process. I think that the audience was fine, so maybe I didn't like what I was doing and I despised them for wanting to watch it. I look back on the first seven or eight years and it's still all a blur. It feels like I'm a very different person in a very different life, that I was on another planet somewhere. Not really engaged in anything. I don't know whether that's partly due to just youth, or it feels like not being very well looking back at it now. I was not a very well person. It wasn't the nature of the work I was doing, because it was quite diverse then, but not very satisfactory work. There were a couple of productions that I really enjoyed, which were both at Bristol, where I felt like something was happening and I was progressing. The rest of the time, it felt like marking time.

When did you leave drama school?

In 1979. I did five years of repertory and stuff, before I did the Ruth Ellis film.[1] There were lots of promises and expectations around. That didn't really happen and I don't know if I would have been able to cope with it, but I carried on with both – film and theatre.

Was doing the film about Ruth Ellis some kind of turning point?

Only in that I hadn't done a feature film before, and that it was a leading role and all that. I was working very instinctively again, with not much time to concentrate on anything else. I didn't find it easy to chat around with people on that. I feel that I have got to be serious about my craft, and yet, should also be light about it. A lot of the time, I don't manage to be light about it.

You take your work very seriously and you are very committed.

But am I? I don't know. You talked about research, and I don't always feel it's necessary. I feel that the audience is doing 50 per cent of the work as well; they're willingly suspending their disbelief. Perhaps one of the most obviously researchable people would have been someone like Viv in *Tom and Viv*.[2] I didn't spend a lot of time studying medically what might or might not be possible, and I sometimes regret that now. It's just like … use your imagination. So I am in a sort of fear state really. When I work on something, I am torn between wanting to not be caught out and also not wanting to do too much.

What kind of performance challenge did those parts give you?

I had no reference points for Ruth Ellis at all. I was exhausted at the end of that. I was doing everything wrong in terms of looking after myself. With *Tom and Viv,* I was much more objective about it. It felt like a wonderful work-out really. It wasn't exhausting or upsetting, because she was the one who was actually expressing what she felt at the time and not keeping it in. Everybody else was being repressed in stuffed shirts, and she was seemingly the healthiest of the lot of them in a way. I took a lot of enjoyment from what she did, forcing people to confront themselves to be truthful. I just felt it was something where I could show colours. It doesn't have to be somebody who is very active; it can be very subtle and small. Some of the things that I've enjoyed seeing have been about tiny journeys in people's lives that completely absorb you, because of the way that they're portrayed.

Is performing an extension of your self or selves?

I think everybody is everybody. Everybody has the potential and that's why something can work; there has got to be some universality there. Your particular circumstances might help you to understand one character better than another in a situation, because of something in your childhood, but you've got to be able to produce more than one thing. You've got to be athletic, and you've got to encourage your capabilities to show as many different facets as possible of existence. I think that I make instinctive choices about work, which hopefully move me on in some way. There have been roles where I have had absolutely no idea how I could do this, but I thought I should – for example in the film *Damage*.[3] She's supposed to be x number of years older, and she's this type of person, or is she? She has to do this, she has to get to this point, and I thought that was something I should tackle. I can't say exactly how it moved me on, except it probably gave me some more confidence to do the next thing.

Earlier on you said that you liked making people laugh as a child. Did you enjoy playing the queen in the television series Blackadder?[4]

Yes, I did. I think most of what I do has some comic element in it. I do think that if you can do comedy, you can do most things.

Do you like women stand-ups?

I think some people have a facility for it, and others don't. If I get any sort of sniff of blokery – someone trying to be like a bloke stand-up – then I'm put right off. It's personal taste – there are some people I am very happy to watch and others I just can't watch. I think we get the best of American television comedy shows. I like French and Saunders. I've not seen many people live, and that would make a lot of difference. I wouldn't want to perform stand-up at all.

What about performing a one-woman show, like Orlando[5] *at Edinburgh?*

Orlando was marvellous, and at times during that, I was feeling very comfortable on stage – when time expands and you feel very in charge. It's also lying back on something – very enjoyable – a lovely moment. It's about the endurance and sustaining something, and the discipline of verse that is challenging – to be able to tell a story clearly through that. *Orlando* taught me about endurance, and that is not in blank verse, that's just two and a half hours on stage.

Are there any future projects that you would like to do?

If Martha Geldman was approachable, I would like somehow to represent her life, but I think the ideal thing would be a wonderful documentary about her. I don't have any particular hankering to play Hedda Gabler or Cleopatra; somebody would have to interest me in the project from the beginning again. Some actors' life ambition is to play Hamlet ... I don't seem to be like that. I wasn't particularly happy doing the classical stuff. Sometimes I felt like I was on a runaway horse. I've hardly done any – *The Changeling* is one.[6] I didn't join the RSC.

Why was that?

They asked at one time, and I was very aware of this trawler net attitude. They weren't parts that I particularly thought were right for me, so I felt dragged in and I chose not to. Also, I thought that I wouldn't get any help from the directors. I'm going on an instinct – it may be a misguided one.

Can you identify any key moments in your life as a performing woman, such as the winning of awards?

The trend is not to be churlish about them. It goes back to the attitude about this gift and you shouldn't kick it in the face. What can awards mean, particularly when you see so many unrecognised talented people? It sets off resentment and competitiveness, with the whole thing feeling contrived.

I can't help noticing an award up there on your shelf.

It's a BAFTA for *Damage*,[7] which are the equivalent of Oscars, but I've never thought of them like that. Oscars get all the attention. We are allowing ourselves more and more to become Americanised and influenced by all that, but now the BAFTAs have got their act together a bit more, so the staging is a bit grander. I remember feeling more familiar about the BAFTAs than the Oscars, because they are so huge and so ridiculous. The funniest thing is that everything stops for the commercial break. It's bizarre; the whole thing is a facade in that it all stops for the commercial, and then they have to have everybody back. It's all show. Key moments though? What is one of yours?

Giving birth in water to my son Oliver.

I don't know what to say about key moments. Certainly, when it comes to awards, I often find it a great downer, because it's all about nothing. What the hell is all that hoo-ha about?

Having said that, didn't the theatre critic Michael Coveney give you some incredible accolade?

Yes, he did. It was extraordinary and completely unexpected, which was very nice having just come back into theatre and knowing why I wanted to do it. It wasn't to win awards; I really wanted to work with Robert Wilson. I wanted to explore this other dimension of theatre and I wanted to feel engaged, using every bit of me. Then for him to say that ...

Did he say, 'the most stunning actress of our time' ... ?[8]

It was something like that, 'in any medium', which I thought was coming it a bit really. I hadn't been on stage forever, and then suddenly it was theatre, film or television. It was there in print, but it didn't mean anything. It probably put a lot of people's backs up. You can't make a statement like that.

Notes

1. Ruth Ellis in *Dance with a Stranger*, directed by Mike Newell, First Films, 1985. Evening Standard Newspaper 'Best Film Actress' Award; City Limits 'Best Film Actress' Award; Variety Club of Great Britain 'Most Promising Newcomer', 1985.
2. Viv in *Tom and Viv*, directed by Brian Gilbert, New Era, 1993.
3. Ingrid Fleming in *Damage*, directed by Louis Malle, Skreba, 1992.
4. Queenie (Elizabeth I) in Rowan Atkinson's *Blackadder II,* directed by Mandy Fletcher, BBC Television, 1986.
5. Orlando in Virginia Woolf's *Orlando*, directed by Robert Wilson, 50th Edinburgh International Festival, 11–31 August 1996.
6. Beatrice in Middleton and Rowley's *The Changeling*, directed by Richard Eyre, Royal National Theatre (Lyttelton), 1988.
7. BAFTA Award: 'Best Actress in a Supporting Role' for *Damage*, 1992.
8. 'I am now convinced she is our very best actress, on film or on stage, and this performance, ... , seals her career thus far.' Coveney, M., *Observer*, 18 August 1996.

Victoria Wood

'The big attraction as a stand-up is that it's very immediate. You walk on stage, tell a joke, get a laugh, and that's two halves of the contract done.'

'I don't feel the need to take on a massive big tour any more, but I can't imagine not performing.'

Performance Context

Born: 1953, Prestwich, Lancashire.
Prior/current commitments: Stage Show, UK Tour.
The tea lady in the Terry Jones film, *The Wind in the Willows*.
Post-interview (selected): Bren in situation comedy series, *dinnerladies*, starring and written by Victoria Wood, BBC Television.
Best of British, a half-hour documentary celebrating Wood's career, BBC Television.
Other: Wood's book, *Chunky*, published by Methuen, 1997.
Video, *Victoria Wood Live*, 1997.
CD collection of songs, *Real Life*, 1997.

Interview

I spotted Victoria Wood reading in the foyer at the British Broadcasting Corporation on 25 September 1997, tired from finishing her tour. Despite this, her wonderful wit sparkled in the cramped BBC sound studio where I interviewed her, revealing her evident love of being a mother.

Alison Oddey: *What do you enjoy about being an itinerant?*

Victoria Wood: Going from place to place and having a different audience in each place makes me able to do it. I once did a twelve-week season at the Strand Theatre, and I found that difficult going to the same theatre every night for that length of time and to a similar sort of audience. But going from town to town, I feel that it's part of a job travelling around being a comedienne in different towns.

Is that in a sense of owing it to play to a whole range and diversity of people?

Yes, to take yourself to the people, rather than expecting them to come to you. I feel that it's our job to travel around. It's not always possible for me to do it, but I really like doing it.

What's the worst thing about being on tour for you?

That I can't have the children with me, or not usually. Before I had them, I used to tour, driving round in the car from place to place doing one-night stands, getting drunk and staying in hotels. Now I come back every night if I'm within two and a half hours' drive, so that I'm there to get them up in the morning, which makes it quite a long day. I do that for four nights a week and then I have three nights off, then I take every fourth week off, so it makes my tours incredibly long as I don't do that many shows, but the span of time is a lot more extended.

So the tour is specifically structured to take on your life as a mother?

Yes, completely. I don't work half-terms, school holidays or sports days! I'm very fortunate. It's quite a struggle to fit both halves together, but obviously people who have a very fixed routine still have to turn up in an office or factory, and that's much harder. I feel lucky that I can pick and choose in the job I'm in.

When you're touring, how important is it to take in the new environment?

I've been touring since 1984 and I've been to every place before. There are no new venues in this country, so sometimes I just turn up in time for the show, or wander around and my tour manager and I will go out for tea. I have a pretty good sense of each town and how it is. I am very familiar with all these places, theatres and sorts of people, so I can make jokes about the town, because I know what I'm talking about. I would never make a joke about a town I had never walked around. When I went to Australia, I arrived at Perth airport and went straight to the theatre. I didn't say anything about Perth, except to say, 'I have not seen Perth, I came straight from the airport and I'll talk about somewhere else.' That is very important, otherwise it's fake and you just change the name of the town and do the same joke. It's not real. Every town and theatre has its own atmosphere, even though towns are now so similar to look at. I walk on stage and I have a sense of what the audience is. I don't know how that affects my performance particularly, but I have a very good sense of what sort of audience they are.

How soon do you pick that sense up?

I pick it up in the wings, just from the noise they are making before you go on. If they are very quiet, you have to go out there and gee them up a bit. Sometimes they are really raucous and you have to calm them down a bit, you get the sense just from that.

Is that part of the attraction as a stand-up – reading your audience and playing with them?

The big attraction as a stand-up is that it's very immediate. You walk on stage, tell a joke, get a laugh, and that's two halves of the contract done. You do that throughout the night, which is very satisfactory. It's not like television, where you write something and six months later it goes on, and then the next day someone will say they liked it. It's a very long and drawn-out process. Also, it's very different from night to night; you have to actually do it, it's not like a play where you can virtually walk through it and almost give the same performance without engaging your mind. If you're telling a joke, you have to tell it. You can't act telling it, you can't just say it, you have to actually tell it, which means that you have to engage that audience that night. It has to be spontaneous and you have to react to the audience as they are that evening. You can't think, 'Oh, it was nice last Tuesday, I'll just do the same thing'; it's always just slightly different.

What do you see when you look at the audience?

I don't see them. I specifically have lights at the back so that I can't see them and they are a black mass. I see latecomers coming down the aisles and I can pick out people as they come in, but generally you look up and with spots in your eyes it's just a black hole. If I can see them it destroys my own idea of them, that they are individual people. I don't want to see them sitting there with their coats on their laps, I just want them as spirits connecting with me!

An amorphous mass?

Yes, but they all have an identity. It's like one animal really; it's like hearing an animal. Sometimes if I've had a quiet first half and my husband happens to be in the audience, he will say, 'I'm not surprised they were quiet, if you had seen them you'd see that they were all about eighty-two and wearing pleated skirts.' I think, well that explains it, but I don't know that at the time.

Why do you still perform stand-up?

Mainly, because it's my job. That's what I do. I've struggled to be a comedienne rather than a writer, or a comedy actress. I specifically picked stand-up as something I wanted to reach the top of the ladder at, and that took me a long time to do. Once I did it, I wanted to carry on doing it, and once I started selling out theatres, then I wanted to carry on selling out theatres. I feel that I'm only being a stand-up if I'm going from place to place, doing a show on my own. God knows, it gets harder to pump out this material because of writing it as well, but there is something almost irresistible about it and I think if I didn't have children I might go around doing it all the time.

Like an addiction?

Yes, but the minute I come off stage I forget all about it, so it's not an addiction that lasts longer than the time you are doing it. I certainly feel I could stop now, but I don't know if I will. I find touring incompatible with family life, not having a wife! If I had a wife, then I would do it more. I feel that I'm doing two jobs, and it's difficult to do.

How do you balance these identities?

They are two things I'm very comfortable with. I don't count being a wife as a job, but being a mother – I really love being a mother. I feel comfortable with that and I don't have that tug of not wanting to be a mother some of the time. I always wanted to be one, making sure they are alright and wanting to be with them as many hours as I can out of my day. I cram my working life into a shorter time than I used to, so there's not that identity tug, but there is that feeling that I deserve to work. I have to work for my own self-respect, as well as wanting to earn a living and be self-sufficient. I don't feel guilty about working, I feel that's very much part of our rights as women; that we should have jobs and children, and nobody should deny us if we are able to do both. I do feel that they need an enormous amount – I don't discount what they need from their own mother, and I am prepared to do as much as I can to make sure they have as much of me as I can possibly give them. Most of the working mothers I know work really hard and are dedicated to their families and to their jobs. We are packing an awful lot in, and it's wonderful to have such a full life. I don't regret the days when I did bugger-all apart from work, coming home and just sitting around. I don't miss those days. Physically leaving the children and going to another town is very difficult. I don't want to do it. It has taken a lot of the enjoyment out of going away, and that is a fact that I work around. I chop my days down, I extend my tours; I juggle everything around them because I've had a career and they are going to be children for a few years. I think it's really important to respect their needs.

How old are your children?

They are nine and five. I feel that they support me, inasmuch as they can, but they would like me to be there and I respect that. When I said to them last week that I had just finished this tour, they cheered! I said that I would be doing cabaret and they said, 'We don't mind you doing cabaret, you only go out for the evening once a week.' My daughter, who is nine, said, 'When are you doing another tour?' I told her not for at least another two years and she said, 'Oh good, a mummy to ourselves for two years.' Babies are really easy because they are just with you and don't mind being minded for a bit, but bigger children have to get their piano practice. I have to take them to their swimming and all these things that I really want to do. So that's why I'm doing television this next year, which is much more compatible as I don't have to go away anywhere. Also writing – then I'm at home.

You're the youngest of four children?

Yes. We were quite spaced out in age so a couple of them had left home when I was quite small. My brother is thirteen years older, so he left home when he was eighteen. I was five, so I didn't grow up with him. My other sister is eight years older, so she left when I was about ten to go to university.

Did you have a close relationship with your siblings who were there?

Not as close as my own two children. My sister, who was two and a half years older, was very different and tended to pair off with the next sister up, because my brother had gone. They were friends, and then I was sort of left at the bottom. They have more in common than I have with them. I was on my own and I wanted to be. We lived in a house with no other houses or friends around us. People from school never came to our house because it was a mile and a half walk, so nobody popped in to tea. My parents didn't encourage that either, so I had a very isolated upbringing in that sense. I ate, read, watched telly or played piano all the time – all very solitary pursuits. I didn't have much to do with other people.

Did your parents come from a theatrical tradition?

No, my father was an amateur musician and played the piano very well. He wrote songs and radio plays, some of which he had performed, and he wrote a stage play. So he did bits and he wrote all the time in his spare time. He was an insurance salesman, but when he got home in the evenings, he just went to his office and wrote. That's another thing, we never all sat there. My mother would go into a room to sew or read, and my father would go into his office and write. He would have loved to have been a professional writer, performer, or something like that. He loved the fact that I did this. My mother has a very good brain, but she has no sense of humour to tell the truth! She is very serious, but she has a good way of putting things. She makes me laugh, because whether she is trying to be funny or not, she is funny!

Can you track down your original desire to perform?

I had a very strong feeling of wanting to be famous. I knew that before I was five. I remember sitting in the garden, thinking, 'I want to be famous.' I was about four then. That's a very strong memory and that was my driving force. Fame was the first thing and it was all to do with getting attention. I used to sit at home and write these comic songs, imagining that I was performing them. I used to sit twisted round where the audience would be, practise funny things and write funny pieces. I used to write things about the girls at school, read them to them, and I really liked the focus and attention that put on me, because I always felt I was a bit anonymous, or I didn't fit in or I wasn't popular. I wasn't unpopular, but I was one of the boring mass of girls in the middle. I would look at other girls and wish I was them. That was the one thing I could be – to be funny, which was certainly a way of getting attention.

Performing to gain attention and affection. So the comedy follows the fame?

I didn't think of stand-up because I didn't know of the job, and I'd never seen any stand-up, though I had seen Joyce Grenfell. I had seen a woman stand on stage alone, which was a very strong image to me, but when I was about fifteen, I joined a youth theatre and started acting, which I was good at. I was always in trouble and being smacked about – I had a chaotic existence, and when I discovered acting, I really latched on to the place and the people. I loved it and the theatre was part of my stagestruckness, as it was a theatre and not a theatre within a school. Then I thought I would be an actress, go to drama school and that was perfectly acceptable; nobody batted an eyelid when I said that. I wanted to be a comedy actress, because I could see even then that I wasn't going to be a great Shakespearian actress or a classical actress. I didn't look right apart from anything else. Then, when I went to university to do drama at Birmingham, I got such an inferiority complex the minute I walked through the door. I was met by two very gorgeous-looking girls, two tall blondes, who are now very good pals of mine, but I felt I didn't know the things they were talking about. Instead of asking them what they were talking about, I just blanked out. It's a terrible fault in me that I won't get stuck in and compete. I just go into a decline really, thought they were all snobs, just went away and ate baked potatoes in the canteen. I did that for three years, but while I was there, the people were very rude about my accent, saying, 'Don't bother with it dear.' I do have a very ambitious streak, and instead of just sitting in the canteen eating baked potatoes, I did audition at the BBC, and got some jobs singing and playing the piano. I got my Equity card, so I was on local telly quite often, and did about ten broadcasts before I had left. Then I auditioned for *New Faces*,[1] which was a very big hot talent show in 1974 – Marti Caine and Lenny Henry were on it. Then I got an agent and a manager, so I switched at some point. I realised that singing songs at a piano was actually the way forward, rather than just writing to all the reps, saying, 'Please can I be in your Shakespeares and Agatha Christies?' I wouldn't have been any good anyway. So by the time I left university, I was already on telly and had a very high opinion of myself, thinking that fame and fortune were just round the corner! I'd done well on *New Faces*, which had a spin-off series (*Summer Show*), which was a diabolical sketch show, and then nothing happened. Although I had an agent, there was no interest in me. I didn't really fit in! I did these songs at the piano and I didn't do anything else. I didn't look glamorous and I didn't wear dresses. People always complained that I didn't wear dresses or do my hair ... I didn't want to! I didn't have a very good act, so the first years were really awkward, because I felt there was something I could do, but I didn't know how to do it. I didn't know how to get jobs, and I didn't know how to structure an act. So it was a pretty dull performance. It was really scary after that, because I didn't have the sense to move to London. I just waited in my Birmingham bed-sitter, thinking something would happen, but it didn't. There was nowhere to work. In the early 1970s, there was the big working men's club circuit with all the big famous comedians, and there was also a sort of cabaret club circuit with people like Bob Monkhouse and Shirley Bassey. I couldn't have got into either of those places. There were no comedy clubs; there was a bit of fringe theatre, but it was only theatre rather than people like me. There were a couple of people standing out like Jasper Carrot, Max Boyce and Billy Connolly. There were people doing one-man shows on their own, but I didn't fit into any of these categories. I couldn't sell tickets, as I wasn't known. I just had to sort it out for myself, which is what you have to do, to be yourself. It took me about four or five years to come through with an act with an identity and a voice.

Now, in 1997, you are the act and identity for other women stand-ups to follow. Are you interested in other women stand-ups?

I'm not specifically interested in women more than men. I just look on them both with great interest. I've come to accept that there are very few and there have always been very few, and there must be sociological reasons for that, because nothing is to stop you. I don't think an audience has ever cared if you are a man or a woman, as long as you can engage them with personality.

It's still a short list of women thirty years on, which is quite bizarre.

You would expect a pyramid, with the bottom end having lots and lots coming through, but there aren't. French and Saunders were around in 1977, so that's twenty years that they have been around, and yet, there are no or very few women double acts going around. There are certainly very few women selling out at the top level, selling out on a tour. Jo Brand is working middle-sized theatres; French and Saunders could sell out if they wanted to tour. Jenny Eclair is known, but the average person in the street wouldn't know who she was really. Nobody has broken through to that great middle ground that we all need to crack if we want to make money. I'm struggling to think of a few ... Caroline Ahearne ... Donna McPhail ... Even if it takes ten years to become a comedienne, there should be people of thirty or thirty-five, who would be very big now with their own shows.

Can you describe what performing actually gives you?

I don't know what it gives me now after so long. It used to give me the most tremendous buzz, a mixture of scariness and adrenalin. I did get that again when I played Australia and New Zealand, particularly Australia where I'm not known. I went on as an unknown comic, although they knew I was famous at home, feeling that I was earning my living. I didn't have anything except my own skill as a comic, so that was a big buzz for me. It was almost like starting again, except with twenty years experience behind you. I do feel I have an easy ride here when I play big theatres and there's a big rush to get tickets. It gives me, apart from the huge satisfaction of having achieved my ambition to be one of the top comediennes in the country and to sell out, a really nice feeling. I have always felt in my life that I talk and people have no idea what I'm talking about. On stage, you set the agenda, and know that people have experienced what you've felt too. It's a good solid feeling of communication with people. You are plugged into a bunch of people, which is a feeling I haven't had much of, not feeling part of a group or anything. However, that's just my own feeling from my own childhood and how I was brought up in that strange way, not fitting in very well. It doesn't last a minute past walking out into the wings, then it's gone. That's why so many comics are alcoholics or take drugs, because they have to carry on that feeling.

That feeling of terrible loneliness.

It's such a cliché, but it's so true. In the last few months, I've just started to dread that walk from the dressing room to the stage. It's two years since I started the tour, and I get very tired. I'll be standing on stage thinking, 'If I stop talking now, there will be a great silence and what the fuck is going to happen!' You start to get really anxious about it. Then I know it's the time to pack it in and have a break, when I start feeling like that. The first few months of the tour with a new show are lovely, and you work up a routine, which has certain high points and you know where the big laughs are going to come. It's really exciting, good fun and you ride on that wave of good will. You can push your performance then. It's not that you are struggling to get their attention or to get them to listen. They are listening, so you can be quite extreme in the things that you say and the way you behave, which is nice to be able to do.

Why has it been important to achieve your ambition?

Because I am a person who likes to see things through, and I'm always very disappointed in myself if I don't achieve what I've said I will do. Sometimes to a point of stubbornness I think. I had such a time in my early twenties of people saying, 'We like you, but we don't think you are ever going to make it.' I thought, 'Right then I will.' I was determined to do it, and every time I broke the box office anywhere I thought, 'That's it, I've clocked up a little point for myself.' It was very satisfying – a sort of revenge – and I didn't hurt anyone. These people probably never even remembered the things they said. Comedy is so subjective. It's very airy-fairy, it's not like running a race and you are the fastest one, but there is something very concrete about selling tickets. The more people want to see you, the more tickets you sell, and it's just a very 3D way of acknowledging your own success. The Albert Hall has five thousand seats. I've sold it out for fifteen nights and you can't take that away from me now. I can go on stage tonight and die on my arse, but I could still say, 'I sold all those tickets in that year.' It just means a lot to me.

It sounds like a need to prove yourself.

Yes, but I don't have it now, because I feel I've proved myself! I don't feel the need to take on a massive big tour any more, but I can't imagine not performing. I can imagine just writing at home, but I wouldn't want to do it all year round – never get out, put on a bit of make-up and costume. That's why I do these cabarets, which are a nice earner, a challenge and I enjoy them. The most fun is doing a television series, because you're doing it with a group of people and there is a team of technicians. I'm hoping to write a television series to be recorded next May.[2] I've had more fun doing that than anything else really, but it doesn't feed me the same way as it would doing it all the time.

Has this journey of performing and writing enabled you to explore yourself through the work?

I don't think I did explore myself; perhaps in plays I have unconsciously. The first plays I was writing in 1978–79,[3] and then with *Pat and Margaret*[4] there were elements of my own life in that, but I don't think I did. I brought in observations of life, put them into my act and made a show out of it. I do steer off personal things in my own acts. The first time people could see me was in *The South Bank Show*,[5] and you wouldn't really gather from the stage act, who I was really. I don't think I ever did find myself through working. I feel that I know myself now, because I've had counselling and God knows what for the last few years, which has really helped me. I don't actually think of myself as an actress. I think it's a strange job pretending to be other people, which is why I love stand-up comedy. You're not pretending to be somebody else, you are trying to be yourself, and the more you are yourself, the more successful you will be – generally speaking. I could not find any satisfaction in the life of an actress. I enjoyed one day's work on *Wind in the Willows*,[6] playing a tea lady, but at the end of the day's filming I'd hate to go back tomorrow and do it all again.

Stand-up gives you more control and must be an empowering experience.

It is, and that may be why women have not been so drawn to it. It's a very male thing to want to dominate a group of people. Men do it in society much more than women in a group of mixed people. A man tends to talk everybody else down or be one to take control of the group. It may be why some women have felt they need to be very sexy to be acceptable, dominating by more covert methods; but I never tried to do that. I never tried to be sexy; I washed my hair and put a nice suit on, but that was all. I think it is a very male thing to want to do that, but then I think I have a mixture of both genders in me – most comics do. I think it's quite common, if you look at somebody like Ken Dodd, he's not a macho man at all. A man would feel comfortable with him and a woman would not feel threatened by him. Woody Allen is little and weedy, Jackie Mason is middle-aged and grumpy – he's not a sex symbol. People that we like as comedians do have to fit in the middle between men and women to be acceptable to a mixed audience.

Would you say in your experience up to date that there are any problems peculiar to being a stand-up in the late 1990s?

Not that I'm aware of particularly. I find it odd the reverence that has grown up for comedy in the last few years. I was never very comfortable with that, because I couldn't see why everyone was so keen on it suddenly, and everybody thought they had to do stand-up. Then I think that was just a phase and people dropped back to what they were doing. I think it is a timeless profession, and I felt very plugged in to a tradition of people trudging from town to town telling jokes. That's kept me going when I've been in some great barn of a place on a Sunday when it's raining. I've walked down the steps to get on stage, feeling that lots of people have walked down these steps to do this job, and that's actually cheered me up.

Because you are a part of that?

Yes, absolutely. I'm part of the music hall. If I'd been around in the 1930s or 1940s, I would not be doing this job. Nobody then was ever required to do two hours of material all by themselves. You had to do twelve or twenty minutes, and you could do the same thing all over the place for years and years. That's why we all know these old golfing sketches, because people just did that one thing and now they are all burnt out, knackered. I've done six brand new two-hour shows in my career since 1984. The first time took about three months. I usually do my old show and I'll put in a new block of material, and then the following week, I add more new stuff and take out more old until by the end of about four shows, I've got a completely new show all tried out. Twenty minutes is a lot to learn. I'll do a new twenty minutes one week, and then I'll learn another for the next week.

Do you discuss it with anybody when you are in that process?

I only discuss the structure with my husband. He watches it from the outside, so he has a good sense of the whole show, whereas I'm in the middle – I'm the hamster on the wheel trying to get to the end! So he is very useful, but I don't discuss anything to do with content. If I've just written a good joke I phone him up! I don't share it with anybody that I like. I only try it out on the audience. If it doesn't work, I cut or change it, and try it again the next week.

Can you identify key moments in your life as a performing woman in the widest sense?

I think the first part I played on stage when I was fifteen and hearing the audience laugh, and having a very strong sense that I knew what I was doing. That gave me an immense amount of confidence that I had not had before. That was one important moment. The first time I played the piano at a party, where there were lots of BBC producers – I must have been a little drunk – but I sang my own songs and one of them said, 'You must come and audition at the BBC, we'll expect you tomorrow morning.' I didn't take any notice, but next morning the phone went – 'Where are you?' I went down and that's how I got these jobs on television, so that was really important. They were two key moments, and everything else has been icing.

Is there anything in your personal life that has been key?

The births of my children were absolutely the best. The whole thing from being pregnant the first time, has been the most exciting thing, and what I always wanted to do. I absolutely adore my work, but the first thing is having a baby and the next thing is filling the Albert Hall. In actual fact, I felt I worked better afterwards, concentrated better, because there was less time. Breastfeeding meant that there were only short gaps for writing, which stopped a lot of time-wasting that I used to do. The first night I ever did a cabaret after Grace was born, when she was eight months old, I just drove home and thought, 'Oh, and she is here as well, fantastic!' So what if you have to get up at five, that's life!

To date, what is your most significant achievement in the performing arena?

Breaking the record at the Albert Hall for solo performance. It was a sell-out for fifteen nights, beating Eric Clapton's twelve!

Notes

1   *New Faces*, talent show, ITV, 1974.
2   Wood's first situation comedy, *dinnerladies*, six-part series, BBC 1 Television, 1998. Wood plays the part of 'Bren', alongside her long-term acting colleagues Celia Imrie, Duncan Preston and Julie Walters.
3   Wood's first play, *Talent*, 1978, had its premiere at the Crucible Theatre Studio, Sheffield, 8 November 1978. *Talent* won Wood two awards: The Plays and Players Award and the Evening Standard Award for the 'Most Promising Playwright'. Subsequently, *Talent* was adapted for television and broadcast in 1979, starring Wood and Walters. For this, Wood won an award from Pye Television for 'Most Promising Writer'. This was followed by a sequel, *Nearly a Happy Ending* and a third television play for Granada Television, *Happy Since I Met You*.
4   In 1994, Wood completed the screenplay *Pat and Margaret* in which she starred with Julie Walters. This was transmitted as part of the BBC's Screen One Autumn Season. The script of the screenplay was published by Methuen.
5   While on tour in 1996, Wood recorded an episode of *The South Bank Show* with Melvyn Bragg, as well as live footage of her stage performance.
6   In 1997, Wood appeared as 'the tea lady' in Terry Jones' film of *The Wind in the Willows*.

Penelope Wilton

'I am a working actress, who has a leaning towards the
theatre, because that's the way my career has gone.'

'You have to want to do it a great deal to keep on,
because it does have its frustrations, disappointments,
judgements and continual criticism.'

Performance Context

Born: 1947, Scarborough.

Prior/current commitments: Madame Ranyevskaya in Chekhov's *The Cherry Orchard*, Albery Theatre and RSC tour.
Deborah in Pinter's *A Kind of Alaska*, Pinter Festival, Gate Theatre, Dublin.

Post-interview (selected): Hesione Hushabye in Shaw's *Heartbreak House*, Almeida Theatre.
Deborah in Pinter's *A Kind of Alaska*, Donmar Warehouse.
Rosemary Horrocks in Bennett's *Nights in the Garden of Spain*, Talking Heads 2, BBC Television.
White Queen in the film *Alice Through the Looking Glass*, Channel 4 Television.

Other: 1997 Irish Theatre Awards 'Best Actress' for *A Kind of Alaska*, Gate Theatre.

Interview

I interviewed Penelope Wilton on 7 May 1997 in her Kensington home and was fascinated to learn more about her extensive career. Penelope had recently finished performing in a festival of Harold Pinter's plays at the Gate Theatre in Dublin.

Alison Oddey: *How would you describe yourself, Penelope?*

Penelope Wilton: I suppose I'm a middle-aged woman now. I'm forty-nine, and I've been acting for twenty-eight years. I've come through a rather tricky time as actresses do when they reach a certain age, because they're not old enough to play the mothers and they're not young enough to play the daughters any more. Then you reach my age and suddenly another world opens up for you – interesting roles for women of my age now. I'm a working actress, who has a leaning towards the theatre, because that's the way my career has gone. Life becomes more complicated as you get older, having disappointments, regrets and enormous joy. All these parts that one plays incorporate all those things that one feels as a woman oneself. I'm a mother as well, so your life and your work collide as with all great writers, and that's what I'm really interested in, doing great work. It's great work because it says something today as it always has done and that's why they are masters –

Chekhov, Pinter or Shakespeare. They go on being done, because they are so relevant to people's lives.

You've recently performed in Chekhov's The Cherry Orchard[1] *for the Royal Shakespeare Company and in Pinter's* A Kind of Alaska[2] *at the Gate Theatre, Dublin – how were these challenging roles?*

Both brought their rewards and their difficulties as roles, and as playwrights. Harold's work is particularly difficult, because he's very precise and usually dramatic in a very still way. It is rather like poetry, his writing, which means that you have to have a freedom within a very tight framework, and you have to find that freedom. You can't let the play rule you; it's like the boundaries are very tight, whereas Chekhov is a much freer writer. The interaction with people is much bolder and it's seemingly more accessible. It actually isn't when you get to know Harold's work, but Chekhov also requires an emotion and a building up of character before you actually come onto the stage to be Madame Ranyevskaya (this hopeless aristocrat), who is letting her whole life go down the drain.

What kind of satisfaction do you get from performing? Is it different from when you started twenty-eight years ago?

I think it's a deeper satisfaction I have now. It has changed in that respect. When you're young and you start in your career, you're just delighted to be working. You practise trying to get better at what you do, and you take pretty well anything that's offered to you – within reason, of course. You have to do things because you have to earn a living as well as do what pleases you. As you become older, you realise that when you act, you can only please yourself. You become much more self-critical because you know more about it, and then, of course, it's more frightening because you know how easy it is not to get it right. I think you dig further into yourself because you have to.

So what exactly is that satisfaction?

I think it's finding the truth in it, having that mountain to climb each evening, and doing it really. I enjoy the doing of acting very much. I also like acting with other people. You can't do it by yourself, so I enjoy working in a company of good actors and producing a work. Also, what I think more important probably than anything is trying to do what the writer wanted you to do, and not what suits you. It's delving in and mining the text to find what Chekhov and Pinter wanted. The play's the thing: the politics, the period and the rhythm of the play, so you stand or fall on the writer. He's actually the creator. You hopefully create in your own smaller way, but you really do serve the writer. That's what all my training years ago at drama centre was very strong to point out, and I think I've always tried to stay true to that. I think it serves any actor in very good stead to do that.

Were you from a theatrical family?

I have family members who are in the theatre. My mother's family was all in the theatre. She was an actress for a short time, as were her siblings. I've been married to two actors, so it's sort of been around. Not that my childhood was in the least theatrical; I just had a normal upbringing, but I went to the theatre. I've always been aware of it, and it's always been something that I've had an enormous love for.

Can you locate the root of your desire to perform, and where it originates from?

Well, I think it's very simple in my case, because I liked stories. I loved being told stories. I didn't perform as a child. Some people are very outgoing and love performing as children. I didn't particularly, I wasn't very good at it. However, I loved storytelling, particularly when I went to the theatre or to the cinema. I think it's a very basic thing telling a story. I think, on the whole, that's what the theatre does best really. You go on journeys with people, and I wanted to do that. As a young person, dressing up and putting on make-up never interested me. Telling a story was what brought me into theatre. When I was about sixteen or seventeen, I went to Stratford and saw plays. I found the whole spectacle, the words and the extraordinary world you were drawn into absolutely fascinating. I like words and I enjoy listening.

Why did you want to perform?

It's a very curious thing. I don't know why anybody performs, frankly. I mean to get up and persuade other people that you've turned into this person. I often ask myself why I do it. I think it's a very odd thing to do actually. Except when I see it and go to the theatre, it doesn't seem odd at all. I sit there in the audience, and I'm always so impressed by people who can do it. They don't seem to be frightened and all the things I am. I don't know why I do it. I think probably because I wasn't very good at anything else. I never wanted to do anything else particularly. I've always wanted to do it. When I was younger I loved making people laugh, but I don't think it came from any deep lack of confidence in myself as a person or anything. Hearing an audience laugh is the most wonderful thing. Now I've got older, I make them cry in the roles I'm playing. As a young actress, I did a lot of comedy. I think it was considered lightweight being able to make people laugh easily. Some performers are limited in what they do, but I wouldn't really call them actors. They're performers, doing a certain sort of performance. They play themselves fright-fully well, which is terribly good, but it's not what I do. I like turning into people, all sorts of people.

Is there a need in you to perform?

Yes. I think there is, otherwise I wouldn't do it. There are times when you don't work and you think the world's forgotten you. If you are a cellist and you're not working, you can pick it up and play it, but if you're an actor it's like having a cello in the next room and the door's locked. You have to want to do it a great deal to keep on, because it does have its frustrations, disappointments, judgements and continual criticism. You can spend a week in a play and perhaps one night there is a wonderful response, and then the next night there's nothing. It's not easy. It's easier working down a coal mine, or physically doing something like that. It has its drawbacks.

I'd like to go back to something you said earlier about the difficulties of performing comedy alongside a perception of it being lightweight work. Is there something attractive about being humorous as a woman?

Well I think there is. There is an enormous lineage repertoire of comedy writers and comedic writing, as well as wittiness. We're very witty as a nation, understating and all those things. I think the repertoire produces very quixotic actors, who can change or turn on a sixpence. I think the English are sated with wonderful comedic writers. We do have a wonderful sense of irony as a nation. Those writers that have allowed women to be very funny, for instance, in Wycherley's *The Country Wife*, the Lady Fidgets and those sort of parts are tremendously funny roles. When I went into repertory, those were the sort of parts that came up. You did Shaw, and Shakespeare's very amusing. Then when I got older, I did a lot of Alan Ayckbourn. I think it is part of our heritage.

Do you like stand-up comedy?

As a young person, they were my heroes. I'm talking about people I used to hear on the radio, really wonderful stand-up comedians, like Jimmy James. I'm not too hot on alternative comedians, except I think they're very clever. I came from the north-east of England, so there used to be a lot of them up there. They used to come to Scarborough and I used to go with my aunt to see them, so I'm very impressed by stand-up comedians. I think they're brilliant – Jack Benny, Tommy Cooper, Frankie Howerd, Roy Castle – I loved them. Those terrible jokes that never went right with Tommy Cooper. Frankie Howerd was more complicated because he was rather political. I loved all that innuendo, sort of rude seaside postcard-type humour, which makes me laugh. You have to be pretty vulgar to like all that, but I do. Mostly men, not women so much, except for Thora Hird or Beryl Reid. I just arrived when revue was on the wane really. Beryl Reid used to do revue, turning into people, performing sketches, which were completely brilliant. I think Victoria Wood is wonderful.

It sounds like those stand-ups were inspirational. Is there anybody else who inspired or influenced you particularly?

When I was young, I saw actresses at the Royal Shakespeare Company like Dorothy Tutin, Geraldine McEwan and Maggie Smith, all of whom are just ten or twelve years older than myself now. They all moved me in some way. I remember seeing Sybil Thorndyke in a really bad play, but she was wonderful in it. I get inspired now. I went to see a wonderful Russian clown, who was absolutely fantastic. I'm very impressed by people who can hold an audience by themselves. I think it's fantastically brave, and brilliant. I loved Max Wall. It's the tragedy of them, often very tragic people – very funny people. I know it's a sort of cliché to say it, but the reason they're funny is because sometimes they go very sad and then they make you laugh again.

Have you done any solo performance work yourself?

No, I find it far too lonely. I couldn't do it for any length of time. I did a play with one other person, *Vita and Virginia*,[3] which was an adaptation of the letters between Vita Sackville-West and Virginia Woolf.

Was that with Eileen Atkins?

Yes. She was playing Virginia Woolf and I was playing Vita. It was their correspondence, which Eileen had put together and we dramatised it. That was fascinating. It was also lovely working with Eileen, who is a wonderful actress. I have worked with some wonderful actresses in my time and they have been very influential in my life. I worked with Irene Worth when I was quite young. She was playing Madame Arkadina in *The Seagull*, and I was playing Masha. She was so encouraging and I was terribly interested in the way she worked. It is quite tricky leading a company for a woman. I found it quite hard when I was doing *The Cherry Orchard*.

Can you elaborate further?

Well, I can't really fathom it, but I've found younger directors are inclined to be a bit sort of macho, if that's the word. They sort of strut rather. I don't think women can be bothered frankly. I have found myself occasionally slightly patronised, and I think, 'Well come on, not only am I an actress but I've run a home. I've brought up children, I cater, I look after people, I take people to school, I make enormous decisions in people's lives, and I act, so don't patronise me because I know about the world.' When I got to be about forty-five, I thought that I couldn't put up with it any more. You have to look after yourself.

Women can accommodate a range of identities at the same time, whereas men in the theatre don't have to do that.

Oh, I think that's absolutely true. I know that they can go into a quiet room and learn their lines. I can now, but when I was younger and married to Daniel Massey, my first husband, he'd say, 'You're always winging it', and I'd say, 'Listen I have to wing it because I've got sixty-five other things that I have to do.' Alice, my daughter, is my first husband's child.

So it has been a case of identities competing and contradicting each other.

Oh, very. I can remember on the first night of *Betrayal*,[4] when Alice was about seven months old and my nanny left. There was a strike at the National, so we didn't know if we'd go up or not. It was a very difficult play with the three characters in it, and at six o'clock I had to be at the theatre. At 5 o'clock I'd found someone to take Alice for the night. I hadn't eaten all day, I'd probably had half a Mars bar. I went to the theatre, did the play, had two glasses of wine after the show and fell down, because I'd done the whole thing on an empty stomach. I was completely drunk. It was all too much. The adrenalin going, a first night, wondering if Alice was alright ... it was a nightmare. Never again. Of course, when you're younger, you sort of manage it with difficulty.

It's issues, such as childcare or your child being ill, that seem to particularly resonate if you're a working mother.

Oh, I can understand that. I used to be like that. I'm not now. It's lovely now. I can go for a walk and not feel guilty. I felt totally guilty all the time. I found once Alice had gone, I had to re-educate myself to go out, because if you work and you have children you do exactly that, you work or you come home. I never went out on the nights I wasn't working, because I felt guilty going out. That was particularly me. I'm sure other people manage it better, but I didn't manage it very well.

Did you turn work down when Alice was younger?

I did – a lot of work. I used to dread being asked to work at times. I was asked to go to the RSC a couple of times, three times I think, but I couldn't take her out of school. I'd put her into a school up there, because my husband was working down here, and that would have meant that I would have been somewhere worrying on the M40. I wouldn't have been in one place or the other. So I didn't go. I was so lucky, because for about the first six years of her life, I was practically at the National all the time. I couldn't believe it, but there seemed to be things for me to do there. When she was little she could come with me sometimes, but when I did a film in Zimbabwe and I was away for three months – that was a nightmare. I couldn't bring her out there. It was the film called *Cry Freedom*,[5] a very anti-South African film, and we had guards and things. This was ten years ago and before Nelson Mandela came out, so I wasn't going to put her into that position. I also had to stay in the hotel quite a lot, and unless you're a great star, film companies don't cater for young children and nannies. I wasn't, so it was all very tricky and I found that very hard. I felt so guilty and I didn't manage it very well. She's fine now and says, 'I don't know why you were so guilty Mum.'

It's as though you are driven to perform, searching for those moments of satisfaction in performance you described earlier. Can you imagine a role which provided that sense of huge satisfaction and describe what it felt like performing this part?

When you do a part you are really pleased with, you are so on top of it that it's like putty in your hands. You can do anything within the parameters of the piece, but you know the person you are playing so well that you have this fantastic freedom. You are so strong – it's wonderful. I felt that sometimes with Mary Tyrone, when I did *A Long Day's Journey into Night*,[6] which was a really difficult part, but sometimes you just feel you are singing. Not very often, but sometimes. It's not just you (it's never just you), it's when everything around you is going well too. It is like a tennis game, so you are never very good if you are just doing it by yourself, because it's all to do with interaction. Sometimes you have evenings like that when it all goes like that.

Could you ever describe performing Mary Tyrone as a psychic experience?

I do know that sometimes it's not you there. That somebody else is speaking. That sounds whimsical, but sometimes the words can take you off. It's wonderful. It's when they sing (when you can make them sing), that you can sing.

Is your ultimate goal to perform good writers' work, and do you admire any women writers particularly?

Yes, to perform new work as well. I admire Caryl Churchill very much and the younger women writers are tremendously good. There is a new generation of women writers in the last fifteen or twenty years, who are wonderful. I haven't actually ever been in a play written by a woman, and I've never worked with a woman director.

That's quite a statement in terms of the length of your career.

Yes, never in my life – I've never been asked. I'd like to, but it is extraordinary when you think about it. Earlier on, perhaps there weren't so many, but there are now and they are younger. They are inclined to know their own generation of actresses, so in a way it's not so extraordinary.

Looking back over the last three decades, do you think things are generally better for women in theatre in terms of status, opportunities and so on?

I think there are more women actively involved in the running of theatres, playing bigger parts than they used to. I think that actresses have more choice of roles, and certainly seem to be much more able to stand up for themselves. I think actresses have always been taken seriously, because they just share the same job as an actor. There have always been wonderful women designers. As far as women directors and administrators go, it seems to me that there are more women. I've never really thought of it as being men and women, because if you act you are on an equal footing with any actor most of the time, so you don't really have the problem of feeling inferior to them because that is just not how it goes. Nowadays, I think young women expect a great deal, therefore, they will find the frustrations more difficult than I did. There are young people who expect to get there just like that, and the biggest worry is that there aren't the opportunities to allow you to go into rep, but that's the same for men too. For women, there are fewer opportunities in the theatre than there were, and I think the theatre is very hard. You should be allowed to play things that you wouldn't always play, so that you can broaden your range and you might fall upon something that you didn't know you could do. I think there is less of that now, than there was in the 1960s when I started.

What are the key moments in your life so far that hold great meaning for you?

Well, a key moment when I was younger was having Alice, which was a remarkable thing. She was 2lb 9oz, and I'd lost a baby before – a baby boy who died. So it was an extraordinary event and she was ten weeks early, so it was enormously traumatic. Now she is 5 ft 9 and fine. That was a very big moment in my life, changing my life completely. Three months previously to that, my mother had died. I had a very stressful time for about four years when she was dying, and losing the first baby. Then I had a period when I didn't do a lot of work, and that was a very difficult period in my life. I was thirty when I had

Alice and it did teach me that there was very little that mattered but survival. It put a lot of things into context and when I got upset later on about losing things, I thought nothing can be as bad as that. These dramas happen in everyone's life. The other one was not a specific moment, but gradually over the last few years I have found that I have become my own person, and I'm not ashamed or embarrassed. I don't think I would have given you this interview five years ago, because I couldn't put into words what I felt about things. I've noticed over the last few years that I've got a confidence not to be so shy. Shy sounds ridiculous in middle age. It's not just about having confidence, but about working with younger people whom I am very fond of.

What is your most significant performance achievement to date?

It's always the one I did last. The one that's been the furthest away from me was Mary Tyrone in *A Long Day's Journey into Night*, which I didn't think I could do because I was a bit young for the part. I was very pleased to have done it and would like to do it again. I could do it better next time.

Notes

1 Madame Ranyevskaya in Chekhov's *The Cherry Orchard*, directed by Adrian Noble, Albery Theatre and RSC Tour, (original production at the Swan, 1995), 1996–97.
2 Deborah in Pinter's *A Kind of Alaska*, directed by Karel Reisz, Pinter Festival, Gate Theatre, Dublin, 1997.
3 Vita in *Vita and Virginia*, directed by Patrick Garland, Ambassadors Theatre, 1993.
4 Emma in Pinter's *Betrayal*, directed by Peter Hall, Royal National Theatre (Lyttelton), 1978.
5 *Cry Freedom*, directed by Richard Attenborough, 1987.
6 Mary Tyrone in O'Neill's *A Long Day's Journey into Night*, directed by Laurence Boswell, Theatre Royal, Plymouth, and Young Vic, London, 20 May–10 August 1996.

June Whitfield

'... I must be an itinerant! I love travelling from role to role.'

'The great thing about radio is that you don't have to look remotely like whoever you are trying to be, whereas in television you are obviously a little bit restricted by size, shape and looks.'

Performance Context

Born: 1925, London.

Prior/current commitments: *The News Huddlines*, co-starring with Roy Hudd and Chris Emmett, BBC Radio series.
Mrs Whitfield in *Tom Jones*, BBC Television series.
Ivy Trench in the four-part serial *Family Money*, written by Ruth Carter from the book by Nina Bawden, Whistling Gypsy Productions, Channel 4 Television.
Irene in *Common as Muck*, written by William Ivory, BBC Television series.

Post-interview (selected): *Like They've Never Been Gone*, co-starring Roy Hudd and Pat Coombs, BBC Radio series.
The News Huddlines, BBC Radio series.
The Mirror Cracked and *Nemesis*, Miss Marple productions, BBC Radio.

Other: 1985 – OBE Award.
1994 – a British Comedy Lifetime Achievement Award.
1998 – CBE Award.

Interview

June Whitfield's quick-witted answers to my questions after a radio recording of The News Huddlines *at the BBC Radio Theatre, London, on 15 May 1997 offered light relief, having queued for hours for a place in the auditorium.*

Alison Oddey: *I've just watched a recording of* The News Huddlines,[1] *which you have been appearing in since 1984.*

June Whitfield: Yes, this is my thirteenth year and it's great fun. I love it.

You have obviously worked in so many different mediums – television, film, theatre and radio. Why does performing in radio comedy particularly appeal to you?

The great thing about radio is that you don't have to look remotely like whoever you are trying to be, whereas in television you are obviously a little bit restricted by size, shape and looks. On radio, however, you can try to be (if you are short and square like me) tall and thin.

You've had a very wide-ranging career; have you worked with many women directors during that time?

Yes, one wonderful one, Enyd Williams, who is a BBC drama director. She is the one who produces all the *Poirot,* and she also produces *Miss Marple.*[2] I'm her Radio 4 Miss Marple and we've already done five of those, and we've got another one coming up – *The Caribbean Mystery,* which is fairly soon. Liz Anstey is another radio director, and I'm doing a thing with her soon.

How would you describe yourself?

I'm certainly not a stand-up and I'm probably a bit old to be a strumpet (I'm seventy-one), so I must be an itinerant! I love travelling from role to role. I'm basically a character actress and the more I can do of that the better.

You describe yourself first and foremost as a character actress, not as a comedy actress?

Well, character comedy actress if you like, yes. I can't remember at what stage it was in my career when I suddenly had to appear looking like myself. That was a big transition, because before it had always been wigs and glasses, and now I seem to be drifting back towards the wigs and glasses for various parts. I was Aunt Drusilla in the film *Jude,*[3] which was in costume, and then a landlady called Mrs Whitfield in *Tom Jones.*[4]

Where does your desire to perform originate?

The desire was really in my mother, who would have been a very good actress, but her father would not let her, so she spent a tremendous amount of her life doing amateur work. I went to dancing classes at the age of three and a half and elocution lessons; I was in all the local pageants, dancing competitions and all the things that kids go through. She was not a pushy mother, but it was something that I assumed that I would do. That's probably very arrogant, but I never thought of doing anything else. My father was a Yorkshire man and if I took him a contract, he'd say, 'You are keeping up with your shorthand and typing aren't you, just in case?' Quite right though! Wise man.

You must enjoy it to be working the way that you are.

What else could I do that would give as much pleasure? How many people are there in jobs that they really enjoy? This is what keeps one going. People ask me when I'm going to retire, but I don't think that you really ever retire. Sometimes you look on it as a bit of a challenge, thinking, 'Can I still learn that? Am I still capable of doing that?' Then you do it, proving that you could do it, and so it's that sort of thing. I'd really given up doing pantomime, which I'd done for quite a few years with Roy Hudd, Terry Scott and Frankie Howerd. I'd given that up, but then somebody offered me Wimbledon, where I live, and I thought that perhaps I'd do one more![5] I've properly stopped doing that now, because twelve shows a week is quite heavy going, and to have got through the season for a couple of years – I don't want to push my luck!

Is the challenge of performing a part important?

Yes, to a certain degree. It's something a little different, and it's new sets of people.

Has the challenge changed over the years?

No, a job's a job really. In the last couple of years, I have done more straight stuff than I've done for years and years. I started off at RADA, but I was always into comedy then, which I still think comes from basically a lack of confidence in yourself. I think that if I do that, they'll laugh at me, so I'd better do something they will laugh at. That's what starts it and even at dancing classes, when we did a public show at the end of term, I was always the ballet dancer who tripped up or fell over, so I think it was put upon me from an early age.

Do you know where that comes from particularly?

My father had a marvellous sense of comedy. He used to recite monologues, which were very funny, and so maybe it came from him a bit.

In comedy, you've won the Lifetime Comedy Achievement award.[6]

Yes, it's amazing. It sounds as if you are dead doesn't it! Get it in quick before she goes!

You've worked with an impressive list of comics – do you think there is something attractive about a woman who is humorous?

That's a difficult one. When you say attractive, I'm not so sure. When I started there were very few women stand-up comics, because I think there was at that time a great resentment from men. Both men and women thought that it wasn't really a very nice thing to do – women to tell jokes and things like that. It wasn't quite the done thing, so in that sense it has changed a tremendous amount.

For the better?

Who can say? It's very reasonable that women should be in comedy, but I'm not sure that I go along with some of the young comics, women and men, who just rely on either bodily functions, or real filth and swearing. I don't particularly find that hysterical. I always think it's a bit 'behind the bike sheds' humour. It's been going on for years, but now suddenly, it's called entertainment.

Do you have any favourite women stand-up comics that you like particularly?

The awful thing is that I haven't really seen many women stand-up comics. I love Dawn and Jennifer, but I haven't actually seen them doing an act. I've worked with them and I think they are brilliant, but I don't think that sort of stand-up comedy particularly appeals to me, so I wouldn't go out of my way to see it.

Can we go back to comedians being rather insecure people, and that's why they do it.

I'm sure of it – a lack of confidence in themselves. A lot of boys start because they are worried about bullying or school. I think their insecurity comes from the fact that they reached the top, and if you do that, there is only one way to go. Every show has to be as good or better than the one before, and I think that it is a tremendous strain if you've got a series and it's a success, and then someone says do the next one. It is very difficult because, unless they write their own material, which so many do now, they rely on the writers, the presentation and the people around them. So there is an awful lot to think about if you are actually heading a show, which doesn't apply so much to the people like me, who are around those people.

Such as Absolutely Fabulous,[7] *in which you've had huge acclaim, despite all that you've done before.*

That's thanks to Jennifer Saunders.

In terms of the writing certainly, but the performance is your own. You are that mother.

That's sweet of you, but the few lines are Jen's – she's wonderful. It's the fact that mother just comes in with them now and again that makes it funny. If it was a whole show around mother, I don't think it would be quite the same.

You're a mother yourself? Is it one daughter you have?

Yes, Suzy Aitchison, who is an actress.

When you were bringing her up, did you find it difficult being a working mother?

I always think that a mother, who has a nine to five job every day, sees a lot less of her children or child than an acting mother, because after Suzy was born I didn't do any theatre. I did television, radio and the odd bit of film, so everything came to an end. Usually, you are at home in the evening, soon after they are back from school. So I don't think I was missing any more or less than a working mother. That is the one thing about theatre that I find so tying. Your whole day is geared towards it, and that is the reason I don't do it now. I know perhaps one should, but there is life outside the theatre. Once, when I had a conversation with dear old Donald Sinden, I said to him, 'You love theatre Donald, don't you?' and he said, 'What else would I do in the evening?' Well, I can find other things to do in the evening.

Is that also a practical reason why you do more television and radio?

Yes, I think so. I have turned down theatre. I always feel slightly guilty, but then I think that it's my life!

Is that guilt in relation to the public wanting you to do it?

Or people who say you should do theatre, but I think for me there are more cons than pros.

So what is the satisfaction that you get from performing?

I don't know. I think that it's habit as far as I'm concerned. I've been doing it for so long.

Obviously there is that, but if you think of moments when you've been really pleased.

Obviously, you are flattered when people say they like what you do, or you get letters to this effect. However, if you have been around as long as I have, and a lot of people have grown up with you, you are part of their life in a way with television, radio and things. You take part in some comedy and you get a letter from somebody, who says they were feeling so miserable, but then they listened or they saw the show and it really made them laugh and feel better. I mean that's marvellous. I had such a funny letter from a lady. She said, 'I haven't laughed so much since my husband died.' I know what she meant, but it did make me laugh. Not the sort of sentence you should write to somebody who is on *The Huddlines*. It's a joy to work with people like Roy Hudd, Chris Emmett, Jennifer Saunders and Joanna Lumley. I've been so lucky with the people that I've worked with, and the more you work, the more confidence that you get.

Is there an actual need in you to perform?

No, I think that if I didn't perform professionally, I don't think I'd do it in an amateur way. In other words, it isn't something I have to do.

Performing a live radio comedy programme involves an audience in the same way as theatre, so do you see them as a group or are you aware of individuals out there?

I can't see. I know I'm wearing my glasses, but I can just about pick out Albert, Irene and Vera, who are people who come every week and the front row I can just about do. When Tim, my husband, comes, I spend hours looking for him – he's probably at the back somewhere. I don't see that well. Faces, of course, I can see. With *The Huddlines* audience, you feel that they are always ready to respond. They are usually people who have heard the show, after all it has been on the radio for twenty-two years! So they know what they are about to get, whereas if you go to the theatre and you know nothing about it at all, it is in a way harder work.

In a sense, you could say this is almost like one big family.

Oh yes, very much so. We used to love the Paris (when it was at the Paris cinema), because that was a little more intimate, but the BBC in its wisdom sold it off. I don't think anybody has occupied it yet.

Who has inspired you or influenced you particularly as a performing woman?

I don't think that it's inspiration as much as learning. You learn something from everyone you work with. Whether you mean to or not, you can pick things up from them, so I don't think it is inspiration exactly. I can remember as a child going to all the cinemas and seeing all the great Hollywood stars, like Bette Davis, Barbara Stanwyck and Rosalind Russell, but Judy Garland was the one who made me think, 'Oh I would like to do that.' I soon realised that I was not going to be Judy Garland, but I never really thought, 'That's what I want to do' as you hear so often from actresses. So I feel there is something lacking in me really! I've always thought, 'That's what I do.'

What did you like particularly about Judy Garland?

I loved musicals, the singing and the glamour I suppose, which I gather wasn't for her, poor woman.

Somebody said to me, 'June Whitfield, she's become a real cult figure.' What do you think about that?

I've been called an icon. I thought it was something you found in a church! I think there aren't too many of us still going strong in their seventies. Dora Bryan is, of course, and she's absolutely fantastic. She does a one-woman show and she is worth a dollar a minute – she's wonderful. I'm sure there are more that I haven't seen. I don't really think I could do that, I prefer to work as a team with people around me. That's one thing I don't like about being the fairy in a pantomime, because the fairy comes on in a front cloth and says something to further the plot, while there is something going on behind, but usually she's alone. It's lovely when she's got King Rat to argue with, but very often she comes on, says something and then goes off, which is boring. It's much more fun to talk to somebody.

As we approach the millennium, do you think that there are problems peculiar to women starting out in the profession now?

I think it's a pain, I really do. I feel so sorry for the young, because there is a great lack of manners about some of the younger directors or people in advertising. They will get a whole group of girls in to see which one they want to advertise their soap powder or whatever, and I believe they can be so arrogant and rude, which isn't necessary. The competition is tremendous, and the other thing is that as far as films and things like that are concerned, if you are not prepared to take your clothes off and simulate sex you might as well not bother. It's appalling. Maybe the young aren't worried, but I think it does worry them. Maybe it's going through a phase and it will turn around again, and everybody will be in crinolines!

So the image of actress as strumpet still applies?

The funny thing is that my grandfather would not allow my mother to go on the stage. He thought actors were all rogues and mountebanks. God, I don't know what he'd do now. I'm sure that the girls who do take part in the films where they have to strip off, don't rush about being what is laughingly known as loose women. It's just that they think that they are doing the right thing for the job at that time. There's this thing of the director saying, 'You must stretch yourself.' Well, thank God, I never had to stretch myself that far, that's what I say. I think women are not doing badly at the moment. Really with the Spice Girls' 'Girl Power' (I think there's been quite a lot of girl power), but there's no reason why there should not have been. French and Saunders, Victoria Wood, Julie Walters, Tracey Ullman came along with a whole new approach, writing their own material, and I think they are brilliant. If you write your own material and you are prepared to go and stand up at the Comedy Store or somewhere (and get shot down or cheered), good luck to you, because I don't think I'd ever have the nerve to do that.

Maybe it's the sense of making your own thing happen more.

I think it is with those girls and they do it extremely well.

Can you identify any one or more key moments in your life up to this point as a performing woman in the widest possible sense?

A key moment has to be *Take It From Here*[8] on the radio. Although I'd done a tiny bit in radio before, I was working in theatre a lot of the time. I had no idea of the popularity of radio, because in those days it was as popular as the best television show is now. So when I got that, that must have been a key point, because that's when my name was known. Not my face, but possibly my name. Another key point had to be working with Terry Scott, because I spent so many years working with him.[9] Then another one is *Absolutely Fabulous*, because although I had been working all the time, my husband says if your face is not on the box, they think you're dead!

Was that the first time you had actually performed with Jennifer Saunders?

No, I did a sketch with them in 1988. Jennifer said that she had always wanted me to play her mother, so when the pilot of *Ab Fab* came up, the mother was there for all of thirty seconds. However, Jennifer promised that if it went to a series, she would write mother in, and true to her word she did.

You've worked with so many different comics …

Yes, Roy Hudd once described me as a 'comic's labourer', and I think it was Frankie Howerd who described me as a 'comic's tart'. I worked with Noel Coward in one of his musicals – *Ace of Clubs*[10] – who was a wonderful man. I have met so many delightful people and been lucky enough to have enjoyed a career spanning fifty years and still running.

Notes

1 *The News Huddlines*, BBC Radio series, co-starring with Roy Hudd and Chris Emmett. In March 1994, this became the longest-running light entertainment comedy series performed before a live audience.

2 In 1993, Whitfield created the role of Agatha Christie's 'Miss Marple' for the first time on radio in *Murder at the Vicarage*. This has been followed by *A Pocketful of Rye*, *At Bertram's Hotel*, *The 4.50 from Paddington*, and *A Caribbean Mystery*.

3 Aunt Drusilla in the film *Jude the Obscure*, directed by Michael Winterbottom, 1996.
4 Mrs Whitfield in *Tom Jones*, directed by Metin Huseyin, 1997.
5 Whitfield's last season was with Rolf Harris in *Cinderella*, playing 'Fairy Godmother', Wimbledon, 1994–95.
6 In 1994, Whitfield was awarded a British Comedy Lifetime Achievement Award.
7 Mother in *Absolutely Fabulous*, BBC Television (Three series), written by and starring Jennifer Saunders with Joanna Lumley, 12 November 1992–17 December 1997.
8 In 1953, Whitfield joined the radio series, *Take It From Here*, with Jimmy Edwards and Dick Bentley, in which she created the classic character 'Eth' in the famous family 'The Glums'. This ran until 1960.
9 Whitfield's longest partnership was with Terry Scott from *Scott on ...*, through *Happy Ever After* to *Terry and June*. They played together in over 100 episodes.
10 Doreen Harvey in Noel Coward's *Ace of Clubs*, Cambridge Theatre, 1950.

Sheila Hancock

'I still have to fight not to be driven, not to find myself
doing a job because I'm trying to prove something.'

'I know England very well now, because whenever I go
on tour, I always explore wherever I am.'

Performance Context

Born: 1933, Isle of Wight.

Prior/current commitments: Mrs Squeezum in *Lock Up Your Daughters*, an adaptation of Henry Fielding's comedy by Bernard Miles, Chichester Festival Theatre.
Sarah Meadows in *Kavanagh QC*, written by Matthew Hall, ITV.

Post-interview (selected): Dorothy in *Close Relations*, BBC Television.
Then Again, comedy revue, Lyric Theatre, Hammersmith.
Vassa in Gorky's *Vassa*, Albery Theatre.

Other: Associate Director of Cambridge Theatre Company.

Book: Hancock, S., *Ramblings of an Actress*, Hutchinson, 1987.

Interview

What attracted me to Sheila Hancock was the duality of both intellectual and artistic preoccupations in her life, which struggled against each other for their rightful creative place. It seemed fitting to talk to this actress in the library at the University Women's Club near Hyde Park on 18 July 1996. Her role as the mother of three daughters in the television series Close Relations[1] *(as is true of her own life) was a memorable experience.*

Alison Oddey: *What are you currently doing in terms of performance work?*

Sheila Hancock: Well at the moment, I'm just deciding whether to do a musical at Chichester called *Lock Up Your Daughters*,[2] which was based on Henry Fielding's *Rape on Rape*. It was done originally in the 1950s and is now very dated. Whether I do it is conditional upon whether they will look at the original and rewrite. So that's the stage I'm at, and I want to have a fairly big hand because at the moment it's unacceptable to me as a woman. The script is a prettified version of ravishing and all that sort of thing, whereas the original restoration play was much sharper, much more satirical. I've just finished doing an episode of *Kavanagh*,[3] and I've just lost a wonderful part in a television series. Somebody else got it (Billie Whitelaw), but it was much competed for, because there aren't that many roles for women of our age. It was written by Debbie Horsfield,[4] and is one of the best roles that has been written for an older woman for television for as long as I can remember. But the competition is hot when you get a role like that for older women, and I lost at the last lap.

So you have to feel happy with the possibilities of a role. You're selective in what you do.

Oh, I'm incredibly selective now, I really am. I hate doing theatre for a start; I loathe theatre. Therefore, it's got to be something that I really feel passionate about, and it's got to be for a limited run.

You loathe theatre … ?

Yes I do. I loathe the demands of it. Almost invariably when you do theatre now, if there's the possibility of a West End transfer, you have to do it for a long run. I much prefer working in the repertoire system at the National, or what I'm inclined to do, and, indeed, what I will be doing in March 1997, is to work somewhere like the Lyric, Hammersmith, where you work for a very limited run. In fact, nearly all my theatre work has been at the Lyric, which is not only my local theatre – I can just walk to the theatre – but it is also a short run. I've done long runs all my life and I haven't got the stamina for them, and I get so bored. When you get older you can't spend too long doing the same thing. I've always been a bit like that. I like change in my life. I find over a year absolutely unbearable and over six months almost unbearable. I mean if I do this, I will only do three months. It's awful; it's very harmful to the theatre for people to have the attitude that I've got. But then I reckon I've paid my dues. I'm sixty-three, so I think the youngsters can do the long runs.

So is that a result of your life experience in the theatre up to this point?

My life experience full stop really. My life is more important than my career, it always has been. I'm what you call a working actress, I'm not a career actress. I've never had a structure, which is probably why I'm not Judi Dench or anything like that. I came out of RADA, I drifted around, and if I'd been sensible I would have let people know what I was doing. I would have been a comedy actress, or a musical actress, or a television actress, but I've always darted about, and people never quite know where to place me. If I had been sensible and listened to what my agents told me, I would have made a lot of different choices to the ones I have. I didn't go to America when I could have done (because of my children), and therefore I didn't get an international career. My choice was not to do that. I preferred to be with my kids.

How many children have you got?

Three, well I've got two of my own and one stepdaughter. They're all grown up now. That's no longer a problem, which is why I'm going to Chichester. I wouldn't probably have done that when they were little, unless it coincided with school holidays and I could take them with me. To go back to your original question – am I choosy? Yes, I am incredibly choosy. Latterly, I won't play anything that is demeaning to women, unless that is the point of it. I'm not saying I will only play heroines and lovely ladies who have a positive end, like some feminists want you to. They always want things to have a positive end and not be negative about women. I don't see that. I did a thing on television called *Jumping the Queue* by Mary Wesley,[5] where the character ends by committing suicide. Now a lot of feminists thought that was very defeatist. I actually thought it was real, so therefore I would do it. I thought it was making a point about the hopelessness of women in the situation that that woman was in. I wouldn't do some of the things I did when I was younger, which make women out to be absolutely ridiculous.

So, really throughout your career, your choices have been completely governed by being a working mother with children? Why did you go into theatre in the first place?

It seemed the most sensible thing to do from my background. If I had my time again, knowing what I know now, I wouldn't. I was a bright girl before the Education Act, and I got a scholarship to grammar school. I felt a bit out of my depth, but nevertheless, because of that, fought very hard and was usually top. My headmistress, who was a Quaker, which I've latterly become, tried to persuade me to go to university. I honestly did not know what university was, so I said, 'No.' The choices for women at that time were to be a teacher, which you went to university for, or nursing, and a few oddballs went into the theatre as a way of getting away from their backgrounds. My sister was already a variety artist; she'd been to Italia Conti and was a chorus girl, and latterly had her own act. Therefore, I'd been backstage to a lot of theatres and seen how liberating it could be. My parents worked in pubs as well, so I kind of got the flavour for entertainment; they used to entertain in the pub. I played *St Joan* at school, and it brought me the kind of admiration that I craved for. I was very plain, very spotty and awful. The boys from the other grammar school were asking me out, because I was obviously alright in it. In fact, I think I was probably pretty good really, because I was a deeply religious child at that time. I'd been to convents earlier on, so therefore the kind of passion of *St Joan* would have appealed to me. I tried for RADA, but I had no coaching, although the elocution teacher tried to help me with my accent. I got a Kent scholarship, as it was very difficult to get grants to go to drama school. Drama school was like a finishing school, all fee-paying, and just a few scholarship people like myself there. I was very much out of my depth when I went to RADA. It was a mistake. If I had my time again, I would have gone to university, and I might have gone into theatre much quicker. When I went to the Royal Shakespeare Company in the 1980s, I think almost the entire company were graduates except for me. Certainly when I became director of the tour, I was without a doubt the only director working there who hadn't been to university. My greatest joy is that my daughter's just got her degree at Cambridge, so I'm living through her.

Are there any other contributory factors to wanting to become an actress?

Yes. It was teachers. There was one particular teacher, who actually got me a little part at the Guildhall playing Scrap in *Dear Octopus*, because I think she recognised potential talent, and took me to the theatre. I only went to the theatre about five times in my entire youth. My Aunty Ruby used to take me to pantomime, and she took me to the ballet once. Essentially, I wanted to show off, to be recognised, to say, 'I may be playing but you jolly well clap me.' If I look back, I'm afraid that I had no nobler motive than that, but it's changed since then.

As a child

I'm interested in how your perception of theatre changed, and what brought about these changes.

As a person, I matured a great deal, and began to look beyond my personal ambition. I developed a political and social conscience. I do regard the theatre, film and television as a possibility of enlightenment, if not of change. I guess when I felt that most passionately was when I was artistic director of the RSC tour, when I had a missionary zeal, and wore everybody out. I was so boring about it being everybody's birthright to have this amazing writing brought to them, which I had discovered very late. It wasn't until I went to the RSC that I really became fanatical about Shakespeare. That was when I visibly saw the power of theatre, because we would go to places that had never seen Shakespeare and were very anti-Shakespeare. They were grilled into coming to our marquee, and went out transformed. I don't say that lightly. You could tell by the letters that they wrote and the workshops that we did. We were trying to release people's own creativity and their own right to their language, which is becoming impoverished in schools very often. It was a miracle. I feel that very strongly. I was on the drama panel of the Arts Council for a while, and that again opened my eyes to the value of the work that I didn't know about. I lived in a very rarefied theatre atmosphere. Then I found myself doing assessments on groups that went into mental hospitals and saw the most amazing work done – in Theatre-in-education – as well. I just thought it was vital to our society and should be not cut back, but hugely expanded. Call it drama therapy, music therapy, whatever you like, but just to unlock people's imagination and creativity is so enriching. Therefore, that began to take over from wanting people to clap me. I get satisfaction out of approaching it like that now, whereas I didn't get a lot of satisfaction about being clapped. It's nice to be clapped, but it's very transitory.

So it's a different kind of performing satisfaction now?

Yes. When I'm actually on stage, I want the show to work. I want people to have a good time, to be moved, or whatever. It's really nice if I'm in something that has moved people on. You're not going to do that with all of the audience.

Is the satisfaction to do with engaging with the audience?

Yes. I've always liked engaging with audiences. I suppose that's why I most enjoyed working with Joan Littlewood, because she's a great director. Having said that, I also do like just giving people a damn good time, which is probably what this next project will do, if I do it. It's not going in any way to change people's view of society. It will hopefully give them a good time and an insight into a certain period. That's the other side of me, that I do like making people laugh and I do like to entertain them and have fun. Having said that, I'll probably then want to do something a little bit more serious.

It's a significant achievement to have directed at both the RSC and the National. Were you the first woman to have achieved that?

Well, I was the first woman for ten years at the RSC,[6] and the first woman to run a company, which was the regional tour. I was the first woman in the main house at the National. I battered on Trevor Nunn's door for quite a long while before I got it, which was only because none of the boys would do it. The RSC tour is the least attractive part of the operation, or it was then. It was bloody hard work. Not a lot of glory associated with it. I turned it round quite a bit, because I insisted on certain things. At the National it was terrifying, because I chose to do an extremely difficult technical show. I insisted on meeting the stage hands right at the beginning, before rehearsals started, because I knew that I had a complicated show and I wanted to ask their advice. I guess it was a sort of female approach in a funny way, and it worked. They couldn't have been more wonderful with me in the end, whereas they were quite bolshy with some people. It was pretty scary.

What was particularly scary about it?

I think the cross of being the first woman. I didn't want to fuck it up for other women, I've always been very conscious of that. I felt that at the RSC as well, when I used to sit in on meetings, when Genista MacIntosh[7] and I were the only women around. One was very conscious that you could frighten the horses. Trevor Nunn was enormously supportive. They now have many women working there (not as many as they should), but they do.

Despite success as a director, you continued to pursue the performing path.

Well not long after that, I contracted breast cancer. I think there was no doubt that a lot of it was to do with stress. It was after that period, and because I was so fanatical, I drove myself much too hard. It was a combination of two things. It was a combination of passionately wanting the tour to work and be taken to the people. We went to prisons and I did endless workshops. I was always around giving notes. Nowadays, the actors all say that I was lovely to work for, but they hated me at the time, because they would give what they thought was a good performance and I would say, 'I want notes tomorrow because it wasn't perfect.' I look back and I'm horrified at the way I treated them. It was too much. It was exactly the same at the National. I was in the company. I was performing Madame Ranyevskaya in *The Cherry Orchard*,[8] I was in *The Duchess of Malfi*[9] and I was understudying in my own production of *The Critic*, so I was there every night. I was working the most awful hours, and things were dodgy at home at the same time as well. In the end, I just collapsed and then I was gravely ill. I thought I was going to die. I kind of link directing in with that; I'm not emotionally cut out for it. Being an actress too, I get terribly fraught if actors are having problems. I know now that actors always have problems, and they always get out of them. Towards the end of any production they always blame the director. I do it myself. It's a kind of ritual that we all go through, but at that stage I found it so upsetting because I loved my company. I'd hand-picked them and I thought they were all so talented. I adored them personally, and I got involved with their private lives, because it might affect their performance. I'd be running around trying to sort out their love life and it just broke me. Now I've just begun to think I might direct again, because I think now I've changed hugely as a person and I would be able to be much more detached than I was in those days.

I had a sort of image when you were describing yourself in that period as a kind of 'great mother'.

Yes, I was. That leaves you open to abuse. Everybody relies on you if you're not careful. You take away people's independence. The fact that I was constantly giving notes to people, I realise didn't allow them to grow in their parts. They had the right to make a mistake, discover they'd made one and put it right themselves. I never thought they would, and I wanted every single night for every single audience to be magic. I was lucky inasmuch as I think most of the company was as passionate as me by the time we'd finished.

Are you still a perfectionist?

Yes. I am, but I'm conscious of it now. I know the disease, and I stop myself. I certainly try not to be a perfectionist with other people. It's less easy with myself. The last show I did at the Royal Court, which didn't work at all for a lot of reasons, was a disaster. Normally, I'd have been rushing around in circles with anger against either the critics, director, or the other actors, and I didn't. I was quite sanguine about it. Some you win, some you lose. I did my best and I was sorry for the author, but it was just one of those things. That was a huge step forward for me. Normally, I'd have been in a right state.

It sounds like the collapse and the breast cancer became a major turning point.

Looking back, it obviously was. It didn't seem so at the time, it seemed awful at the time. I think what I did was start thinking about my life more, and not being driven quite so much. I still have to fight not to be driven, not to find myself doing a job because I'm trying to prove something. I have to stop and think, 'Why am I doing this? Is it still to tell Daddy that I'm clever?' I do think, for my generation particularly, that was a very potent thing. Wanting to please, or being frightened of, a father.

When I met you in the bar at the RSC in the 1980s, I was with a close friend – the actress Susan Leong – who was performing in a play, Typhoid Mary *by Shirley Gee, with Juliet Stevenson in The Pit. My impression of you then was as you've just described.*

We used to meet up, Juliet Stevenson, Harriet Walter and various other people, because we were finding the laddish directors tough going, particularly in terms of interpretation. I was having a real battle with *A Winter's Tale.*[10] I was playing Paulina in that and she always seems to be seen as this terrible nagging woman, and I didn't see her as that at all.

Has anybody particularly influenced you as a performing woman?

No, not really. There weren't people like me. I didn't fit in. I couldn't be myself until Joan Littlewood changed it all. I wasn't allowed to be like me. I used to run around in flat shoes because I was too tall, trying to flatten out my cockney accent. I was just pretending to be something else.

Are you yourself now?

Oh yes. I'm what I've become. I'm not what I was. Now, I don't give a fuck what people think about me, I really don't. I'm not frightened of any type of people. The people that I respect are usually clever people. I've huge respect for my husband's first wife – Professor Sally Alexander – who is a socialist historian.

What is it then that makes you still perform?

I think it's a sickness, a disease really. I have so often decided that I won't do it any more and I'll write. That's my great ambition – to write. I've got two chapters of a novel, which have been sitting in a drawer for two years, and then a job comes up, and I can't resist it. Then I do it, and I think, 'What the hell am I doing this for?' It's the same pattern and I repeat it over and over again.

What is the lure of the job?

It intrigues me, the research aspect and the rehearsal period. I love rehearsals. I just don't like performing any more. I find myself doing it and I wish I didn't.

My ideal scenario is that I should not do it any more, and I should write. I should write so many hours in the morning, go for a little walk and then go to exhibitions. I mean this is my ideal. I see bits of London that I haven't explored for a long time, or I go on holidays and explore.

Are you exploring in a different way via these opportunities that keep presenting themselves?

Yes. I mean the joy of theatre is exploring new worlds. I do love that, I do love getting in other people's lives. One of the roles I most enjoyed recently was playing Dowager Duchess in *Dangerous Buccaneers*,[11] a television series. We filmed at Castle Howard, and I had to be the top of the aristocratic pile. That's a world I not only don't know very much, but actually sort of faintly dislike really. I plunged into it and I ended up with huge respect for that sort of woman, who holds together a dynasty. I did a lot of delving in the archives of Castle Howard and came across some amazing women – past duchesses. I learned a great deal, got rid of a lot of prejudice in myself by getting inside this woman's mind, who wasn't a particularly sympathetic character, but I loved her in the end. I could see exactly where she was coming from. I think this is one of the joys of our profession. I'm always amazed how little most people know about anybody except their own circle, which is what leads to the most appalling prejudice and bigotry. Playing those parts gives you an enormous breadth of knowledge about society. I think that's why I love actors. They do have an enormous compassion, and an understanding of an awful lot of things in life. It's always such an irony that we're depicted as luvvies and stupid, because most actors know more about things than the average person, and certainly more than the average journalist.

Does the word 'strumpet' – in the sense of morality of the theatre – hold any resonance for you? Has the image of the actress moved on a bit?

Yes, I think it has. I'm amazed at how very proper younger actors are. They've all got mortgages and tied themselves down to all sorts of funny things. I think we were much more outsiders when I started in the business, we were very much more rogues and vagabonds than we are now in actuality. In terms of strumpet, would that I'd had the chance! As far as I'm concerned it hasn't been like that at all. But then, I've never been that type. I guess for beautiful girls, the temptations and the demands were much more difficult than for me. When I was young I worked all the hours God sent on weekly rep; I didn't have time or energy for anything else but work. My background was very straightforward and you behaved and that was that, so I didn't have much strumpeting I have to say. Sadly, I wish I had. However, an itinerant certainly – a lot of itinering.

Have you enjoyed being an itinerant?

Yes. I love travelling. It was difficult when my kids were young. It was a strain dragging them everywhere, but now I love hotels, digs and new places. I'm always going off main roads and seeing what's down side roads. I really enjoy that aspect. I know England very well now, because whenever I go on tour I always explore wherever I am. I'm less happy with touring now – I like being in my home, but I still will go off for a one-off thing and I enjoy that very much indeed. I've loved working abroad on the few occasions when I have. I'm avid for new things.

In the same way that you haven't been easily categorised as an actress, you've never settled into one particular kind of direction.

I can easily be distracted. I'll be doing something quite soberly, and then something will spark my imagination and I'll fly off. It's a kind of joke in the family, 'Oh dear, Mum's got one of her things. She's learning something or doing something.' That's why I keep working, because my self-discipline is very poor. The only way I finished my book[12] was an editor phoning up and saying I must have that chapter by tomorrow. I really do have to be brow-beaten.

So, why aren't you realising your ideal image of writing daily?

It's probably fear of being mediocre. I know I'd be mediocre. Comparing myself with other people, I know I'm better than him, but I'm not as good as her. I can't be as good as her, because I've no education, which is always my excuse. I look back occasionally at the two chapters I've written, and I think it's quite funny and interesting. But why don't I finish it? I could find time.

There's a sort of contradiction in yourself somehow. You don't care what people think, and yet, it's exactly that which prevents you writing. You've obviously got very high goals.

I don't care what people think of me as a person, but I do care what they think of anything I create. I suppose that's the division. I don't care if they think I'm vulgar or silly, because I know what I am now. I know my failings, and I know, to a certain extent, my qualities and abilities. But I do loathe being condemned for my work, particularly at the moment in theatre. It's such an ephemeral business. If you're certain people then they'll rave about you. I mean Judi Dench can do no wrong. Maybe she can't do any wrong, but that is the rule. Ian Mckellen, to a certain extent, can do no wrong. You know they'll still be great actors whatever they do. And yet there are other actors, people like Penelope Wilton or Alison Steadman, who are amazingly good actors, who don't come in the list of critics' great actors. I'm not saying I should be on that list, but I'm saying what I observe about our profession. So you think they're not going to recognise what one's doing anyway, so why does one beat one's head against a brick wall? Writing is so different to acting. That's why I want to do it. You do a great performance one night, and who remembers except a few people who might be there? Writing a book, it remains.

What are the key moments in your life so far as a performing woman?

Well, the tour, without a shadow of doubt. Seeing people transformed. We had this group of people from Barnsley, miners and their wives, who kept popping up at all the other venues. It was during the strike. They'd never been to Shakespeare before, but they were just besotted with it. So that was good. Working with Joan Littlewood was amazing, and the musical[13] I did with her was one of these extraordinary things. On the first night I stopped the show with this little number that was thrown in. Joan made me do it because they wanted to change the set behind me. I didn't have a song at that point in the show; I was just a small part. On the first night they wouldn't let me go. It just went on and on. It was only one chorus to cover this scene change. I do remember being flabbergasted by this. Then it was one of those wonderful overnight success things. The first night of *Rattle of a Simple Man*[14] was quite funny, because again I was very unaware in those days of the success I was having. After the first night performance, I was with two gay friends of mine, and we had to push my Morris car down St Martin's Lane. I remember that as a very treasured moment because we were all a bit pissed by then, and I remember Tony, who'd been at RADA with me, leaning on this terrible car that had broken down, saying, 'You've cracked it, you've done it you cow.' There was my name in lights, but it was only a moment. My dad had come to the show, and my dad always used to cry if he was pleased, and he was crying with emotion in my dressing room. It had obviously been a big personal success.

Your daughter graduating at Cambridge must have been a key moment in your life.

Oh, absolutely. Oh, that is mega. Watching her graduate in the Senate House. I went with my eldest daughter and we were sobbing out loud. Just sobbing with delight. All the other parents were behaving impeccably and beautifully. I just wished that my parents could have been there. That was absolutely amazing. Most of my key moments are to do with my children. They are my greatest joy without a shadow of a doubt. Other sadder moments have been life-changing. I think a life-changing moment for me was reading *The Female Eunuch* without a doubt. That was the most transforming moment for me as a woman to read that, because that was the first time I'd ever really thought about what women were, and then meeting Germaine Greer as well. I respect and admire her so much. I still do. She's still shocking, amazing and life-changing, and just transformed my life. I think all my feminism stemmed from the minute I put that book down. It just opened my eyes to so much. Joan Littlewood was life-changing for me as well, because Joan released on stage for me the right to be myself, to use my own experience. I had been trying to be what actresses were at that stage – conforming, being nice, refined – and Joan was the first person who said, 'Be a clown.' She was also the one who made me realise the value of comedy to enlighten, enrich and contact people. I evolved from her this real desire to communicate with an audience. I'm one of those directors who rushes around every bit of the theatre, making sure people are audible, which a lot of directors don't. I'm determined that my set should be able to be seen from all angles, which again a lot of directors don't. Joan taught me that you've got to be conscious that you're trying to reach people.

Did Joan Littlewood initiate a starting point for your development as a comedic actress?

Yes. I'd done a lot of comedy in repertory and I think I'd been quite good at it, but what she did was make me realise the intrinsic funniness in my own personality. The fact that I could be a bit quirky, a bit gauche as I was at that stage particularly, and to use that to bring myself through a part. You did a lot of ad-libbing, a lot of improvising, and a lot of it was me. Doing *The Cherry Orchard* with Mike Alfreds[15] was influential, because he works in a similar opening-up way to Joan, although in more detail. Another person who was hugely influential, in terms of language, was John Barton. He was very patient with me, because I didn't have a university background. All the others knew what he was talking about and I'd keep saying, 'What do you mean?' That was the first time I came across this sort of academic analysis of Shakespeare's text, how enriching that can be and how it gives you clues to the way of doing it. The combination of him and Cicely Berry, the voice coach at the RSC, was very potent in my understanding and appreciation of Shakespeare. Trevor Nunn as well.

Have you ever been a stand-up?

No. I wish I had been really. I did revues, and I'm doing another revue, which will be a bit like stand-up in a way. No, I was the wrong generation for that. The transition from what I was in sitcom, which was built around this tizzy persona, to women on television today has largely come from stand-up and women who write their own material. In my day, one didn't do that. It never occurred to me to write my own material. It occurred to me to ask other people to write it for me, when I did a sort of revue format on television, but they were men. Women weren't around, they weren't writing. It's an extraordinary jump … from having to be conventional-looking to play Viola or Rosalind – you had to be a pretty, beautifully-spoken girl. It would have been unheard of for somebody like me to play Viola or Rosalind. Whereas Juliet Stevenson or Fiona Shaw who are not conventional-looking are acceptable immediately. It's wonderful that it has changed.

Notes

1 Dorothy in *Close Relations*, BBC Television, directed by Michael Whyte, 1998.
2 Mrs Squeezum in *Lock Up Your Daughters*, an adaptation of Fielding's comedy by Bernard Miles, directed by Steven Rayne, Chichester Festival Theatre, 10 October–2 November 1996.
3 Sarah Meadows in 'Blood Money' episode of *Kavanagh QC*, written by Matthew Hall, directed by Jack Gold, ITV, 10 March 1997.
4 *Born to Run*, written by Debbie Horsfield, directed by John Stewart, starring Billie Whitelaw and Keith Allen, BBC Television, 1997.
5 Matilda in *Jumping the Queue*, by Mary Wesley, BBC Television, 1989.
6 Buzz Goodbody was the first woman director at the Royal Shakespeare Company, working there from 1970 until her death in 1975. Hancock was Artistic Director of the RSC Tour, *A Midsummer Night's Dream*, which was originally part of the small-scale tour in 1983, and then performed at The Other Place as part of the Stratford Season 1984.
7 Genista MacIntosh was the Planning Controller for the RSC in 1983.
8 Madame Ranyevskaya in Chekhov's *The Cherry Orchard*, directed by Mike Alfreds with Lilia Sokolov, Royal National Theatre (Cottesloe), 1985.
9 Julia in Webster's *The Duchess of Malfi*, directed by Philip Prowse, Royal National Theatre (Lyttelton), 1985.
10 Paulina in Shakespeare's *The Winter's Tale*, directed by Ronald Eyre, RSC, Stratford, 1981 and Barbican, 1982.
11 Duchess of Trevenick in *The Buccaneers*, four-part serial, based on Edith Wharton novel, written and adapted by Maggie Wadey, directed by Phillip Saville, 1995.
12 Hancock, S., *Ramblings of an Actress*, Hutchinson, 1987.
13 *Make Me an Offer*, directed by Joan Littlewood, with Roy Kinnear, Theatre Workshop, Stratford East, 1959.
14 *Rattle of a Simple Man*, with Edward Woodward, Garrick Theatre, 1962.
15 See note 8.

Brenda Blethyn

'The characters I'm playing are not me,
I'm just performing them.'

'It's curious, because *Secrets and Lies* was only my
third film, and yet, I've been in the business for
twenty-four years.'

Performance Context

Born: 1946, Ramsgate, Kent.
Prior/current commitments: Cynthia Purley in Mike Leigh's film *Secrets and Lies*.
Dawn in *Girls' Night*, written by Kay Mellor, Granada Films.
Post-interview (selected): Mari Hoff in *Little Voice*, Scala Productions, Miramax Films.
Alice Mooney in *Night Train*, Subotica Films.
Ida Stubbs in *In the Winter Dark*, R. B. Films.
Julia Montgomery in *Daddy and Them*, Free Hazel Films.
Other: Nominated for Golden Globe Award for 'Best Supporting Actress' in *Little Voice*, 1999.
Awards for *Secrets and Lies* – 1997 Oscar nomination 'Best Actress'; 1997 British Academy Award 'Best Actress'; 1996 Golden Globe Award 'Best Actress'; 1996 Cannes Film Festival 'Best Actress'; 1996 London Film Critics Award 'Best Actress of the Year' (selected).
1994 'Best Comedy Actress' for television role in *Outside Edge*.
Awarded Honorary Degree of Doctor of Letters, University of Kent at Canterbury, 1999.

Interview

Brenda Blethyn's wonderful anecdotes and impersonations of well-known directors flowed naturally out of her descriptions of the rehearsal process, which never failed to make me laugh when I interviewed Brenda in my Canterbury home on 1 July 1997. Her Oscar-nominated performance as Cynthia in Mike Leigh's film Secrets and Lies *won world-wide critical acclaim, supporting an already distinguished career.*

Alison Oddey: *Is there a family theatrical background?*

Brenda Blethyn: No. My parents were both very witty people. We weren't rich by any means, but we were rich in communication and affection for each other. We would entertain and amuse each other. We'd laugh a lot. My mum was a very funny woman, and even now, when we all get together, if one of us comes out with a 'Mumism', then the others will laugh. She left an indelible impression on us all. They're both dead now. When we look back we don't think about being poor, but we laugh and find something funny about it all.

That is a real gift she's given to us, to be able to cope with adversity with humour and it makes you stronger.

A remarkable quality to learn from your parents.

Yes. They taught us humility and a sense of humour. To see the ridiculous side of things and the ridiculous side of oneself, more importantly. Just to laugh at yourself.

I know that your sister and brother live locally – are you from a large family?

Yes, I'm the youngest of nine. It's great, although sadly one brother has died. We're pretty close and have a lot of affection for each other.

Aged six

Were you brought up in Ramsgate?

Yes, born there. Dad used to take me to the cinema. There were four local cinemas when I was growing up; it was wonderful and I loved going. If I was naughty, which I wasn't very often, then I couldn't go to the cinema. It was the big Hollywood films that seemed so remote and so fantastical. If I had thought then, that one day I would be there, I wouldn't have believed it.

I read somewhere that you have a partner who keeps your feet on the ground.

Oh yes, he's great. I've been with Mike about twenty-two years now. We always seem to be able to put things into perspective.

What attracted you to either the theatre or performing?

I learnt quite early on that I could make people laugh by *pretending* to be silly. I can remember when relatives came to stay for a two-week holiday in Ramsgate with us, I worked out ways of making them really fall about laughing, but pretending that I didn't know I'd done it. It was like a secret joke. They must have thought I was a bit daft, and they'd try to play jokes back on me, so I went along with it. I do that now; that's what acting is. When I started school my attention span wasn't all that good, but when we did drama I couldn't wait to get back to it, I wanted more and more of it. Just something I enjoyed. I went to Thanet Technical College and did Office Studies, which was a sensible thing to do. Acting was something I did at school and would probably never do again.

So what was the turning point, when did you go to drama school?

Not until my mid-twenties. I left school when I was seventeen and went to work in a bank in London. Then I joined amateur dramatics and found I really loved it. I worked for British Rail for a while and they had a drama group. Once a year there was a British Rail amateur drama festival at Manchester and for a couple of years I won 'Best Actress' award, but it still never seemed a professional option. I was married just before I was twenty, and when that broke up – six years later – I applied to Guildford. Fear of rejection put me off for a bit, but I did go. They invited me to join them on a two-and-a-half year course. Before the end of my course, I was offered a job with the Bubble Theatre Company, which I accepted. I also got my Equity card. It was difficult then – you had to have a job before you could get a card, or you had to have your card before you could get a job. Some repertory companies could give out two a year, and I got a job with a card. Guildford released me and I didn't have to go back and finish my course.

Is it possible to say where the root of your desire to perform comes from?

It might be to get attention.

Does it give you pleasure to make people laugh?

Yes, it does give me pleasure to make people laugh – it must be like scoring a goal at football. It's free, it's healthy and very good for you to laugh, especially if you can laugh at yourself.

When you talked about being at school and finding drama, I got a sense of you feeling at home with that.

Yes, I did. It felt comfortable and I liked it. It's like putting on something that fits really nicely. I know my work is appreciated, but that is like a gift I have. I am the custodian of that gift. It's not me. I'm just in charge of it. The characters I'm playing are not me; I'm just performing them. I didn't write them. Mike Leigh's things are a bit different, but I still don't own them. They are different people in their own right.

But you have had a part in creating them, haven't you?

Oh a huge part, but they are not me. My work has obviously gone into it, but I'm still creating something that is nothing to do with me. In fact, you are creating an entire character with Mike Leigh, and because the work is so thorough it's even more removed from oneself. You have to look at the person utterly objectively. You don't have to like them.

No, but you have to find something from inside yourself to feed those performances.

Yes, but do you think that in order to play a murderer that you've got to go and murder someone? I've only got 5ft 2in and brown eyes to present to anyone. Every character is going to look like me, but still the total life experience of the character you are playing is not you. You draw from your imagination what makes this person tick, what makes them get up in the morning; of course, you've got to do that. But you are still creating someone else and try to give them a whole identity. People always think you've got to draw upon yourself – I don't think so. Do you think that in order to play Hannibal Lecter that Sir Anthony Hopkins had to go and kill a few people for his breakfast?

The South American theatre practitioner, Augusto Boal, argues that an actor can play any part, because all emotions are universal.

Well, of course, we are all capable of anything. We are all capable of murder, sadness or whatever. In fact, when we had just finished *Secrets and Lies,*[1] it got to me. Looking at the character made me sad, because she had had a tough life and is frowned upon by most people. It has been difficult for her to make ends meet each week and she was lonely. I would have complained a lot had I been in her position, but she didn't complain much in the film, in her history and in what I know about her. It depressed me playing her. I'd be driving home in my lovely Mercedes to my lovely house in the woods, and Michael would have a meal waiting for me. I'd say, 'Why am I doing a Mike Leigh film?' He would say, 'Oh, for fuck's sake, I wish you'd stayed at work and sent Cynthia home!' I get depressed because there are millions of people like Cynthia in the world, who are not driving home to a nice meal. So, whether it's a devised piece or a scripted piece, I don't think there is necessarily anything of me.

We're watching Cynthia, empathising with her character, whilst marvelling at Brenda Blethyn's ability to perform this character.

In my work I try to be as convincing as possible, like the character or not, and I try to the best of my ability to be real.

We do sense that reality in Secrets and Lies, *even though we have never met Cynthia in life.*

Also, while I'm doing an improvisation, I've got a third eye here which is Brenda's watching over Cynthia and I might think, 'That was a good line, Brenda.' However, at the same time it demands total commitment and concentration. For instance, when she says, 'I've never been with a black man in me life', and then there is that realisation. *I* found that amusing, whether anyone else would or not, is irrelevant. You've still got to be absolutely sincere about it.

You have worked with some of our top directors, particularly in theatre, such as Peter Hall, Bill Bryden, Peter Wood, Greg Hersov – what is your experience generally of working with women directors?

I haven't worked with many. I worked with Jane Howell on *Henry VI*[2] and I really enjoyed it. I am one of those people who are a little bit afraid of Shakespeare, because it doesn't sound like realism, and it is foreign to my ear. Into production week she said, 'I'd like her to be from Yorkshire.' Panicking, I said, 'We've been rehearsing for two weeks with me sounding like this', but she said, 'Well, can we just try it?' It was totally liberating. Suddenly it was completely someone else. It was probably getting in my way, going back to what we said earlier, in that I was thinking it was me doing it rather than the character. I loved that.

Does gender make a difference in any way?

It depends on the talent of the person I'm working for, and also what I think they think of me. If I feel that somebody is less than satisfied with my work, not necessarily the work in hand, but any of my work, I am not very good. I have to feel that they have confidence in me. At the end of the day, of course, I feel a certain pride, but in the making of it, I feel I've got to deliver the goods I'm being paid for. You've got to do what the customer wants. That's not to say you are not trying to be creative, but you have to assume that's what's wanted anyway, otherwise you wouldn't have been cast.

Do you have any desire to direct?

Yes, I would like to direct, but it would probably take me forever to get round to doing that because of fear of failure. I think I would be okay at it, but I worry that I would be a bit of a bully. I think I'd be the kind of director I wouldn't like to work for! It's something to do with whenever I'm first working on a script I am rather aggressive, but that's only because I'm trying to master it, and tame it into submission. I suspect, if I was directing, I might be a little bit aggressive only because I'm trying to master it.

So this is your own experience of directors?

I've worked with some directors who can be positively beastly to people, but they rarely are to me for some reason! Peter Wood, who I've worked with lots of times and who taught me a great deal, has a bit of a reputation for picking on somebody and being unpleasant, but he's a very good director. One of the best theatre directors I've ever worked with was Greg Hersov at the Royal Exchange in Manchester. He was rather like a hippy, a big huggy bear type. He was a bit dishevelled and didn't say very much to start with, and I used to want to lend him a comb. Then he suggested something to me and I thought, 'You pipsqueak, telling me what to do.' (Despite everything I've just said about always listening!) This was on the second day and I thought that I shouldn't have done the job. Two weeks later, I hung on every single word he said. I've seen a lot of his work, and it's always wonderful. I did *A Doll's House*[3] with him there, and I consider that to be my best stage performance. He was great. That was ten years ago, or so.

Is that your most significant performance achievement?

It is certainly what I'm most proud of. It's a classic, and has been seen many times, which means being held up to comparison inevitably. I succeeded in finding that world they lived in and the constraints upon them. I felt I entered that world and understood what made Nora get up in the morning, what made her feel warm, what made her shudder, what her fears were and her passions. I felt I understood what made her walk out of the door in the end.

You've obviously received international recognition as Cynthia in Secrets and Lies, *but having watched your work over the years, it wasn't surprising to me that you performed so well.*

Thank you. It's curious, because *Secrets and Lies* was only my third film, and yet, I've been in the business for twenty-four years. I think that it's the international recognition that has made the biggest difference, especially winning a Golden Globe. It's got the Hollywood stamp of approval. It was a huge exposure being in a film with five Oscar nominations, but winning at Cannes and a British Academy Award was absolutely fantastic. However, I don't think it puts everything else I've done to shame, because I'm pleased with my theatre and television work.

Is there the same satisfaction to be gained from performing in theatre, film or television?

I think it's more to do with the characters that one has been asked to do. If you can open the audience's eyes to them – to have some kind of impact is good. Just to trigger the brain off in one direction or the other is important to me. As soon as you read the script, you can know whether it's a worthy piece of work, usually. Things can change in production of course, but that's one of the gambles. It's great if you can make somebody change their mind about particular types of people. Even comedy, like *Outside Edge*,[4] with that put-upon middle-class woman, who you think has got everything. She's got a lovely house, but she hasn't got that closeness with her husband that she wants; he's a bully. The other two have got all that affection but no baby, so not everyone has got everything in the world. There are things all of us hanker for and we are not going to get, so you've got to put up with that.

You mention Outside Edge, *for which you got a 1994 'Best Comedy Actress' award. You've got so many awards and you've done such a real diversity of work. You are obviously attracted to comedy in some way.*

To be honest, other people are more attracted to me playing comedy. I get offered a lot of comedy. However, in every single thing I do, I see both sides.

I cannot see anything funny without seeing the dark side of that. We are going back to when we were kids. We were taught to see the ridiculousness of things and the funny side of the tragedy. Look at Cynthia – such a tragic woman, but you sit there and you laugh at her. It's the same with *Outside Edge*.

Do you enjoy watching women being funny?

There are not many female stand-up comics that I like. That I *know*, to be more precise. Jo Brand is one of the exceptions. I think she's really funny, but it's something to do with the fact that she appears not to be acting. She is performing, but it doesn't look as if she is. I was about to say Lily Savage, but he's a bloke! If it was a woman, I don't know that I'd find it so funny. I love watching Roseanne Barr. I find Dawn French very funny. Everyone thinks of Josie Lawrence as a stand-up comic, but she's never done it in her life. She's an actress, but she's often thought of as a stand-up comic because of the Comedy Store.

Is there anybody in particular who has inspired or influenced you?

No. Dad always used to say, 'Always do better than your best', and one strives to do just that. I don't know how you can apply that to acting. There are other things involved – like being punctual, doing your homework, knowing your lines and being courteous to other people you are working with. Washing, personal hygiene! There are all those things to take into account.

If you had to think of any key moments in your life so far, what would they be?

One was at a school party. In the months leading up to Christmas, the pupils would all take in a jelly or a tin of peaches. This was in the 1950s. A blancmange powder or a bag of nuts, just maybe once a week or once a fortnight if your parents could afford to do that. So when Christmas came there was enough to have a school Christmas party. You didn't have to wear uniform and you could wear a party frock. I didn't have a new one. I had a nice one from last year, a bit tight with the hem let down! Dad said, 'Don't you worry Bren, you'll be the prettiest one there.'

Are there other key moments in terms of your career?

When I was making *A River Runs Through It*[5] with Robert Redford. It was a Scottish character and I worked on the Scottish accent. I went to a voice coach here to make sure it was just right, and I think it was good enough. When I got there, one of the first things he said to me was that he'd decided he wanted it all non-specific middle-America, me included. I thought, 'God, how am I going to sound American?', working with everyone in it, all Americans. They weren't going to use me for two weeks and I spent all my time in Livingstone, Montana talking to townsfolk. I spoke with my American accent all the time so that I would get used to it, even when I was off-duty. So having got over that obstacle and after a few days filming, they'd gone to see the 'dailies', as they call them there. I was in the make-up trailer and someone called out, 'Bob's coming over with his entourage, he's looking for Brenda', and I thought, 'Oh God, this is going to be humiliating.' Is he coming to say, 'You're off the picture?' He came in, unsmiling and said, 'Brenda I've just seen the rushes. I could see what you were doing was good but the camera thinks you are wonderful, I just wanted to tell you that', and he went out! I truly thought he was going to say, 'If you want to stay on this film, you've got to pull your socks up.'

You expected him to say that you weren't up to scratch, which brings us back to your dad and 'Always do better than your best.'

Sometimes when I'm working on something, I'll come home and Mike will say, 'How's it going?' and I'll say, 'Oh, terrible.' He now says, 'Oh that's good', I say, 'Why?', and he says, 'Well you always say that and it always turns out alright, so that's a good sign.'

How would you describe yourself?

Coward.

Why do you say that?

I'm a bit weedy sometimes. I am a survivor certainly. I have a big pain threshold. I suppose it's the struggle to be successful. Before all this furore over *Secrets and Lies* I'd never been out of work. It's necessary for me not to be idle, to pay my way, to make a contribution, not to be a waste of space.

Your work has taken you all over the world. Is being an itinerant part of the appeal of performing?

Yes, but it is often a bit of an eye opener or a bit sobering when it comes to fruition. I would quite like to work from home for a bit. I treasure my home and Michael more and more, especially with what has been going on with me lately. It's all rather insincere, all that adulation. I'm just doing a job, going to work. It's rather comforting to come home to sincerity, even if it's rather blunt. I've often worked away from home, but generally in England I can come home at weekends. When I was in New York I was there for three and a half months, and then another three months when I made *A River Runs Through It.*

But generally, you enjoy touring.

It varies with me. Primarily, the important thing is the job. To concentrate my day towards doing that show in the evening. That's why I'm there. I'm not there to sightsee. I'm there so this audience, who can't get to London, can see the play. I will be concerned that there is somewhere for me to rest properly, where I can get good food, and how long will it take me to get from the hotel to the theatre, and can I walk home? I have a ritual. I'm not someone who can rush into the theatre at the last minute, and get ready. I can't do that. It's therapeutic to me. I take time to do make-up, much longer than I need, and I'll always make sure I sit quietly beforehand in my room alone. I have to do that just to focus myself. Some people don't have to do that, and I envy them. Gosh, don't I sound boring?

Not at all. What do you enjoy most about being a performing woman?

Making a living, earning money, doing something surprising. Like playing Mrs Cheveley in Oscar Wilde's *An Ideal Husband.*[6] It would not be something I'd automatically be cast in. Just to surprise myself as well, and to keep a standard up. You are only ever as good as your last job. I'm one of these people who thinks I'm never going to work again! I know a few people like it.

So even with your current success, you still question whether the work will keep coming in?

Yes, there is stuff lined up for next year, but nothing is signed on the dotted line and supposing I lost an eye, what then? Supposing I go around a lamp-post – there are lots of things that could get in the way. I'm talking about even if everything goes normally, lots of things can ambush you.

You've won numerous awards over the years – what do you think of awards?

I was asked in Korea if I felt film festivals should be competitive and I said then that they should not be and that it should be a celebration of film, because for every winner out of thirty films you have got twenty-nine losers. I don't think that is healthy. It should all be celebrated, but having said that, it's done my career a power of good! I do think personalities get celebrated rather than the job. I would bet my house that had Timothy Spall been doing a promotional tour of *Secrets and Lies* he would have had an Oscar nomination, but he didn't. I have people come up to me and say, 'You were so wonderful, you were fantastic, I think you are wonderful, I can't wait to see the movie!' I'm getting offers of films from people who haven't even seen *Secrets and Lies*, so it's like celebrating the achievements without having seen what the fuss is about. It seems like you have to have done something or won something to get into the race for a prize.

It's also a case of the critics' taste ...

I've seen shows the critics have absolutely panned, but I've really enjoyed. The opposite as well. So it's only a matter of opinion, not like being an athlete and running the race quicker than the other – then of course one is better than the other. This is a matter of opinions.

Where do you keep your awards?

On the mantle, but they look rather unattractive. They are there because a photographer came to my house once and they were all over the place, but he put them all on the mantle with candles either side, like *The House of Usher*! He lit them and took a picture. It was like a shrine. It amused us so much that they are still there! That's where the prizes got put. It's not a decision, it's a cliché – 'on the mantle'. They are just dumped there. My room upstairs needs re-plastering so I'll put them there, so I won't be embarrassed and have people coming in and looking at them. In my loo is my letter of congratulations from Virginia Bottomley! It makes us laugh.

Notes

1 Cynthia in Mike Leigh's film *Secrets and Lies*, co-starring Marianne Jean-Baptiste and Timothy Spall, 1996.
2 Joan La Pucelle in Shakespeare's *Henry VI*, directed by Jane Howell, film for BBC Television, 1983.
3 Nora in Ibsen's *A Doll's House*, directed by Gregory Hersov, Royal Exchange, Manchester, 15 October–14 November 1987.
4 Miriam Dervish in *Outside Edge*, written by Richard Harris, directed by Nick Hurran, co-starring Josie Lawrence, Timothy Spall and Robert Daws, Carlton production for Central Broadcasting and a Central programme for ITV (Three series), 1994–96.
5 Mrs Maclean in the film *A River Runs Through It*, directed by Robert Redford, Allied Film Makers, 1992.
6 Mrs Cheveley in Wilde's *An Ideal Husband*, directed by James Maxwell, Royal Exchange, Manchester, 2 July–8 August 1992.

Alison Steadman

'..., as a character actress. I've always wanted to play
characters, where I'm disguised and nothing like me. I
enjoy the dressing up in the way children dress up in
their mothers' clothes.'

Performance Context

Born: 1946, Liverpool.

Prior/current commitments: Maria Helliwell in J.B. Priestley's *When We Are Married*, Savoy Theatre.
Voiceovers for radio commercials and television.

Post-interview (selected): Lady Fanciful in Sir John Vanbrugh's *The Provok'd Wife*, The Old Vic.
Christine Peacock in *The Missing Postman*, BBC Scotland.
Completed Mike Leigh's new film in 1998.

Other: Olivier Award for 'Best Actress' in Jim Cartwright's *The Rise and Fall of Little Voice*, Royal National Theatre, 1993.

Interview

I met Alison Steadman on 13 November 1996 in her dressing-room at the Savoy Theatre, London, prior to a matinee performance of J.B. Priestley's When We Are Married.

Alison Oddey: *How would you describe yourself in terms of a performing woman in the widest context?*

Alison Steadman: First and foremost, as a character actress. I've always wanted to play characters where I'm disguised and nothing like me. I enjoy the dressing up in the way children dress up in their mothers' clothes. I like doing accents and I like doing voices, so I've done a lot of radio work over the years, because I can be all these characters vocally but not physically. I'm more a character actress, and I don't particularly enjoy being interviewed as myself, so I'll usually try and avoid that situation. I didn't become an actress to make public appearances and open fetes.

Why did you become an actress?

I always think that there are people who are born with certain characteristics, for example, my grandmother was a very anarchic character. When I was a child, she used to dress up and fool around just for fun. She was a very artistic woman. She was a milliner, she could make dresses, she could garden and she used to do woodwork. She was a real nutcase. If times had been different she probably would have made a very good actress, but because of her circumstances and social background it never happened, but she used her creative thing in other ways. The other thing is that I'm the youngest in the family. I've got two sisters ten and twelve years older than me, so I was an afterthought. I was quite spoilt, not money-wise but attention-wise, and I was the delight of the family always. I think everyone was truly delighted when I was born as it was just after the war in 1946. Suddenly the war was over and here was this baby. Mum and Dad loved children, so I was brought up in an atmosphere with lots of love, attention, fun and laughter. When I was quite young I could impersonate voices from television. Very often now I can hear my mum saying, 'Turn off the television, now come on Alison, do us some voices', and I'd entertain them. Then when I was nine we did a school play and I can remember the teacher saying to Mother, 'Your daughter seems to be quite talented. Maybe she ought to be an actress.' This was the first time I had heard of an actress! This idea got planted in my head and from then on it grew. I used to impersonate the Scottish woman next door when we lived in Liverpool, where you only heard Liverpool accents, as it amused me. Maybe all those things came together. At grammar school I found the work very tough (my son is dyslexic and I don't know whether I am a bit), but I always found reading out loud very difficult, which is odd for an actress. That has been a difficulty for me, particularly at read-throughs. It's always a bit stressful, but if I get a big speech, I have to go through it before I go to the read-through, because otherwise I get so panicky. When I was doing a read-through for *Pride and Prejudice*,[1] we read six episodes in a day, which was a big deal. We got there to a huge rehearsal room at the BBC, and there was this great table – right the way round the room. There were about eighty people there and this was the first time anyone was going to hear me read Mrs Bennet. I had been cast – I don't have to audition now – people just ask me to do things. I hadn't met the director, I knew the producer but I didn't know most of the actors in it. I just walked in and wanted to say, 'Sorry, I've changed my mind!' and walk out. I thought, 'Oh my God, this is my worst nightmare and it's all here in this room!' I was a wreck the whole day so I launched myself into it. I thought, 'Just think of the character, don't think of anything else!' Then it was fine, but it was such an ordeal. You feel that you're being judged. You pray that you will come up with a good performance and your idea of the part.

Where do you think this performance that you can produce comes from?

I love people. I love watching people, and I like to think I'm quite an understanding, caring person. We are all so different and I enjoy trying to understand what makes people tick. I just enjoy investigating the human being – I find it fun.

So is there a need to perform? What drives you on?

If someone said to me, 'You can't act any more', my life would be very empty. I'd like to think that I could retire tomorrow, walk the dog by the sea, which I love, but if that was the only thing I had, I would miss that terribly. You've always got to remember with actors, that however modest you might be, there has to be a side in your nature which craves recognition, wanting to show off. You like to get the odd award, you like to be asked for your autograph, growing and building until that's a part of your life. People look at you in the street, recognise you and come up to you. It's great to be loved in life by your family – it gives you a good feeling of well-being, and this is a similar sort of thing. There have been times when I've been a bit low in my private life and I've been in a show in the West End, feeling rock bottom after the show and having to walk out into the street, get into the car and drive off. I've wanted to go to a party because I didn't want it to finish. I am very prone to loneliness; I'm terrified of loneliness. Ever since I can remember being a toddler, I can remember a fear of being alone.

Do you know how this sense of loneliness originated?

When I was ten, my sister got married, and I felt devastated by her leaving home. Then my other sister got married and left home, and I was left alone with my parents. After this jolly house being filled with boyfriends or young women coming in and out, I had this strong sense of loneliness. They had

As a child

gone and the house was so quiet. It felt like things had come to an end. I find it very difficult to live on my own.

Even though you could always phone someone, or invite people round?

Yes, but I'd still be 'alone'. I would not choose to live alone. I liked life best when my children were quite small and the house was always full of kids. However, that period of time has passed, as they are much older now. One is fifteen and one is eighteen.

Have you found it hard to be both actor and working mother?

My children are very important, and I turned a lot of work down because it was inconvenient. I found it very difficult to go back to work when they were little, because I loved just being a mother at home with them. It was very hard handing them over to the nanny – I cried my eyes out. But the nice thing about being an actress is that it is changing all the time – for instance, the hours change or the job changes. My job may take one week, two weeks, six weeks and then I can have six weeks off. So I was able to balance my time between working and spending time with them, because I didn't want them to grow up remembering childhood with different nannies and never with me. I did, and still do, enjoy being with them. I saw it as constantly weighing up jobs as to whether I could cope. I remember when my son was about eleven, I was offered and accepted a job in theatre, and whilst we were sitting together I said, 'I'm going to do this play', and he said, 'Oh no, how long for, you'll be out every night.' I suddenly realised that I had thought he was old enough not to worry. I felt really bad, but it's swings and roundabouts.

Can you describe what it feels like physically or emotionally to perform?

You go through various stages – rehearsals are a battle. Usually, the harder the rehearsals, the better the reward in the end. If it's all been plain sailing very often it means you are not going to get much out of it. I think back to rehearsals where I've gone home and had a weep because I can't get it right, or I've no confidence, or don't agree with something that's happening, but usually out of that will come something really good ultimately. Like the 'no pain no gain' thing. Then you get a fear when approaching a preview, and you really do think, 'Why am I doing this?' I have been in situations where I could quite happily just run out of the stage door and never work again as I'm so scared. I took over a part at the Royal Shakespeare Company years ago when I was playing Elmire in *Tartuffe*.[2] The actress dropped out at very short notice and they asked me to take over. I was left with two and a half weeks' rehearsal, which is alright, but the RSC normally gives you six weeks' rehearsal.

So when I turned up everybody had learned their lines brilliantly, so they said, 'We'll just go through the scenes with Alison.' They were performing in these wonderful voices – it's all difficult language in Molière. I thought, 'Oh my God, what have I got into – I'll never catch up.' I went home and cried my eyes out, threw my script down and thought I'd have to tell them I couldn't do it. Of course, I did and it was a terrible struggle, but I got there and the first preview we performed terrified me. I remember the music before the show, which if I hear it now, strikes terror in my heart! I got through the performance, and at the curtain call I was on the verge of tears because it had been such an effort to get there. Back in my dressing room, I knew then, it would be okay. Still a few more days of terror, and then the ultimate feeling of being actually able to enjoy the performance, having got over the initial fear. It's a bit like having a baby – the horrible stage of feeling sick and weepy, and what have I done! Then you get to the stage where it's okay, then you get terrified of the birth when it gets nearer and when you give birth you feel relief and think, 'Did I do that?' Wonderful, it's all over. Then you have the joy of it.

When you're offered work, how important is the performance challenge factor within the decision?

It's very important. For instance, with this play, *When We Are Married*,[3] I've personally had a difficult year – one of the most difficult of my life. My mother died in July. She had cancer for twenty months, and I was very close to my mum. My father died five years ago. It was a very difficult time, watching her go downhill, along with my marriage problems and the fact that I no longer live with my children. When I was offered this job, I read it and thought that this is a good funny play; I can absorb myself in it. I don't want any more pain and angst. I want something uplifting. You've got to feel that you've got the energy and commitment to do it. This job, I felt I could handle it, that it would be a comfort to me rather than an oblique challenge where I'd be tearing my hair out. This was a play that had such warmth and humour that it is a jolly experience. During the second week of rehearsals my mother died, so before that I was backwards and forwards visiting her. Then when she died I had to come straight back into rehearsals, but I could cope with it. It opened after her funeral, so it was a testing time.

You've played a lot of comic roles over the years.

I like comedy. We've been talking about theatre, but doing radio work with an audience is another thing. There you don't have time to ponder, think or get anxious – you just do it. With an audience you normally get the script that morning, go through it, sort it out in two hours, rehearse a bit, and then you are out there. You have to come up with the characters and voices, which is very good. I used to be terribly serious about everything, and if a voice didn't come out of my head and heart then it was wrong. This was partly down to my training, where they said if you weren't beating yourself with a birch twig every night, then you actually weren't really an artist! I went to East 15 [drama school] in Loughton. Doing radio work took me out of all that. The fun of it is coming up with a voice, and that's what changed my approach. It took me back to when I was a child doing all those voices.

Do you think there is something attractive about being humorous as a woman?

There is something attractive about anyone who is humorous, not particularly women. I know it's said that men find it easier, but nowadays more and more comediennes are coming along. It probably is harder for women, because in the past there haven't been many women, and women are more and more fighting their way in the outside world. I love watching stand-up; I love Jo Brand. I couldn't do it myself though! It's not my scene.

Over the years, have you become more self-questioning as a performer?

Yes, I think so. My first professional job, when I was at drama school, was to play Sandy in *The Prime of Miss Jean Brodie* at the Lincoln Theatre Royal.[4] I was very nervous about it. The idea of playing a Scottish girl did not worry me at all. The accent was the least important thing – I just turned up. But now, if I was asked to play someone Scottish, I would be down at the BBC accent library, getting tapes, researching the area. I wouldn't assume that I could just 'do' Scottish. The older you get the more you realise that it's got to be much more specific, and you have to be careful about what you do.

Do you see a difference between performing yourself and performing a character?

It's always me – you can't disguise yourself enough, because it all comes from the core, particularly in improvised work. For instance, Beverley in *Abigail's Party*[5] is a million miles from me, and so is Candice Marie in *Nuts in May*,[6] but there are elements in those characters that are in me as a person, which helps me understand what makes those women tick. In some ways, it's a release of something maybe repressed in me that comes out. There is a core element of that in it, and also in all parts you play; you can fulfil something that is not happening in your own life by performing and pretending. If someone had said that to me twenty years ago I would have called them names! But now, in hindsight, I can see that there is a lot of truth in that. My experiences in life of meeting people get absorbed and locked away somewhere in my memory or subconscious, and when I come to do a character, it comes out from nowhere.

Are women more positively represented in the theatre? Are there more roles?

It definitely has improved. Apart from just the acting, there are more women producers, directors, camerawomen, and there are girls doing the sound. You see it all the time, really young women. I did a pilot, a few months ago, for a comedy series and the producers were two women in their early twenties. It's very encouraging to see that. Now there are more women writers as well. It's still not an equal balance for men and women, but I don't go around thinking there are no parts for women. It's not true any more. I think it's great that on film sets you see girls doing the jobs, which you never saw years ago. In the past there have always been too many actresses, but I'm encouraged by the number of women going to film school. Look at Jane Campion's *The Piano*; years ago you would not have got that. Even women documentary-makers, and that's great.

Do you have any desires about performing that you would like to achieve?

I've never been terribly ambitious in the sense of having a career plan. Partly because of my background, being a grammar-school girl. I really don't think that much was expected of us. It was an academic grammar school, but there was no drama, school plays or anything like that. I launched into a profession that I knew absolutely nothing about. I'd barely seen a play on stage when I went to drama school. I went to the audition and I remember they were talking about Chekhov and I had never heard of him. So I launched into this profession not expecting a great deal. I knew I had this ambition and drive to become an actress, but my father didn't want me to have false hopes of wanting to be a famous actress. He wanted to ground me in the real world. He wanted me to enjoy the time at drama school, get something from it, and see what happened. I've always had that attitude anyway. It's always been a surprise to me to be offered work, and every time I got another job, I was thrilled. I never expected a lot, because I knew it was a difficult profession. I've actually always despised people who threw dinner parties and invited directors to try and impress them into offering them a job. I've always seen that as distasteful, and I've always wanted to achieve something because of the work I can do rather than because I've been nice to somebody! I hope just to carry on acting and getting nice jobs. People ask me if I want to go to Hollywood and make a film, but I don't see that as particularly attractive. I see it as horrid to be in a strange country with all those pressures on you. I'd rather be here with my friends and family and enjoy myself. Why sit in a lonely hotel in Beverly Hills when you could be at the Savoy Theatre!

Are there any key moments in your life so far that are particularly memorable?

I won an Evening Standard award for *Abigail's Party*[7] when I was due to give birth to my son, so that was quite a day. I think the best thrill – real genuine thrill – is when my sons were born. It was like falling in love a hundred times over.

What is your most significant achievement as an actor or performer?

It was a big thrill getting the Olivier Award for *Little Voice*,[8] to play that part, which was one of those parts I thought I'd never do, and I was terrified. It was very rewarding to be nominated for this award and I honestly didn't think I would get it, because Judi Dench and Wendy Hiller were nominees, so I was totally surprised. However, I don't like to think of awards as being that important, because my whole philosophy and training has been that we are in it as a team, but it still is a terrific thrill when you get an award. Particularly the Olivier Award, because it is quite prestigious. You go home and put it on the mantelpiece and feel so high, but then after a few days come back down to earth. You've got to move forward all the time. The more that's expected of you the harder it is. In some ways I sometimes still feel like a beginner, but mainly I'm much more settled than I used to be. I've always been under-confident. I am a mixture of being over-confident in lots of ways. For instance, I can meet people and talk, but in other situations I am a complete wreck. I am a funny mixture. When I was a child, I remember if I was upstairs and friends of my parents came to visit, I used to spend ages and ages trying to get the courage to walk in the living room to say hello. I knew that every eye would turn on me to say hello, but that was an ordeal! I was alright if I opened the door to them and they came in, but having to enter a space – it's a bizarre contradiction.

Is being an itinerant part of the appeal of being a performer?

Yes, in a sense. I would hate to do the same thing in the same place. The fact that my life constantly changes, is interesting, exciting, refreshing, frightening, means you can't get bored. I could not bear a life being in the same job in the same place every day. I have worked in an office, which I enjoyed, but only because I knew it was temporary and I would be moving on.

Notes

1   Mrs Bennet in *Pride and Prejudice*, directed by Simon Langton, BBC Television series, 1995.
2   Elmire in Molière's *Tartuffe*, directed by Bill Alexander, Royal Shakespeare Company, Barbican (The Pit), 1985.

3 Maria Helliwell in Priestley's *When We Are Married*, directed by Jude Kelly, Chichester Festival Theatre and the Savoy Theatre, 1996.

4 Sandy in Spark's *The Prime of Miss Jean Brodie*, adapted by Jay Presson Allen, directed by Richard Wherrett, Theatre Royal, Lincoln, 1969.

5 Beverley in Leigh's *Abigail's Party*, directed by Mike Leigh, Hampstead Theatre, 1977. BBC Television production, 1977.

6 Candice Marie in Leigh's *Nuts in May*, directed by Mike Leigh, BBC Television, 1975.

7 Evening Standard Award for 'Best Actress' in *Abigail's Party*, 1977.

8 Olivier Award for 'Best Actress' in *The Rise and Fall of Little Voice*, directed by Sam Mendes, Royal National Theatre (Cottesloe), 1993.

Julie Walters

'Acting is part of what I am and who I am.'

'I've been very fortunate, but there is always that
escapist creative thing I'll always be searching for.'

Performance Context

Born: 1950, Birmingham.

Prior/current commitments: *Julie Walters is an Alien*, television documentary, Meridian Television.
Jackie in *Girls' Night*, written by Kay Mellor, Granada Films.
Marjorie Beasley in *Intimate Relations*, written and directed by Philip Goodhew, Handmade Films.

Post-interview (selected): Petula in television situation comedy *dinnerladies*, written by and starring Victoria Wood, BBC Television.
Bernie in *Titanic Town*, Company Pictures.
Marjory in Alan Bennett's *The Outside Dog*, Talking Heads 2, BBC Television.

Other: BAFTA Award 'Best Film Actress' for Rita in *Educating Rita*; Golden Globe Award; Variety Club 'Best Film Actress'; Oscar nomination.

Interview

It was sheer enjoyment talking to Julie Walters at the Grand Hotel in Brighton on 18 July 1997, when her sharp earthiness provoked laughter and compassion. At the time of meeting, Julie was involved in promoting the film Intimate Relations, *in which she played the role of Marjorie Beasley.*

Alison Oddey: *What performance work have you been doing recently?*

Julie Walters: I did this programme called *Julie Walters is an Alien*[1] in New York and in Miami. It was a light-hearted documentary about the city, which involved learning to work in different jobs – for example, being a reporter for NBC, which nearly gave me a nervous breakdown, and being a park ranger in Central Park, and then as a doorman at the Four Seasons Hotel. In Miami, I worked with the police and with a chap who rescues animals from people's gardens like alligators and snakes. The programme, *Julie Walters is an Alien,* has a book going out with it in the autumn, which was my idea. I haven't written it; I've just edited it and put my stamp on it, because I'm writing a novel at the moment. I've only written eight thousand words in a year. I love it and I'm completely obsessed with it; it's like acting only better.

What do you mean by that exactly?

I quite like writing, because I like telling stories. That's partly why I like acting; it's the storytelling part of it that's exciting. For the theatre it's more exciting than for film, because you are not in charge of the storytelling in a film. I did write this daft book called *Baby Talk* when I was pregnant, about the comic side of pregnancy. It was a diary, and this was nine years ago now. I really enjoyed writing it. It wasn't a great piece of writing but it was good fun, and they wanted me to write another book. The history is that they wanted me to go into paperback, but my daughter had become ill in the meantime, which meant loads of publicity about her all the time, so I didn't want to do it any more. So the people who bought the paperback rights had a meeting about eighteen months ago and suggested that I write a novel. I got a bit frightened at first, but was told that all I needed were some interesting characters. We talked about an incident that happened in New York, which I thought would be a good springboard for a story. I became completely obsessed with the characters – where they came from, what they were about, how they behaved, and getting them in a room. All that thing about the characters having their own life-force is true. Once you have made them, you can't make them do things that would not ring true. So it's like acting – you have complete control over them, and you can make the adventure of them very exciting. The only time I've ever felt that excited was working with Mike Leigh, which is a similar thing. It's like a magical mystery tour, but you don't know where it's going to go. You make the character and you don't know what's happening with them. You get a sketchy plot, which they basically follow, but how they follow it is another matter. But it's really been the most exciting thing for years and years.

It's fascinating that a number of women I've interviewed are both performers and writers – for example, Sheila Hancock, Kathy Burke and Meera Syal. What does writing give you that is different from performing?

It's very single-minded. The wonderful thing about acting is that you deal with other people's creativity as well, and you come together, which is exciting. I like teams. But with a book you don't have to deal with anybody except yourself and the editor. I like making contact with him and I read to him over the phone, because I'm frightened of showing it to him in print in case he misunderstands it! I read to him every so often on the phone, which he says nobody else has ever done! I quite like reading it as well, which you can do whenever you feel like it. Totally, ongoing. An acting part is restricted because you have to interpret someone else's work. That's why Mike Leigh's way of working is the most similar, because it is your creation. The words that come out are yours, not anybody else's, but then he will put you with some other character, which is exciting. However, the novel is totally mine, and I can make whatever I want to happen. It's my own secret, private little world. It has the same escape value as acting has, where you can escape into another person, but with writing there is the whole world I can escape into, which means escaping into each of them every so often, depending on what's happening in the scene. I describe everything as scenes, because I've been brought up as an actress. So that's it, it's total escapism and it has been wonderful to have it alongside other work, because I can just go back to the hotel and get the book out. It's not like work at all, whereas acting is like work because I've done it for so long, twenty-odd years. This is like the first time you act – I want to do it all the time – I don't need a break from the book.

So you don't get the same satisfaction from acting now – it's more a job of work?

Yes, it is a job of work and I'm more jaded about it all. I've explored so many of the characters that are in me, as well as the bits of myself that are used in parts, that that side of it isn't so exciting. A lot of scripts that come through I am not interested in. I have got to earn a living, but I'm in a fortunate position where I can turn things down. I tend to choose things now that are as different as I can get them to be, because I've been in the profession for a long time and I do get a lot of work and respect. I'm very lucky. I haven't got anything to prove any more. I've fulfilled a lot of what I wanted, and the business has been very good to me in every sense – financially, professionally and everything.

Was motherhood a turning point for examining your need to perform?

Oh yes, it usually changes things and it changed me massively. Maisie is more important than anything. You've got to look after yourself. There is that analogy of when the plane is going to crash and you've got to put your own oxygen mask on first, then your child's; you've got to survive. Acting is part of what I am and who I am. When I first went for my interview at Manchester Polytechnic to train as an actor and a teacher, they said, 'So you want to become an actress?' I remember being quite taken aback at the time, saying, 'No, I don't want to become one, I am one, that is what I am as a person. Whether you take me on and I get employed is another matter, but I am an actress.' I totally believed that and I think it is not something you can go and train for, although you can train to be a type of actor (which is a behavioural thing – the way people behave in certain situations), but there is more to interesting acting than that. Now there is a big move against that, a move towards taking off layers rather than putting them on and being. Being yourself in other people's situations, which is what some actors do very well. It can be just as absorbing, except that everything they do is going to be more or less the same. But why do we want to do it?

So what is it that makes you still want to do it?

Well, because I'm a bloody show off! I enjoy things just as much like opening a bloody village fete; it's often as much fun as going into a read-through! Maybe that's because Maisie is involved; it's easy and without stress. There are genetic reasons: for a start my grandfather used to learn court cases and recite them to people in the bar as local entertainment. So he must have been some kind of actor to do that. I love conveying drama and telling stories, which I think is a genetic thing. I used to think there was a flaw in me – that feeling of not being good enough as a child – of thinking everybody else had the answer to how life went, and wanting to do it like they did it. So I love watching other people. I used to impersonate and mimic people lots as a child, but I don't enjoy doing that now. I used to entertain people at school with impersonations of teachers, rock stars and actors. But as I got older it was how people looked at things emotionally and dealt with them that I found more interesting. So I think the sum of that and the sum of what is genetically there. I think some people are genetically extrovert and like being the centre of attention. Also, my parents were very funny and I think that's a way of dealing with fear and with life generally. Not letting it get on top of you by putting things in their place with humour.

Are you from a theatrical background?

No, only in that way. My brothers are teachers, which is a similar thing. I am the youngest with two older brothers.

Is not feeling loved part of the reason for performing?

No, I was fiercely loved by my mother, who is dead now. I don't want to put her down, but she had a way of pushing us on by saying, 'So and so is doing this, and so and so is doing that. What is the matter with you?' We were constantly trying to please her, and I think there is something in that. Teaching is a performance definitely, getting people to believe you. That is part of acting – challenging people to believe you.

Where does the desire to perform originate from?

I always wanted to act, but I can't really locate it. My earliest memories are being behind the curtain and coming out to perform to my aunt who lived with us, when I was about three or four. I can remember being knocked down when I could only just walk. I think actors have very good memories of their childhood. There is a childish nature to acting of playing and pretending, and there is some link with the intensity of childhood.

You were born in Smethwick and your mother wanted you to be a nurse.

Yes, she had us all labelled. My eldest brother was the academic, and my middle brother was the sportsman. I was never going to be academic, so she suggested that I try teaching or nursing; something that you only needed five 'O' levels for. I didn't dare voice that I wanted to be an actor. I couldn't actually because there was no context to put it in at home, and when I did it was met with, 'What are you talking about, an actress!', because we didn't go to the theatre and we didn't know anybody in the theatre.

So nursing was your mother's suggestion?

It must have been, because it didn't come from me, and it was something she wanted me to do.

Did you take that on to please her?

Yes, and I'd been asked to leave school, so I thought I'd better do it.

Asked to leave school?

Expelled seemed a bit strong! I was in the sixth form and I was never there. They told me not to come back and gave me a letter to give my parents, which I put in the bin of course. I went home and said, 'I may as well leave school because I want to be a nurse. It's what I'm going to do.'

Did you do all the training?

No, I did half of it and then went to Manchester. I enjoyed nursing from a performing point of view. I was always entertaining the patients and making them laugh. I loved it when the senior nurses went off and I could have a good laugh with them. I loved that side of it, but was terrified that anyone would die if I was there, and I'd have to deal with it!

Did you feel that Manchester gave you something that was extra to the desire to perform and your self-acknowledged identity as an actress?

Well, it just gave the right space – that's what it did. It was like struggling along in the wrong gear, very insecure and not good enough, but then you get the right gear and think, 'Oh life is so much easier, I'm in the right place.' I loved it. I think my own feeling of not being good enough as a kid is a human condition; I don't think that's just me. I think we all have a little bit of 'Am I good enough?' and I think mine fitted in with my mother's huge drive of wanting all of us to be the best at everything, and having to please her. So there was a mixture of that, and a mixture of being totally fascinated by other people. How they did things and wanting to be them, which I don't have any more. I love the storytelling, which may be genetic. I'm someone who likes to escape as well.

How would you describe yourself in terms of a performing woman in the widest sense?

Oh, I don't want to really; I don't know. I don't like to categorise myself as I'd like to think it was endless. I'd like to think there is a huge universe out there full of characters and things so that I could be anything. The book has given me another voice to do this and the editor has said that people will be surprised and shocked at it, and so I thought there is a part of me that I'm not allowed. The profession and the media keep you in a sort of category whether you like it or not. It's hard to move from, so it's quite nice to write something that nobody is going to expect.

You strike me as wanting to reinvent, to discover and explore all the time. Are you striving to find something else?

Yes, but I don't feel discontented. This is a very contented time of my life. I get stressed out by many things, but I don't feel discontented by work. I've been very fortunate, but there is always that escapist creative thing I'll always be searching for. It depends on how this novel turns out, but I can imagine being quite happy just doing that really and letting the acting go a bit. I've done too much of it! No, I don't think I would let go really. I enjoy that showing off.

I'm not aware of any theatre work you've done since 1991. If a particularly challenging theatre role was offered – would you be interested in it?

I might be, but I think it might be too exhausting. I think, 'Do I need that amount of stress on the first night?' or, 'Do I need to be completely absorbed in something when I've got a nine-year-old daughter?' I'll miss out on God knows how much of her life, which will never ever come back. I was offered something in the West End, Ayckbourn's new play, and I just thought, 'Do I want that? Do I want this kind of life? I'm going to be totally stressed out on the first night.' I'm forty-seven and the family have all died of heart attacks, and I've got a young daughter. So I turned it down. That's something I wouldn't have done a few years ago; I would have felt that I'd better do it. But now I just think, 'No.'

That must be one of the hardest aspects of being a working actress and mother. I don't think that there's any one solution to this dilemma. There will never be a happy medium. It's a case of competing identities and what is most important at the time. For some women, there is no choice if they need the money to survive.

In some ways it would be easier if you needed the money, because that's for the child. It's a much harder decision if it's something you want to do and you feel as if it's important for your career, but you need not do it financially and it would not really make that much damage to your career if you didn't do it. Those are very difficult ones to make. That's also why writing is very attractive. When Maisie comes home, I can just leave it. When I was away doing this programme I was telling you about, as soon as I arrived at the airport I said to the producer, 'I am never doing this again.' I was so upset leaving her and it's worse than when she was a baby. She's older now and our relationship is better; she is someone to talk to. I was so depressed, I was crying myself to sleep. I thought, 'What am I doing?' Especially as I was in Miami and I thought they could have been there. She would have loved it. But she couldn't fly because of her illness. We didn't want to risk it.

Have you done any stand-up performance?

No, maybe it was a road I could have gone down years ago. I've never ever considered it as I like playing parts, but I can imagine enjoying it because I like telling stories. I've never had the desire to get up like Vic[2] and do what she does. I think Vic's the best of them all; she's really clever.

What about performing comedy; you obviously love doing that because you've done so much of it.

I just like a laugh! It's part of what I am and how I was brought up. Laughing is extremely cathartic and very good for you, and puts things into perspective.

You've performed a diversity of roles over the years, which has given you the opportunity to reflect the excellence of your acting ability.

The theatre has allowed me to be more diverse than anything. There are loads of things that I've done over the years that I would never be asked to do on film. Victoria's stuff is about great diversity.[3]

Do you have a preference for performing in theatre, film or television?

There's no doubt that theatre is the most exciting, although I haven't done any for ages. I like films because it's not pressured like theatre is, and I like being in a team of people all doing different jobs. I love that feeling and I like film sets – I do enjoy it. I like them all really. Theatre is very hard work and very anti-family. I feel I'm in a better position to do theatre work now, but I think I'd prefer not to be doing eight shows a week.

Do you think of yourself as an itinerant?

I suppose so, although I've done very little touring. I think I've only toured twice and they were very short. I like the thought of the gypsy sort of thing. I like the fact that you are not mapped out for the rest of your life. I like the thought that I could be anywhere and that excites me. Travelling in some escapist way.

Like finding the different characters in your novel? Not quite knowing where you are going?

Yes, that is important to me actually. It's exciting. I wouldn't like it in the frightening sense.

What have been the key moments in your life as a performing woman in the widest context?

I think being offered a part in a play at the local church hall when I was about nine. A man came round and gave me the part. I went up to my room, and by the time he had had a cup of tea with my mother, I had learnt it. I knew it all. When I went down he was just leaving and I said, 'I've done it, I've got the whole part ready.' When I performed it on stage, my older brother said, 'That's really good.' I was very excited about that, which is probably when I got the first feelings of it.

What else?

I think lying in the bath at home when I knew I was going to be a nurse. I'll never forget lying in that steamy bath and feeling, 'Oh God, I want to be an actress.' It was the first ever time I had admitted it. From being a little thing, there it was now, a clear-cut fact. Nothing to do with fooling about in school. This was what I wanted, when I knew I was about to do something else. It brought it into sharp focus that was what I wanted to do! I just lay in the bath, but felt relieved that I'd said it and got it out of the way. Getting it clear, so that it wasn't muddled. Another key moment was being with a group of boys and girls when I was about sixteen or seventeen and feeling that I had a special place there, and I knew what my role was in the group. I had a special, happy place in that group, because I knew how to make them laugh. I knew I could get their attention, and I knew they wanted me with them. That sort of feeling; it was a kind of performing thing. So finding that identity then.

What do you see as your most significant performing achievement?

Oh, that's very hard. Significant in what way really? I suppose Rita and Mrs Overall combined! They are the ones that everyone knows and Rita internationally. It also depends on those moments when you come together with the audience. Those are moments of perfection.

Can you describe what it feels like to be in that moment?

That is hard to describe; it's a mixture of realising that the moment is there. There is a sort of elation and almost a fear. Utter pleasure, and a feeling of power as well. It's like a relationship with a person, and you feel that there is total belief that the two of you are feeling that one moment together. That's what it is, as well as a moment of total escape. That's what it actually is: total escape, very elating, as if you are totally revealed and accepted; it's something to do with that. Acting is very revealing and makes you very vulnerable. It is something very special like when you meet someone and you love them – you are opened up to them and they accept it. It's that same thing only with an audience.

It sounds like a desire for acceptance as who you are.

I think that's some of it, but I don't think it's as simple as that. That's why it's hard to describe. It isn't one thing, but many things and very complicated. There is a serenity about it. It depends on what you are acting at the time. I can think of times, like in *The Rose Tattoo*[4] and also in Sam Shepard's *Fool for Love*,[5] where the character completely breaks down and opens up to the audience virtually. Opening up in deep distress, for instance, and you are feeling your weakness and taking that, and embracing it. There is something about that, which is like a relationship with a person. That's the nearest thing, like a love affair with a person. That sounds so clichéd, but it is actually like that. It's love with a great many people rather than with one person. I think some people deal with relationships – big public relationships – better than they do with personal ones. I think I can just about deal with a personal one!

You've been with your partner now for some years, haven't you?

Twelve years, love him. It's a lot to cope with really.

It must be difficult with you being so busy, especially filming and going away on location. Do you find that your domestic and professional lives clash very often?

He's very open to it and easy about it, otherwise I think people do have that problem. Somebody said that a good relationship is when two people allow one another to have their dreams. I think that's a very good thing, and I think that's what he does for me.

Has anybody particularly inspired or influenced you as a performing woman?

Influence is difficult. In the early days, the actors in Coronation Street were probably the most influential! I never went to the theatre. Usually people I've met, rather than other actors. That time I worked with Mike Leigh, I found him really inspirational. I did a play called *Ecstasy* in 1979 with Jim Broadbent and Stephen Ray, and it was fabulous. I loved it. I wouldn't say anybody else, although my older brother is probably more influential than anybody.

You've won lots of awards – do you have any particular views on awards?

I've won a few, but you mustn't get too hung up on them really – it really doesn't bloody matter. I suppose it helps raise money for things because if you've got an Oscar, people are going to want you for work, so it helps in that sense, but you must not allow them to judge you, the real you. I think people get upset in that way and think they have been rejected if they don't get it. A lot of it is political, and a lot of the choices that are made are absolutely awful. Some of them are great, some are just dreadful. You think what the bloody hell do they want to give that person an award for? So on one level they are meaningless, and on another it's lovely to get one. I didn't become an actress to win awards; I became one to do parts.

Where do you keep your awards?

I don't know where they are – oh yes, some are on a shelf up the back. I never put them there, but someone has put them up there and they are all filthy. So there are some there, but I don't know where my BAFTA one is – I've lost it. I was so drunk at the 'do' that I never got a plaque anyway to say what it was.

How does that relate to you being drunk?

I think it was because I was sitting under a table when I was supposed to be meeting Princess Anne. I think I've got a Golden Globe in the conservatory, which is handy for keeping the door open as it's very heavy. But I wouldn't display them. It's lovely to win them, but I think that you've got to keep it in perspective. That's my advice to the young!

Notes

1   *Julie Walters is an Alien*, television documentary, Meridian Television, 1997.
2   Victoria Wood.
3   Working with Victoria Wood has included: *dinnerladies*, written by and starring Victoria Wood, directed by Geoff Posner, BBC Television, 1998; *Pat and Margaret*, directed by Gavin Millar, BBC Television Screen One, 1994; *Victoria Wood as seen on T.V.*, BBC Television, 1985, 1987.
4   Serafina in Tennessee Williams' *The Rose Tattoo*, directed by Peter Hall, Playhouse Theatre, 1991.
5   May in Shepard's *Fool for Love*, directed by Peter Gill, Royal National Theatre (Cottesloe), 1984.

Bobby Baker

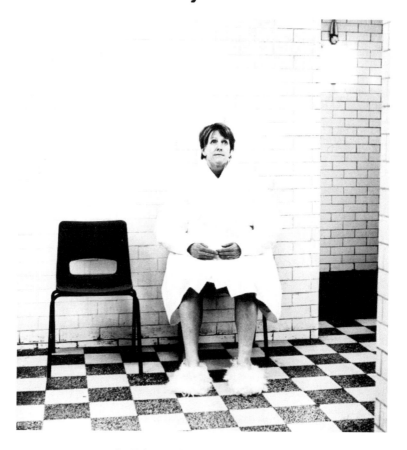

In *Take a Peek!*, Royal Festival Hall,
London International Festival of Theatre, 1995

'... I'm still more interested in making work that is outside theatres,
although I very much enjoy performing in theatres.'

'As a child, I felt very much that women were voiceless and the only way
out of that was to pretend to be a boy, which I did for many years.'

'... I appear to be a very normal middle-aged home counties-type
woman occasionally, but the power is for people to feel lulled into
security in that appearance, and then break out of that in a very
aggressive or subversive way.'

Performance Context

Born: 1950, Sidcup, Kent.

Prior/current commitments: *Table Occasions*, launch of London International Festival of Theatre (LIFT), 1997.
Working on the final two stages of the 'Daily Life' series, *Grown up School*, to be shown in LIFT 1999, and *Box Story*, to be shown in LIFT 2001.
Re-doing *An Edible Family in a Mobile Home*.

Post-interview (selected): Bobby Baker's film *Spitting Mad*, BBC 2's *Expanding Pictures* series. *Table Occasions*.

Other: 1993 – Die TZ-ROSE Award, Theater der Welt Festival, Munich, for *Drawing on a Mother's Experience*.
1991 – Time Out/Dance Umbrella Performance Award, London, for *Kitchen Show*.

Interview

Bobby Baker's clarity of thinking distinguishes her particular journey as a performance artist. I see her standing alone on a table in Table Occasions, *ready for anything. I interviewed Bobby on 18 September 1997 at the Royal Festival Hall in London.*

Alison Oddey: *I recently interviewed the American performance artist Carolee Schneemann in New York, who is currently reconstructing* Eye/Body *in her Manhattan Loft for the Los Angeles Museum next year, which she first did in the 1960s. I know that you're planning to re-do* An Edible Family in a Mobile Home,[1] *which was an extraordinary piece of work in 1976. How do you envisage it in the late 1990s?*

Bobby Baker: I find it fascinating thinking about the concept of doing it, because it would become very different. We are debating whether to find another mobile home, as there are still some in existence, or to do it in a flat. Alternatively, we could recreate the mobile home in an exhibition area in a gallery setting, making it into a pure exhibit, and obviously it will be very different to the first time when I did it in Stepney in 1976. That is the fascination: the idea is becoming more overridden with associations of what's going on now and my relationship to the family, because the family within that piece of work was my own. I was the baby in the family, but was completely decimated and eaten during the opening of the show, so I will be quite intrigued to see how I feel about that now – whether I have moved on in relation to my ideas of family life.

You're the youngest of three children, aren't you?

Yes, I've got an older sister and an older brother, and in the family both those figures have a structural framework, which survives the eating of the family. The mother remains intact throughout, the father decays and gets eaten, the baby is just pure cake, and all you get left are a few crumbs at the bottom of the cot. It's a dreadful image!

It's very disturbing. It will be interesting to see how the imagery alters with time and the experience of making other work.

Yes, it's something we'll need a lot of energy to push through, and I'm wondering whether to leave it until after I've finished the 'Daily Life' series,[2] because there are so many different ideas going on in that, which echo *An Edible Family*, but are a development of it. I quite like the idea of doing a retrospective as well, to get the chance to look back at what I've done over the last twenty-odd years. I feel that when I've finished *An Edible Family*, the 'Daily Life' series and *Table Occasions*,[3] I'm going to start on a very new tack with my work. I'm quite looking forward to that. I don't know what I'm going to do, but something in a new direction.

I know your background is as a painter, but are there any aspects of theatrical or performance tradition within your family?

No, none. Quite a few painters, but nobody that we can ever remember that has stood on stage. I had an aunt, who was a cookery demonstrator, and that's the closest I've got to public speaking. It must have influenced me at some level!

That's interesting in the light of the context of some of your work. What do you think attracted you to the whole concept of performing, and to making a theatrical event?

It was really borne out of frustration. In the early 1970s, I was making these cake sculptures, and I used to make these little meringue figures and dress up like them. I'd take my troupe with me not knowing what to do with them, present them, but I didn't know how to take it further. I was still thinking of myself as an exhibit. This was visual and it became obvious that I couldn't get across the range of ideas that I had connected with the pieces that I had made. It was insufficient to just give them to people to eat. I wanted to add more layers to it, or explore the complexity of the live situation, where I was relating to the audience and people who had come to see work I had made.

I could do this through performance and it led to a clear and new form. Sometimes, as in *An Edible Family in a Mobile Home*, being there as myself, talking to the people who came to see the show and eating those cakes in a very mannered way, but not really performing the way I did subsequently – standing on a stage or in other settings. That's what I became intrigued by, because the possibilities were there and I was playing with ideas. It seemed like playing! That's what I feel I'm doing with *Table Occasions*, although it's rather daunting doing eighteen unique shows, but the excitement is that I literally can do whatever I feel like within that setting, playing with ideas and with my relationship with the audience.

So you needed to have an audience physically present?

Yes. I became frustrated with the idea of making a set of objects, which were then viewed without my presence there. It's nosiness partly, but I want to be there and watch what is going on and what people are thinking of the idea. I want to be part of that relationship and that event, because I think one of the ideas that I started work on at art school was this fascination with a particular moment, with situations that can never be repeated. There's a group of people, certain things happen, and how can that be exploded or developed within different contexts? This is why I'm still more interested in making work that is outside theatres, although I very much enjoy performing in theatres. Once you accept the rules that are unspoken about people's attention being focused on you and on the stage, it cuts out a lot of the practical problems of live work, allowing one to focus on other aspects of ideas and communication. However, I still am intrigued about daily events, small moments and exploring those in different settings.

As a child were you interested in performing in this way?

I was for a bit. I was an exhibitionist and I used to like singing songs that made old ladies cry. I'd be wheeled out at parties, sing a couple of songs and they'd get quite weepy. I loved that, but I stopped doing that. I think that it was a way of expressing myself which came naturally to me, but I became very passionate about painting when I was a teenager and that took over. I couldn't see how you could marry the two ideas and so it's been very intriguing to find how those two strands come together.

If you had to try and trace the roots of that desire to perform, can you recall a first conscious moment of performing?

I remember when I was two, pinching my grandfather's hat and running around in it at a wedding, and attracting a lot of attention from a huge crowd of people. I remember being very happy just running around. I liked doing really shocking things. I remember tipping a whole packet of cornflakes out of a pram. I was sitting in there with my brother, who was hysterically excited by my naughtiness! I think those were the first seeds of subversion and exhibitionism.

Why do you perform?

I ask myself that question quite frequently! I have been painting a great deal this last year and I'm very pleased to have rediscovered that as a means of communicating ideas, but it isn't the same as performance. For instance, the sort of gathering of people in the Purcell Room with me standing on a table is a very similar experience to being a small child showing off. I came initially to performing because I wanted to express ideas that at the time were quite jumbled up. It was only through doing a series of very dull performances that I didn't enjoy or connect with, that I suddenly discovered these moments where I got the same attention and response. I realised that could become a very powerful way of reaching people and putting these ideas across. I want to put them out there and I want to get a response. I want to see people's faces when they see my ideas and then get the feedback. I have done a fair amount this last year or so, doing a series of short pieces for Radio 4 and a series of short films, which go out on BBC 2 this Autumn.[4] I actually loved the process of making that work, because I didn't have to actually engage with the audience as I was making the pieces. It allowed the opportunity to be far more fantastical, to go to places in my mind, which perhaps I could not do face to face with an audience. However, I still missed those real moments where something happens that is unique to that little group between performer and spectator. I think that I'm still exploring it. We did a big tour in the States last year and I was performing in much larger spaces than before, and what was exciting was to perceive the potential or the power of being a solo performer with an audience. I have come at theatre practices in an oblique way. I have discovered the excitement of that moment of connection, the simplicity of movement or speech. I was very exhilarated about having arrived at that point of thinking that I'd obviously got a certain amount of skill now at coping, and I feel that there is potential for playing more with it in a freer way.

As in the opportunities afforded by the next eighteen Table Occasions?

Yes. I always imagine myself just arriving, because the rules are very simple. I have to come into the space, walking on two chairs. I have to wear a particular pair of stiletto heels while I'm standing on the table, and then I can do what I want. I just love the idea of arriving there and not knowing what I'm going to do. I bring all my props in a rucksack (a coolbag made into a rucksack on my back), and then I can just stand there. The reality will be that I'll have to plan things. Perhaps ultimately I'll plan them less, but initially I think I won't take that risk of arriving on a table and standing there for an hour. In fact, it's going to be quite carefully worked out, marking the occasion and picking out points that seem worth commenting on.

Presumably you'll learn from each experience?

Absolutely, that's part of the attraction.

Is the attraction of performing in the risk and excitement of the unknown?

I think so – not knowing who is going to be there and how they will respond to what I'm doing. The shows that I tour at the moment are all very carefully structured in terms of the form, but I allow as much freedom within that as possible to respond to a group of spectators who are there. It's getting the balance, where there is the chance to really take that further, that live moment, without being too hindered by the structure that you have come with. There is never a written text, there is only a set of information that I want to impart, and so I use the words appropriate to that moment. Quite often, I find myself saying the same sentence again and again. For instance, with *Drawing on a Mother's Experience*,[5] I do use the same phrases, sometimes for several performances, and then I abandon that phrase and find something that's relevant to that stage of my life. Pol Baloh-Brown, my co-director, picks up on this, pointing out that I'm frequently fixated on one particular aspect of an event within the performance, which is obviously relating to what's going on in my own personal life. That is the excitement of it, and I can never imagine myself working from a set text, or as an actor taking on another role.

Is there a need in you to perform?

At the moment, yes. I would say that I've done it out of necessity, and it is something that quite a bit of the time I would like not to have the need to do. There are less risky ways of communicating my ideas, and yet, my ambivalence is that the excitement of the risk is part of what motivates me.

Does your reason for performing originate in your family history or out of your personal identity?

I find it hard to put those two together, because my behaviour is so out of type from my upbringing and background, which did accommodate a few painters but largely was a very conservative, traditional background. I don't feel that I've really fitted within that setting, and yet, I have conformed to it through my life in some respects. I have had the two strands and never completely rebelled against it, but it's an odd marriage of opposites and I think that's part of the tension within my work. The fact that I appear to be a very normal middle-aged home counties-type woman occasionally, but the power is for people to feel lulled into security in that appearance, and then to break out of that in a very aggressive or subversive way. I cannot see where it stems from, other than as a desire to break away and be different.

Can you recall a moment in performance, both physically and emotionally, where you were fully communicating with an audience, and felt that sense of empowerment?

I had an experience recently, where I was performing *Drawing on a Mother's Experience* in a tent, in an open-air festival near Kettering. This tent took about 650 people who were sitting on the grass. The stage was slightly raised, and as I do most of the drawing on the ground, they had to keep on bobbing up, so there was this sea of people bobbing up and down! Something happened within that performance to do with a whole range of different factors. People were open-minded, they were very relaxed as it was a weekend festival, so there wasn't any pressure on them. It became almost a communion between us all, and at the end the majority of the audience stood up and there was a cheer, which was utterly extraordinary and very moving. It was so moving for all of us; a lot of people were in tears. It was some shared understanding and also to do with hope. There was an acceptance of pain and a kind of celebration of humanity somehow. Some bond had been formed. What those people gave as an audience was one of the most overwhelming things that's ever happened to me. Performing in a tent as well – the echo and the roar. It was an extraordinary moment and I suppose that's the drug, the addiction to go on searching for those moments and take them further.

Do you think it can ever be a psychic experience? (In the sense that it's completely obsessive and overpowering.)

Yes, and also spiritual. It is what happens in concerts and theatres in our live setting, and yet, I think it can happen with television and radio, even though one is not physically connected. It is a moment of shared consciousness or a pooling of experience and ideas, which can make one feel part of something much larger than one's self. Jung talks about a collective unconscious, that idea of somehow walking very near the edge and yet finding that there is a sort of psychic bond.

What makes the act of performing so satisfying?

I would question the satisfaction, because it's such a fragile part of the whole experience. It's satisfying if one achieves those moments that I described, for instance, in the tent. It's also the danger and the risk that is so tangible that it tends to override that from time to time, but it's like an addiction. The satisfaction will be momentary, although I did experience that with the first *Table Occasion* at the opening of the LIFT Festival this summer in Australia House. I poured a jug of cream from the top of a ladder into a bowl of fruit below. The bowl represented the audience of about 400 people and the cream, sugar, liqueur and jug represented the artists. That moment of fusion when the cream hit the fruit (splattering all over the floor and the people standing nearby) was a fabulous moment of celebration and mess, as people lost their inhibitions and dived in, digging out handfuls of cream-soaked fruit and stuffing it into their mouths. That was a very satisfying, unforeseen moment. The spontaneity was the way people responded to what was happening.

So what is the challenge of performing?

I suppose the search for that connection and bond, as well as a sharpening of one's skills, and yet, the future seems to be a process of laying bare painful truths. That brings me to *Grown Up School* (part of the 'Daily Life' series), which has been postponed now until 1999.[6] It's about violence and aggression. This exploration of that aspect of my own personality has really proved to be very disturbing, because it seems to be almost impossible to know how to grasp that aspect of oneself. The point I want to make in the show is that we all have the potential for evil and violence within us, but how to explore that safely within the context of a show without abusing the audience? I'm pretty stuck on that at the moment, hence my delight with *Table Occasions*, which is a distraction from what I really see is the main thing I want to get to grips with.

Why do you want to make this particular personal exploration?

The idea behind the 'Daily Life' series was that it was a journey for my own need to explore different aspects of my persona and my connection to my life, and that goes through sexuality, spirituality and all sorts of things that are very important. The dark side is very much a part of all of us, which I particularly want to examine within myself.

Is performing a kind of heightening of the self?

Yes, a channelling of certain energies, directing it in a more specific, sharp, focused way.

So the performance arena enables you to present certain personae of Bobby Baker that you couldn't do in your day-to-day life?

Yes, there is a kind of unspoken contract where people accept and want to be part of that experience by coming to see a live show; that they have entered into an agreement of what they are looking for, which doesn't necessarily exist in daily life. One person will take the centre stage.

Has anyone in particular inspired or influenced you as a performing woman?

My idols are Jane Austen and Virginia Woolf. In terms of women performers, I'm also very keen on Nina Simone, solo women singers, and I have to say that Joyce Grenfell clearly must have been an influence since I saw her as a child. There has to be an acknowledgement of the liberation of having a role model of some sort, even if you then go on to change the way you are working. As a child, I felt very much that women were voiceless and the only way out of that was to pretend to be a boy, which I did for many years. To see a woman in a very powerful position performing and getting a great deal of praise and attention must have had an impact on me. My real problem was that I couldn't identify a well-known woman painter, because the history was so poor in those days. I very much like work by younger women artists now. Also Louise Bourgeois ... I have discovered her work recently and some American artists, like Barbara Kruger.

As a performer, you have a very attractive quality in terms of being humorous and being able to touch on the commonality of experiences, so I assume that you must like making people laugh. Do you know why that is?

I think I made people laugh quite a lot when I was a small child, but I didn't think of myself as being funny subsequently. I discovered that people laughed at the things that I did, but it was a very intuitive response to the boredom of some of my early performances. I'd suddenly get this urge to do something completely ridiculous, and I loved the fact that it was clearly a great relief for people watching the show as something unusual and ridiculous was happening. So I discovered it through that, but I initially thought that if my work was funny, people would not then take it seriously, and it was only gradually that I realised the power of having humour as part of the package. I've got a great quote from Freud about the subversion of humour, and I have also noticed by looking at women in my family, particularly my grandmother and my mother, that humour is a way of getting their own back on pomposity. It's something I've grown up with and learnt to cherish.

Swanage, 1954, aged four

Do you like women stand-ups?

I haven't seen very many. I love French and Saunders and Victoria Wood. I did see her live and she was superb. I'm definitely influenced and encouraged by watching them. Maybe that's what *Table Occasions* will become ultimately – a set of stories with me standing on a table.

Does the 1990s image of the woman performer still embrace the image of 'strumpet'?

It seems to me to be harking back rather, and yet, it's still part of that history and tradition of using your body to express ideas. There has to be some acceptance of that history of the way women's bodies are perceived in terms of the way that you can work now. I think in the historical context it's very worth considering, but it does get my back up.

The idea of being described as a strumpet?

I find it interesting to consider, because I did take all my clothes off and get into a bath of chocolate custard to be sprinkled with hundreds and thousands in *Take a Peek!*[7] I was provoking a certain response and engaging with the audience in a provocative, teasing way. I was quite shocked by some of the responses I got to that show, and yet, I'd done it on one level quite knowingly, making use of my sexuality in order to communicate my ideas.

A kind of conscious, self-aware 1990s 'strumpeting' ...

Yes. The fact that I can take my clothes off and do disgusting things in public is very empowering, and quite an aggressive act. It was like climbing into a bath of shit because it implied something disgusting and yet sexual, and so it's taking back that image, owning it and making use of those associations rather than avoiding them. I feel more and more that what I like is making use of the image of myself as a middle-aged woman and subverting that, constantly shocking and breaking down those expectations. I can see a fantastic future, I long to be standing on a table when I am 80 doing unexpected things.

You're in your mid-forties, a time we're told when life begins ...

Yes, it's very exacting, and particularly in terms of the way men perceive women. When I had just turned forty, all male presenters in articles and interviews described me as middle-aged! Initially this really surprised me and made me quite angry, but then I realised what was going on and that it was a way of trying to contain and categorise me in a way that would not happen with men. It would not be part of the criteria for discussion. Since I've realised what the game is, I've realised that I can turn the tables quite successfully.

Can you identify any key moments in your life as a performing woman in the widest context?

When I squashed a tomato with a meat mallet in a performance at Goldsmiths, where I was a student, and I announced to the audience that I was going to squash this bloody tomato, and then did. That was the first spontaneous and intuitive thing that I did in a performance, and there was a shout of laughter and enjoyment. That was a very key moment. There are so many of them like that, which are just delightful. A very key moment was this argument I had going on in my head about whether I could put a tin of anchovies into my mouth, and I felt that I had to do it for *How to Shop*[8] and I couldn't bring myself to try it. I bought the tin of anchovies and I had it for several months, and the key moment was on my own in my hallway putting this tin into my mouth, taking that risk, and looking at myself in the mirror and convulsing with hysterical laughter. I felt that I had taken a huge step for humankind, that I had discovered something very fundamental! That was a good moment, because the danger was doing it in private let alone publicly. Most of the things I do in performing have that element, where I imagine doing them, but I can't bring myself to do it for quite some time because I think it's too extreme, ridiculous or too dangerous. A real key moment was standing on a chair repeatedly in a nightclub. They had a 'floor show' and I kept standing on my chair and shouting, 'sexist crap', and in the end I was thrown out. It was like a jack-in-a-box – someone would tell me to sit down and I would get up again. That was a wonderful moment; I wish I could go and do that wherever!

Perhaps you'll get the opportunity in one of your Table Occasions *this year!*

Notes

1 *An Edible Family in a Mobile Home*, Stepney, London, 1976. This took place in a mobile home, which was open to the public for a week. The entire interior was decorated with newspaper and sugar, and inhabited by a lifesize edible family, who were consumed by the visitors.
2 The 'Daily Life' series includes: *Kitchen Show*, premiered at LIFT, 1991; *How to Shop*, commissioned and premiered at LIFT in July, 1993; *Take a Peek!* Commissioned by the South Bank Centre and premiered there as part of LIFT 1995; *Grown Up School*, commissioned by LIFT, will take place in a London primary school in 1999; *Box Story* will take place in a variety of churches during 2001.
3 *Table Occasions* is a series of solo celebratory performances, each completely unique and created especially to mark a particular occasion, 1997–99.
4 Baker's film *Spitting Mad* was broadcast in November 1997, as part of the Arts Council of England/BBC 2's *Expanding Pictures* series.
5 *Drawing on a Mother's Experience* was first presented in 1988 and marked Baker's comeback to live art since 1980.
6 See note 2.
7 Ibid.
8 Ibid.

Alison Oddey, Bristol, August 1959, aged 4

4
Why Perform?
Themes Arising from Interviews

Out of the research undertaken, various themes have emerged, which can only indicate, (given such a small sample of women), a sense of why these women are so committed to performing in theatre, film or television. It has never been my intention to offer a statistical survey of responses to questions, nor to proffer a psychological study of the research. However, I do want to suggest that these themes justify further investigative analysis into the central question of why perform and what is the satisfaction of such an experience? What does performing provide and offer to these female performers?

Sense of identity

Acting is part of what I am and who I am. (Julie Walters, p. 257)

If I didn't act, I didn't know who I was. (Juliet Stevenson)[1]

It's always me – you can't disguise yourself enough, because it all comes from the core, particularly in improvised work. (Alison Steadman, pp. 250)

I want to argue that performing enhances a performer's sense of identity, defining the self and who she is. Performing provides the opportunity for identity construction or the expression of multiple identities. It enables the possibility of being someone else temporarily, 'the chance of living as somebody else for a little while' (Niamh Cusack, p. 30), allowing the woman to explore alternate versions of her self, to 'find so many people within you, and you never have to think, "This is me"' (Imogen Stubbs, p. 39).

I propose that these women are motivated by their desire for a unitary sense of identity, but are in fact conscious of fragmented subjectivities. As 'performing women', they are adept at performing multiple identities which are socially constructed roles. They are clearly conscious of gender as a 'performative act',[2] not simply in terms of the roles that they play on stage, but in their roles as working mothers, as youngest daughters, wives or partners, and as children wanting to play. These women are performing roles in public life, as public figures or idols, having to live up to the image that the media has created for them. They have been trained to internalise all the roles they are playing, being judged on how believable they are, and if they have moved the audience. It is small wonder then that they ask about the self, questioning their identity. They aspire to the notion of the unitary self, and most of them have a humanist vision of the artist.[3] Performing creates an opportunity to share, connect and communicate the 'universality' of an experience with others, fulfilling a desire to define the self, whilst conveying something truthful about their understanding and interpretation of the condition of the world and of humanity. The performing woman continues to replay situations, whether through the words of the playwright, the stand-up, or the created, collaborative product of devised work.

Some women have described performing as an experience, which works 'through' the performer (Miranda Richardson), as being a 'conduit' (Juliet Stevenson), a 'custodian' (Brenda Blethyn), or as a 'satellite for something bigger than yourself' (Fiona Shaw). 'It's my job'; 'it's what I do' are constant refrains within this collection of interviews. Performing has become a way of life for many women, integrated into their whole being. It is essential in order to sustain and maintain their identity. Many have spoken of feeling incomplete, empty and bereft without that public, communal, creative process in their lives, where the feeling of revealing and exposing the self to be understood and accepted is a prerequisite for living. Having said that, there is clearly a duality within that process of private and public self, of terror and excitement, agony and joy. Somehow the more challenging and terrifying the role, the better the rewards are, which is a sentiment echoed throughout the collection. The needs of the performing woman are ultimately to do with communicating ideas to others, with a strong desire for some kind of feedback or response to that self-expression.

Performing is an exercise in vulnerability, but always with the potential of both giving and gaining satisfaction. Meera Syal enjoys playing 'vulnerable women', 'that have not fulfilled their potential because I resonate with them' (p. 62), which Syal suggests is to do with being a British Indian woman, '... locking into some big universal experience ... when it's right'.[4] It is the excitement of an unknown adventure, exploring the nature of being, and learning from the experience of working with new people on different processes of creativity. It is about living in the world of imagination and telling a story. Fiona Shaw suggests that performing:

… is to render everything you know, and the only way you can get to that hopefully is on the terrible challenge of courting failure … – that it is a pursuit of heaven, (an absolutely false pursuit, which probably can't ever be fulfilled), but sometimes you get a glimpse of it when you don't expect it. (p. 157)

For some women, the satisfaction is to move an audience, to open or change their mind about a character, and to move them forward in a new direction. For others, it is the pursuit of excellence, such as Victoria Wood's record-breaking achievement of fifteen nights at the Albert Hall for solo performance, as compared to Eric Clapton's previous record of twelve. It is also the enjoyment of working creatively with fellow performers as part of a team or company, the experience of communality and being part of a work of art.

However, I want to argue that the ultimate satisfaction is in the momentary, ongoing nature of the experience, where the immediacy of the moment is the 'hit' that is desired, providing a feeling of ephemeral connection, of being 'plugged into a bunch of people' (Victoria Wood, p. 193). The enjoyment is in totally escaping into a heightened, accentuated state of feeling alive, which emanates from a spontaneous, creative energy and engagement between performer and audience, which can produce 'moments of physical electricity' (Heather Ackroyd, p. 102) to be lived off at the time. The performer is nourished by these moments, gaining pleasure from 'inhabiting someone else's story but drawing on my own' (Juliet Stevenson, p. 134), being brought to 'the edges of yourself' (Stevenson, p. 136). That moment when it all comes together, however briefly, is what these women aspire to, whether it is for an unconscious sense of empowerment, a discovery of truth or as an outlet to release repressed emotions.

There is frequent reference to the notion of a performance 'moment', as though performing is about attempting the discovery of a moment of perfection, which makes the process of performing all worthwhile. It is likened to being in love, to having a love affair or relationship with a person, and as a distillation of love in some way or other. The desire to perform fulfils a need to escape real life, to be in a space where nobody can get you and the 'moment' (however charged) is everything. It is as though the performer is 'chasing a moment', trying to make it work, described by Miranda Richardson as a feeling of:

'I could live here on stage, I feel very comfortable. There happen to be quite a lot of people out there, but oh, it's a nice space.' Time expands when you are there. (p. 177)

It is about a public relationship with an audience, where performing becomes a 'fantastically amorous and generous activity' (Fiona Shaw, p. 159) of getting attention and demanding a response. It is wholly dependent on other people's approval and pleasure, a need for someone to care about how the performer is creating the performance, or interpreting the role, and what effect it may have on them. It is described as 'a sickness, a disease' (Sheila Hancock, p. 226), 'a regular sort of fix' (Jenny Eclair, p. 20), '… like needing to be marked all your life' (Imogen Stubbs, p. 38), but mainly as an 'addiction' by many women: 'It used to give me the most tremendous buzz, a mixture of scariness and adrenalin'. (Victoria Wood, p. 193). To continue the metaphor, the 'drug' of performing takes over, producing a 'buzz' out of the adrenalin-charged existence, which promotes a repetitive pattern of need and compulsion. Without doubt, there is a need to perform in all these women (perhaps with the exception of Dawn French, whose need is to work rather than to perform), the driving force of which is a craving for recognition and admiration, a focus for gaining attention. It is interesting that for many the earliest memories of wanting to perform are as young children, who loved to make people laugh, entertaining adults by being silly, telling jokes, mimicry and impersonations. Being funny and making people laugh has an effect; it gained them attention. At least six women recall specific memories of wanting to perform from the age of four or younger:

> We were taken to a pantomime in Stoke-on-Trent and it was *Dick Whittington*. I was about four and they asked for a volunteer from the audience to come and stroke the baddy's head, who had been turned into a dog. I still remember the act. Suddenly, I was on the stage, in the lights with the audience looking at me! I had to go and pat his head to show he was a good dog. I was very frightened as I thought he would bite my hand, but I felt really at home. I don't know why – I just felt at home standing on stage patting his head. (Meera Syal, p. 56)

Others remember a particular instance during their schooldays; for example, Imelda Staunton talks about starting a diary at fourteen when she realised that she wanted to be an actress, and Alison Steadman recalls a teacher suggesting she might be an actress when she was in a school play, aged nine, 'This idea got planted in my head and from then on it grew' (p. 246).

Acting as playing: recapturing and revisiting childhood

> What we do is childish, so in a way we have a lot in common, both the grown-ups and the children. (Niamh Cusack, p. 27)

> There is a childish nature to acting of playing and pretending, and there is some link with the intensity of childhood. (Julie Walters, p. 259)

Why the desire to recapture or revisit childhood? Is there a need for these performers to keep in touch with childhood, making those connections with the imaginative world of make-believe and fantasy? Being a child is about being instinctive, spontaneous, intuitive and improvisational. Being a child means that the possibilities of drama are always present. How much is it to do with birth order, significant age differences, in relation to gender, or the role within the family? Within these interviews, there is a recurrent theme of acting as playing: recapturing and revisiting childhood. Parallel to this is the remarkable fact that the majority of performers interviewed[5] have been the youngest siblings in their families:

> ... being the junior in my family (I am number four), I've always felt a bit like a child in any sort of work situation as well. I'm just beginning at the age of thirty-seven to discover that I'm not a child and that I can make a difference. (Niamh Cusack, p. 26)

This may possibly link to the evident theme of wanting to please, to make people happy, but, on the flip side of that, of wanting to prove themselves as well. There is a desire to prove their worth, whilst wanting to feel special, different and unique with every audience. A number of women refer to their earliest memories of performing being to please their parents when very young. In other words, to give their audience (parents, relations or friends) pleasure. There is no doubt that gaining attention and provoking a reaction from others was often a first experience of gaining acceptance and approval for many – whatever the reasons. As performing women, there still exists some desire for emotional identification, some call, cry or craving for public love and affection from every relationship made with an audience.

Performing offers the opportunity to be childlike, to have fun, and to fantasize about personal identities. It involves the childhood escapades of dressing up, disguise, voices and accents. Imelda Staunton feels that 'this job allows one to extend one's childhood ... being told you are good, that's what we all want' (p. 121). The role, however, is a mask. It is pretending to be someone else and so make people listen. It can include being part of a group, shouting, misbehaving and being shocking. It offers the chance to expose oneself, to be an exhibitionist, and to be subversive as children can be:

> Suddenly I could shout and scream at somebody and it would be okay. Also, I think when I was younger, my brother said that at seven, my outlook was about forty! As I've got older, I've gone back to being the kid I wasn't. I've got a childlike view of the world but I'm pleased about that. (Kathy Burke, p. 82)

The journey towards performance

I have argued that there is a strong desire within the performing woman to change the self, to transform, to recreate and reinvent that person. This is the case for the 'classic actress', playing a role, removed from herself, written by a playwright to be performed. In terms of becoming a character, it is the fusion of writing and language of the part with the experience of the performer's self, fed by the world of imagination. The performer exercises her being by journeying in search of the discovery of creating that character. Performing is concerned with investigation. A role challenges the performer to find the essence of the character through exploration, analysis and every attempt at portraying this person. Various women clearly enjoy the challenges that come with this process of breaking down and working out the character:

> ... the more you confront that character, the more you are drawn into a combat between you and a bit of writing. Suddenly, you find that it's making sense to you and there is something very thrilling about that. You begin to inhabit something, to be able to say the lines so that they are coming from *you* (from a real person), and then the ultimate challenge is to stand in front of people, convincing them, moving them in some way or pulling off the riddle of that character. Almost once you've done that, you want to do something else. (Imogen Stubbs, p. 38)

For many women, the process in the rehearsal room is often more appealing than the performance itself. The process of rehearsing presents the possibilities of exploration, discovery, learning and invention. It enables new relationships with others, solving the 'riddle' of character, and researching another person's life. Women speak fondly of living with a person for a while in the rehearsal space: 'I love the idea that everybody gets a life to lead and I get millions of lives to lead, I get off on that' (Niamh Cusack, p. 30). For performance artist, Heather Ackroyd:

> It's just like a process of sculpting, of making, actively bringing something from an embryonic stage through a metamorphosis to a piece that people see. I don't think it's ever finished. I could never say I have done a finished piece of devised theatre. There are always things, which are inevitably changing and permutating. (Heather Ackroyd, p. 100)

The process of playing (through discovery and invention) with fellow performers is analogous to the process of childhood playing, as well as the notion of a continuous cycle of beginning again, of creating another family.

Itinerant: displacement of roots

It is clear from interviewing these performers that many of them have fond memories of childhood and are not from self-confessed unhappy, dysfunctional backgrounds. However, I want to suggest that the displacement of their cultural or family roots, for whatever reason, may have contributed to their desire to perform. Whether it is the separation of parents in marriage, an unusual upbringing, which is different from the 'norm', or the death of a parent, performing provides an opportunity to live through everything magnified. I want to argue that displacement (whether cultural or familial) may have driven these women into performing.

Kathryn Hunter's Greek parentage meant a 'double culture at home', speaking Greek and attending Greek Orthodox rituals as part of the Greek community. Josette Simon discusses her awareness of being the only West Indian at grammar school, in her year at drama school, and the first leading black actress at the Royal Shakespeare Company:

> but it has been hard at times because you are so often the odd one out. … You are so often the person who doesn't quite belong, made to feel that you are not sure if you should be here and I've never got away from that.[6]

Being the only one affected her identity:

> As a child, I was a silent person and that need to be private has remained. Whatever is going out to people, I don't like people knowing much about me. (p. 50)

Marianne Jean-Baptiste also speaks of being a bit different at school, 'not being accepted by the "in" crowd', so that she '… developed a skill of being self-contained' (p. 92). As a first generation British Indian woman, Meera Syal had no role models, 'I hadn't ever seen parts that reflected who I was, or how I felt' (p. 57). Syal states that writing has focused on who she is culturally, making sense of who she is and 'of my place in the world' (p. 59). For Imelda Staunton, Niamh Cusack, Kathy Burke (all with Irish roots), Victoria Wood and Jo Brand, it is their particular family situations which may have been influential in furthering them towards the path of performance. I repeat that I am not suggesting that these women were unhappy as children, but that they may have felt displaced culturally or within their own family background to the extent that it may have had some bearing on the 'performance' directions they have chosen to follow.

'Crabs, pongos and fish heads'[7]

A number of the women interviewed come from an armed services background, for example, Jenny Eclair, Juliet Stevenson, Dawn French and Imogen Stubbs, growing up as child itinerants in one way or another. These early experiences meant that they needed to gain access to different groups of people swiftly, adapting to new situations, and yet being able to move on quickly to the next. This is parallelled in the pattern of an actor's work life, which is constantly changing, insecure and never settled. It is a known fact that actors often spend time in their present job discussing and worrying about what the next job will be. In conclusion, I do not wish to overstate the theme of displacement, but it is an interesting aspect of research, which relates directly to why women want to perform.

Performing, motherhood and 'being'

> There's something really odd about the fact that I could play a mother of two living in Hammersmith, married to a director. I could play my life and that would fulfil something, but just to live my life, which could be identical to what I'd be playing (and I don't need the money so I'm very privileged), could be less fulfilling than pretending to be that. (Imogen Stubbs, p. 39)

The roles of performer, mother, wife or partner, and household manager present a constant juggling act of identities to be balanced and rebalanced. I want to argue that there is something nurturing about performing, allowing the occurrence of dream-time and a fantasy world. It enables the woman to become whatever she wants and not to be tied by definition to any one label. Performing allows women personal control, particularly where they are creating their own projects. For the performance artist, it becomes more a dialogue about the relationship between the 'self' of the artist and the 'self' being presented. Bobby Baker discusses the idea behind the 'Daily Life' series as:

> ... a journey for my own need to explore different aspects of my persona and my connection to my life, and that goes through sexuality, spirituality and all sorts of things that are very important. (p. 273)

Of the performing women in this collection sixteen are working mothers,[8] eleven of whom have children under the age of ten. The identity of 'mother' comes first at some point or other for all these women. There is an acknowledged need and necessity for both identities, 'I cram my working life into a shorter time than I used to, so there's not that identity tug ... and nobody should deny us if we are able to do both' (Victoria Wood, p. 189) Imelda Staunton argues that each identity feeds the other, one having the upper hand, and Imogen Stubbs openly acknowledges that she would 'explode' in the single identity of mother, 'What can be more fun than having a baby, and yet I still went back and did two plays' (p. 40). Many women have turned down jobs which would have taken them away from their children for long periods of time, such as Alison Steadman when her children were little, or Penelope Wilton: 'I used to dread being asked to work at times. I was asked to go to the RSC ... three times ... but I couldn't take her out of school' (p. 204). There is clearly a pull between the identities of mother and performer:

> ... I am a mother first, but I still get to the job. I cut corners in a way that a man wouldn't, and the person who always comes out worst is you. You manage the play, manage to give your child an extra half hour, and you are a neurotic mess at the end of the day because you had no time to refocus. (Niamh Cusack, p. 33)

Women often make choices about their work as performers to accommodate their home life. The issue of touring and travelling is particularly agonising for many performers with young children, 'It was a strain dragging them everywhere' (Sheila Hancock, p. 228). Victoria Wood's tour arrangements are specifically structured to embrace her life as mother, juggling everything around her children and never working school holidays, half-terms or sports days. There is no doubt that some performers, such as Victoria Wood, Julie Walters and Dawn French, have the power to set their terms and conditions of working in relation to their role as 'mother', for example, never rehearsing at weekends.

Motherhood is an important part of many of the performers' identities, and they are conscious of the split subjectivities within and beyond performance. Being a working mother concentrates the time of performing, and has significantly changed many women in terms of their attitude and approach to being a performer. They have become more rooted, less self-obsessed, more focused and clearer about their priorities, re-evaluating what matters in their lives. Meera Syal argues that having a child has made her 'a better performer', and practically informs all her work decisions. The same is true for Imelda Staunton, giving her 'another focus apart from yourself, and acting is very self-focused' (p. 128). I have been particularly interested in the women performers with young children, and how they combine these identities within their own lifestyle. This is a subject which is barely discussed, as we live in a country which likes the idea and image of 'mother and child', but does not support the reality of it. Without the provision of essential support structures of childcare in the workplace, the performer/mother must attempt to achieve '... some kind of balance to keep yourself sane' (Juliet Stevenson, p. 132).

The multifarious creative talents of the performing woman

It appears that for a number of the women interviewed, it is important to be able to fulfil themselves through more than one creative, artistic outlet. There is a need to be involved in different kinds of creative activity. These include writing in various forms, for example, a novel (Meera Syal, Sheila Hancock, Julie Walters); a play (Kathy Burke, Marianne Jean-Baptiste); reviews, articles, screenplays or books (Imogen Stubbs, Jo Brand, Sheila Hancock, Dawn French); and guest editing a magazine (Jenny Eclair). Directing is an activity pursued by many, including Kathy Burke, Fiona Shaw, Kathryn Hunter, Heather Ackroyd and Sheila Hancock – the first woman to have directed at both The Royal Shakespeare Company and The Royal National Theatre in the 1980s. Many of these women are multi-talented, for example Marianne Jean-Baptiste has composed the musical score (with Tony Remy) for Mike Leigh's film *Career Girls*, and Heather Ackroyd has created a number of visual art installations.

For Sheila Hancock and Kathy Burke, it has been about being able to perform, write and direct, which is evidently an exploration of various ways of working to address and discover a means of communication. Having a free-wheeling experience of performing, writing or directing is hard in a patriarchal culture that asks for a single definition of who you are and what you do. (See Meera Syal on the problems of being both writer and actress, pp. 59–62). What I find particularly interesting is the contrast of creative experience to be gained from both performing and writing. Both activities require an audience in the end (with its show of appreciation and approval), but the processes are almost two extremes of the creative spectrum. The activity of performing demands a live interaction with somebody else, whereas writing requires isolation. I am not proposing that there is anything odd about the desire to do both, but simply acknowledging from my own experience the differences these two activities offer. For most of the participants, writing serves as a secondary function to performing, although it clearly provides a different kind of fulfilment from performing. The act of writing is a facilitator for another kind of creative space to express a view, opinion or fantasy, which can never be catered for alone within the prescribed roles written for women within theatre, film or television.

Writing is generally a single-authored experience, and does not require any negotiation with others about what to do with the work. It is a clear statement of expression, which is directed at a reader, and yet, does not demand any contract or contact with another. I propose that the solitary nature of writing represents the private and introvert, and yet, there is clearly a pull towards the extrovert and being part of a team in these women. I also detect the pull of wanting to be different, and yet tired of being pointed out as different. There is the public persona, as given through the filter of the media, against how they see themselves. The outward image of the performer is the way that she is identified publicly, via the product, against the mechanics of acting, stand-up or performance art. The private self is how they really see themselves, which encompasses where they come from, what motivates them, and their family. The media commentate on the composite personality, which is the least truthful. Through the media, another person is fabricated – the composite of the person on stage and at home. Then, there is the identity of women as women, with all their multiple personalities, which begs a complex question about when performing is your job, where and when do all those personalities begin to infuse your own personality?

Stand-up: performing comedy

In a recent performance seminar at the University of Kent, a group of second-year drama undergraduate students and I were discussing whether Bobby Baker's performance of *How to Shop: the Lecture*[9] qualified as stand-up or performance art. It was resolved that Baker certainly stands as herself – a 'performative' personality – alone on stage, talking to an audience. Baker is not performing a character or a role, but the presentation does have the trappings of theatre: props, video footage on a large screen, and the standard Baker 'costume' of a white overall. That is, until she is transformed into an angel hanging from a tall, mechanical hoist looking down on the audience.

The stand-up stands completely alone on stage, in a space with a microphone, speaking to an audience. There is the performer, the 'routine' or material to be performed, and the live audience. It is a one-to-one relationship, up close and personal. There are no 'characters', play script, costume or make-up to hide behind, just the stand-up and verbal invention. It's immediate. There is a direct response from the audience to the stand-up each time she speaks. It appears to be terrifying to those who perform in a different genre, particularly the prospect of standing on stage alone. There is no one to turn to, no one to rely on, or work with in performance. The stand-up is responsible for all aspects of the performance. Stand-up involves the expression of an individual woman's perspective on the state of the world, and being funny.

Why perform stand-up?

Stand-ups are overtly political, producing their own work, which involves both writing and performing. The strength of the woman stand-up is that she owns her own words and asserts her identity from within the work; she is the agent of her own humour. Women in comedy, writing their own material, control and create the multiplicity of selves that are performed to the audience, which supports Susan Carlson's argument that comedy is 'the location for multiple definitions of female self, sexuality, and relationship'.[10]

Jo Brand had an early desire to make people laugh and felt frustrated with the fact that men get listened to far more than women in social situations. Brand argues that comics often have similar emotional crises and backgrounds: 'It's push from the inside of you that makes you almost want to tell people about what a shit time you've had' (p. 113). Brand's stand-up pleasure in shocking people and behaving badly originates in a difficult adolescence. For Brand, performing stand-up enables her to speak out and express anger, '... it's a very definite outlet for saying that there are lots of things that piss me off, and I know that piss other women off' (p. 110). Brand has a personal anger, as well as a general animosity at the amount of misogyny directed at women. Brand is mainly motivated by a protestant work ethic, by a political ideology, and by her sheer enjoyment of making people laugh. It's important to Brand to be funny.

Jenny Eclair has created a 'comedy persona' (p. 17) – an onstage 'self', which enables her to let it all go, when performing means 'complete freedom' (p. 17). For Eclair, performing stand-up is '... a sort of pathological need for attention' (p. 17), providing her with an adrenalin rush, which makes her feel alive on stage: 'It's very much the girl in the playground, hanging upside down without pants on, which is sort of "look at me, look at me"' (p. 19). Eclair describes her humour as 'silly, toilet humour' and states that 'if the human race didn't fart we probably wouldn't have a sense of humour (p. 21). Eclair projects a camp, 'queeny' image in performance: 'It's Joan Crawford crossed with the local supermarket check-out woman – the shrieky one. It's a combination of Elsie Tanner and all those larger than life soap opera people' (p. 22).

Like Eclair, Victoria Wood's driving force came from a need for attention and being funny. Performing for the girls at school was one way of getting attention, and her intention was clear, 'I specifically picked stand-up as something I wanted to reach the top of the ladder, and that took me a long time to do' (p. 188). Standing alone on stage represented strength for Wood, and she still finds it irresistible, '... going from place to place, doing a show on my own' (p. 188).

Performing stand-up is an empowering experience, allowing the performer to dominate and to control an audience, 'She stands up to be counted.'[11] As Brand suggests earlier, the act of domination tends to be a male activity, so the woman stand-up is challenging a stereotypical role and the patriarchal tradition by making the woman the speaking subject. However, Wood, Brand and Eclair dominate their audiences by using different methods, such as Eclair's covert way of being sexy in order to be acceptable, or Brand's style of self-denigration. What Wood loves most about performing stand-up is trying to be herself. She no longer needs to prove herself as she is the top comedienne in the country, and cannot imagine not performing.

Women comediennes write and perform from the personal, their task being 'to devise, develop and project a self in a process of dialogue with the audience. In doing so, she transforms the autobiographical process itself into a public event'.[12] The female comic's sensitivity to the realities of daily life lends itself to the content of her comedy, albeit in very different ways and styles of performance. Women's sensitivity and need to express their emotions may partly explain why women stand-ups do not hold the same status as men comedians, and why there are fewer of them. As Brand suggests: 'If the woman has a bad gig she thinks it's her fault, whereas the man has a bad gig and thinks it's the audience's fault' (p. 114). Male comics appear to be more surreal in style and content, reflecting the male characteristic of being more detached and less open in expressing emotions. Brand argues that audiences were more open to women performers in the 1980s: 'However, since comedy has become more populist and people from every class have come to see it, it has regressed a bit to women being assessed purely on their appearance' (p. 116).

The comedy actress

There are curious contradictions in the image of the confident, empowered comedy performer, who lacks confidence in herself, and the performer who wants to be funny, yet desires to be taken seriously at being funny. June Whitfield, one of our most experienced comedy actresses, has stated that being into comedy '... comes from basically a lack of confidence in yourself' (p. 211). Sheila Hancock comments that Joan Littlewood was influential in making her '... realise the intrinsic funniness in my own personality' (p. 230), acknowledging the value of her quirkiness and using it in various roles. Alison Steadman is happiest in comedy roles, whilst Brenda Blethyn sees both sides to playing comedy roles, 'I cannot see anything funny without seeing the dark side of that' (p. 240). Similarly, Julie Walters argues that performing comedy is 'part of what I am and how I was brought up. Laughing is extremely cathartic and very good for you, and puts things into perspective' (p. 261). Humour is viewed as something positive and healthy, beneficial for warding off melancholy, and diffusing pomposity. Imelda Staunton believes that, 'It lets people in a bit more somehow, gives access, but it's absolutely within your control' (p. 125).

Most interviewees saw performing comedy as requiring great skill, yet not having the equivalent status of performing tragedy. Miranda Richardson believes that '... if you can do comedy, you can do most things' (p. 182). Imogen Stubbs discussed the quick categorisation of performers being labelled 'a straight actress or a funny person',[13] and yet she argues that everyone can be both. Stubbs states that if you don't look funny, or have a certain kind of look, it is difficult to be cast in comic roles. Jane Horrocks suggests the reason for there being so few women comedians is an attitude that women shouldn't be funny, and that the men 'have an easier time doing it' (p. 70). Dawn French makes the interesting observation that it is acceptable for actors to cross into comedy, but far less so for comedians to perform drama. French suggests that in the late 1990s, comedy is '... going away from the political' and becoming, '... much more surreal ... a sort of surreal movement happening inside comedy' (p. 170).

Minor themes

Finally, I wish to identify some minor themes, which are separate in their own right, but have only been used to pepper the collection in the end. Across the interviews, there are snippets of conversation in relation to the themes of 'Attitudes towards and relationships with audiences', 'Working with directors', and 'Differences between theatre, film and television performance'. Television has different demands for actors, which means that money and instant fame hold more appeal for many newcomers entering the profession. It appears to be a widely held belief amongst performers that television has undermined the craft of acting.

Contradictions and some conclusions

... Women have not been absent from his-story, but have often been elided with the private and domestic, with child-rearing, marriage and the family. Authorship and ownership, representation and presence, have become crucial issues in the new her-stories.[14]

This research shows evidence of performers having a compulsive need to perform, indicating that there is clearly something which drives them as 'performing women'. Much has been written about performing and performers, but this collection of 'her-stories' is presented as raw material to be analysed further and used in a number of ways. There are certainly questions raised about actresses performing 'women' characters as fictions of the masculine psyche versus actresses for whom performing is an expression of 'the feminine'. If when I was interviewing, I had focused on questions examining the performer's relationship with her mother or father – 'Are you performing for Daddy?' – I suspect that I would have been charged with a reductive psycho-analytical agenda and no one would have agreed to be interviewed! Nevertheless, this might be an interesting area for future exploration.

One of the fascinations about this research is the contradictory nature of the performing experience. A number of actresses articulated a desire to be taken seriously as performers, and yet wanted to be light about it. This is also paralleled in the stand-up comic's wish to be taken seriously in her work, whilst wanting to be funny, but on the other hand, not wanting to take herself too seriously. It is interesting to note how these performers are often quite self-disparaging, suggesting a future argument to be explored concerning anxieties about identity and esteem being linked to the desire to perform, which is peculiar to women's comedy. The overwhelming difference between the actress and the stand-up is the actress's desire to work in an ensemble or company, as opposed to the stand-up standing alone on stage, which seems to signify strength and is admired by many women. It is interesting to note that Joyce Grenfell appears to have been consistently influential in the lives of many of these women.

It is apparent that the language used to describe the actress in the seventeenth century has certainly changed. Some performers were very clear about not wanting to be called an 'actress', and made a point of using the term 'actor' throughout the interview. However, nobody proffered the term 'woman actor' in discussion, and 'performer' seemed a natural term for many to use in discussion. The performing woman has multiple identities, which are ever changing in a constantly shifting cultural climate. Performing is clearly recognised by these women as a job of work. Performing allows these multiple identities to emerge within the work, but they must also be recognised in reality too.

Finally, I must mention the question about 'key moments' in the performing lives of these women. This originated from my own thinking about what I had achieved so far, what I wanted to do, and what I valued most – the priorities in my life. The performers gave spontaneous answers to this question, whatever came into their minds first. I have no desire whatsoever to analyse these responses, but am very clear that interviewing these women has certainly been another significant 'key moment' in my life, and I applaud them all for giving their time, passion and commitment to this book. Without them, there would have been no journey at all.

Notes

1 From an unpublished part of the interview with Juliet Stevenson.
2 Butler, J., 'Performative Acts and Gender Constitution: An Essay in Phenomenology and Feminist Theory' in Case, S-E. (ed.), *Performing Feminisms, Feminist Critical Theory and Theatre*, p. 277. (See pp. 275–9 for relevant argument.)
3 I am aware of the problematics of this debate in terms of gender studies (the idea of a unified 'woman' has long since died), and in relation to how these women performers speak about performing.
4 From an unpublished part of the interview with Meera Syal.
5 Fifteen known out of twenty-four; two unknown.
6 From an unpublished part of the interview with Josette Simon.
7 Royal Air Force slang for children in the armed services.
8 See note 3 p. 10.
9 Bobby Baker, *How to Shop: the Lecture*, co-directed with Pol Baloh-Brown, The Purcell Room, Royal Festival Hall, October 1998.
10 Carlson, S., *Women and Comedy*, University of Michigan, 1991, p. 161.
11 Gray, F., *Women and Laughter*, p. 149.
12 Ibid.
13 From an unpublished part of the interview with Imogen Stubbs.
14 Cockin, K., in introduction to Part One: 'The History of Women in Theatre', *The Routledge Reader in Gender and Performance*, p. 20.

Selected Bibliography

Carlson, M., *Performance: A Critical Introduction*, Routledge, 1996

Carlson, S., *Women and Comedy*, University of Michigan, 1991

Davis, T., *Actresses as Working Women, Their Social Identity in Victorian Culture*, Routledge, 1991

Donnell, A., and Polkey, P. (eds), *Representing Lives: Women and Auto/biography*, Macmillan Press (forthcoming)

Goodman, L., *Sexuality in Performance*, Routledge (forthcoming)

Goodman, L., with de Gay, J. (eds), *The Routledge Reader in Gender and Performance*, 1998

Gray, F., *Women and Laughter*, Macmillan Press, 1994

Howe, E., *The First English Actresses: Women and Drama 1660–1700*, Cambridge University Press, 1992

Oddey, A., *Devising Theatre*, Routledge, 1994

Zarrilli, P. (ed.), *Acting (Re) Considered*, Routledge, 1995

Index

A Long Day's Journey into Night 205, 207
A River Runs Through It 240
A Streetcar Named Desire 40
Abbot, Christine 167
Ackroyd, Heather 7, 98–105, 281, 284, 288
Acting, Devising and Performance, definitions of 4, 162, 257, 281
Ahearne, Caroline 192
Aitchison, Suzy 212
Alexander, Professor Sally 226
Alfreds, Mike 230
Allen, Woody 195
Alternative Comedy 170
Amy's View 147
An Edible Family in a Mobile Home 267, 269
An Ideal Husband 242
Anita and Me 61
Anna Lee 36
Anstey, Liz 210
Arden, Annabel 149
Arts Council *223*
Ashcroft, Peggy 49, 124
Atkins, Eileen 203
Auden, W.H. 133
Aukin, Liane 149
Austen, Jane 274
    Pride and Prejudice 246
Ayckbourn, Alan 202

Baby Talk 256
Baker, Bobby 7, 266–77, 286, 289
Ball, Lucille 19
Baloh-Brown, Pol 271
Barr, Roseanne 240
Barton, John 132, 134, 230
Bassey, Shirley 192
BBC 78, 186, 196, 246
Bechtler, Hildegard 162
Beggar's Opera 122
Bennett, Alan 126
Benny, Jack 202
Berry, Cicely 132, 230
Bhaji on the Beach 60, 61
Bird, Antonia 124
Blackadder 182
Blau, Herbert 4
Blethyn, Brenda 95, 232–43, 280, 291
Boal, Augusto 237
Bourgeois, Louise 274
Boyce, Max 192

Brand, Jo 6, 8, 19, 23, 70, 78, 106–17, 173, 192, 240, 250, 285, 288, 289
Brecht, Bertholt 139
    In the Jungle of the Cities 145
    The Caucasian Chalk Circle 9, 87, 131, 136
Bristol Old Vic Drama School 179
Broadbent, Jim 264
Brook, Peter 132
Brueghel, *Dulle Griet* 138
Bryan, Dora 215
Bryden, Bill 237
Burke, Kathy 64, 76–88, 256, 283, 285, 288
Bush Theatre 83
Butler, Judith 3

Cabaret 70
Caine, Marti 191
Cameron, Rhona 6, 23
Campion, Jane 251
Career Girls 97, 288
Carlson, Marvin, *Performance: A Critical Introduction* 4
Carlson, Susan, *Women and Comedy* 289
Carrot, Jasper 192
Cartwright, Jim 70
    Little Voice 70, 74, 252
    Road 70, 74
Cassidy, David 171
Castle, Roy 202
Castledine, Annie 149
Central School of Speech and Drama 48, 167
Chaplin, Charlie 146
Charleson, Ian 127
Chekhov, Anton 200
    The Cherry Orchard 200, 203, 224, 230
    The Seagull 203
    Three Sisters 29, 33, 43
    Uncle Vanya 119, 128
Chichester 219, 221
Churchill, Caryl 146, 205
    Serious Money 65
    The Skriker 146, 151
Clapton, Eric 197
Clarke, Alan 70
Cockin, Katharine 8
Coleridge, Samuel Taylor
    The Ancient Mariner 155
Comedy Store 70, 240
Common as Muck 78

Coogan, Steve 117
Cooper, Tommy 202
Cooper-Clark, John 19
Covency, Michael 184
Covington, Julie 127
Coward, Noel 216
    Ace of Clubs 216
Crewe & Alsager College 100
Cry Freedom 205
Curtis, Richard 169
Cusack, Niamh 24–34, 279, 282, 283,
    284, 285, 287
Cusack, Paul 27
Cusack, Sinead 27
Cusack, Sorcha 27

'Daily Life' series 268
Dangerous Buccaneers 227
Damage 182, 183
Davis, Bette 214
Davis, Tracy, *Actresses as Working Women*
    6
Dawson, Les 21
Dear Octopus 222
Death and the Maiden 142
Dee, Jack 22, 23, 115
Dench, Dame Judi 124, 147, 173, 220,
    228, 252
Devising Theatre 1
Diller, Phyllis 64
Dionisotti, Paola 132
Directors, working with 68, 71, 74, 83,
    86, 124, 136, 139, 149, 150, 179,
    224–6, 230, 237, 238, 264, 292
Dodd, Ken 195
Donelin, Declan 60
Double, Oliver, *STAND-UP! On Being a
    Comedian* 5
Drawing on a Mother's Experience 271,
    272
Dunderdale, Sue 124
Durkheim 109

East 15 Drama School, Loughton 250
Eclair, Jenny 6, 8, 15–23, 70, 114, 173,
    192, 282, 285, 288, 290
Ecstasy 264
Eddison, Robert 37
Edinburgh Festival 57, 183
Electra 157, 159
Eliot, T.S. 154
    The Waste Land 154, 155, 157, 162
Emmett, Chris 213
Enfield, Harry 78
Evans, Lee 22, 23, 115
Everyman 149
Eyre, Sir Richard 9, 129

Feminism 111, 221, 230
Fool for Love 263
French, Dawn 7, 9, 111, 165–75, 240,
    282, 285, 287, 288, 291
French and Saunders 23, 59, 64, 78, 114,
    170, 182, 192, 212, 215, 275
Friday Night Live 108

Galvin, Joan 79
Gambon, Michael 52, 129
Garland, Judy 214
Gate Theatre, Dublin 199, 200
Gee, Shirley 226
    Typhoid Mary 226
Geldman, Martha 183
Gender 22, 148, 156, 280
Girls' Night 64
Goldsmiths College 276
Goodness Gracious Me! 56, 60, 63, 65
Globe Theatre 68
Grass House 102
Gray, Frances, *Women and Laughter* 5
Greer, Germaine 230
    The Female Eunuch 229
Grenfell, Joyce 64, 112, 191, 274, 293
Grounds, Tony 171
Grown-up School 273
Guildhall School of Music and Drama
    29, 222
Guys and Dolls 9, 29, 119, 127, 128

Hall, Sir Peter 237
Hancock, Sheila 218–31, 256, 282, 287,
    288, 291
Harry, Debbie 72
Harry Enfield and Chums 86
Harvey, Dan 99, 104
Harvey, Jonathan 83
Hayman, Carole 60
Hayridge, Hattie 6, 22, 114
Heartbeat 25, 33
Henry, Lenny 191
Hersov, Greg 237, 238
Hill, Harry 22, 115
Hiller, Wendy 252
Hird, Thora 203
Hislop, Ian 37
Hopkins, Sir Anthony 236
Horrocks, Jane 66–75, 291
Horsfield, Debbie 219
Hoskins, Bob 127
How to Shop 276, 289
Howard, Alan 132
Howe, Elizabeth, *The First English
    Actresses* 6
Howell, Jane 124, 237
Howerd, Frankie 202, 211, 216

Hudd, Roy 211, 213, 216
Hunter, Kathryn 9, 143–52, 285, 288
Huseyin, Metin 78

Ibsen, Henrik 156
  A Doll's House 30, 124, 159, 238–9
Impact Theatre 100
  The Carrier Frequency 103
Inner London Education Authority 91

Jackson, Glenda 132
James, Jimmy 202
Jean-Baptiste, Marianne 7, 89–97, 285,
  288
Johnson, Terry 60
Joseph and his Amazing Technicolour
  Dreamcoat 48
Jude 210
Julie Walters is an Alien 255
Jumping the Queue 221

Kalman, Jean 155
Kaut-Howson, Helena 147, 149, 150
Kavanagh 219
Keaton, Buster 146
Kinnock, Glenys 113
Kirby, Michael 4
Kruger, Barbara 274
Kyle, Barry 48

Lapotaire, Jane 132
Lawrence, Josie 240
Lecoat, Jenny 19
Lederer, Helen 19
Leigh, Mike 71, 86, 93, 233, 236, 256,
  264
  Abigail's Party 250, 252
  Career Girls 97, 288
  It's a Great Big Shame 86, 87, 93
  Life is Sweet 71, 72
  Secrets and Lies 90, 93, 94, 233, 237,
    239, 240, 242
Leong, Susan 226
Lepage, Robert 156
Littlewood, Joan 223, 226, 229, 230, 291
Lloyd, Marie 5
Lloyd, Phyllida 60, 149
Loach, Ken 86
Lock Up Your Daughters 219
London Contemporary Dance Theatre
  91
London Lighthouse 108
Lorca, Federico Garcia 146
Love, Courtney 174
Lumiere & Son 100
Lumley, Joanna 72, 213
Lynch, Calam 26

Lynch, Finbar 26
Lyric Theatre, Hammersmith 220

Machinal 159
MacIntosh, Genista 224
Manning, Bernard 111
Manville, Lesley 32
Marcello, Magni 149
Marquis, Don 22
  Archy & Mehitabel 22
Mason, Jackie 195
Massey, Daniel 204
Mavis Davis 72
McBurney, Simon 68, 87, 136, 139, 150
McCracken, Esther 37
McEwan, Geraldine 203
McKellan, Sir Ian 228
McKenzie, Julia 127
McPhail, Donna 6, 23, 114, 192
McQueen, Steve 171
McTeer, Janet 124
Meckler, Nancy 149
Miller, Arthur 53
  After the Fall 54
Miller, Graeme 100
  The Desire Paths 100
Mirren, Helen 52
Miss Marple 210
Mitchell, Katie 99, 103, 149
Molière 85
  Learned Ladies 25, 31
  Tartuffe 248
Monkhouse, Bob 192
Morecambe and Wise 112
Mortimer, Bob 170
Mr Jealousy 93, 95
Mr Thomas 83
Mr Wroe's Virgins 82, 87
Mrs Overall 263

Never Mind the Horrocks 69
New Faces 191
Nunn, Trevor 36, 224, 230
Nuts in May 250

Oh What a Lovely War 43
Olivier, Laurence 146
One of Us 57
Optik Theatre 104
  Short Sighted 104
Orlando 183
Orton, Joe 85
  Entertaining Mr Sloane 85
Outside Edge 239

Pacino, Al 124
Pat and Margaret 194

People Show 100
Performer
    four types of 3
    the first English actresses 6
    the over-rated value of training 19–20,
        107, 193, 187–8
Performers
    audiences, relation with 281–3
    of comedy 291
    creative talents of 287–9
    and identity 12, 279–80
    in the different media 2, 3
    as itinerants 7–8, 285
    and the journey towards performance
        3, 284
    and motherhood 2, 286
    and the need to perform 282, 286
    and the performance moment 281
    revisiting childhood and playing 282,
        283
    as stand-ups 5, 289–91
    as strumpets 6
    working in a company 9, 281
    why perform? 1
Piaf 128
Pimlott, Steven 26
Pinter, Harold 199, 200
    A Kind of Alaska 200
    Betrayal 204
Poirot 210
Polka Theatre 91
Prozac and Tantrums 16
Pryce, Jonathan 132

RADA 38, 67, 92, 122, 124, 140, 145,
    158, 211, 220, 221
Rape on Rape 219
Rattle of a Simple Man 229
Rawlins, Adrian 100
Ray, Stephen 264
Redford, Robert 240
Red Lion Pub Theatre 85
Redgrave, Vanessa 30, 40
Reeves, Vic 170
Reid, Beryl 64, 112, 203
Remy, Tony 97
Reisz, Karel 33
Richardson, Miranda 176–84, 280, 281,
    291
Richardson, Ralph 30, 37
Rickman, Alan 96, 124, 132, 158
Ring Round the Moon 145
Rita, in *Educating Rita* 263
Rodenburg, Patsy 32
Rogers, Mary 82
Ronnie Scott's 96
Royal Air Force 166, 167
Royal Court 70, 225

Royal Exchange, Manchester 238
Royal National Theatre 9, 87, 94, 96,
    119, 124, 131, 136, 155, 205, 220,
    224, 288
Royal Shakespeare Company 9, 25, 26,
    52, 68, 96, 99, 132, 134, 149, 158,
    200, 203, 222, 223, 224, 226, 248,
    285, 288
Russell, Rosalind 214
Ruth Ellis 181
Rylance, Mark 68, 74

Sackville-West, Vita 203
Saunders, Jennifer 72, 83, 168, 172, 212,
    213, 216
    Absolutely Fabulous 72, 74, 83, 212, 216
Savage, Lily 95, 240
Savoy Theatre 166
Sawalha, Julia 72
Sayle, Alexei 170
Scher, Anna 80, 81, 84
Schneemann, Carolee 267
Scott, Terry 211, 216
Scrubbers 84
Shakespeare, William 25, 46, 47, 68, 148,
    202, 223, 229
    A Midsummer Night's Dream 26
    A Winter's Tale 226
    Antony and Cleopatra 52, 141
    As You Like It 25, 26
    Henry VI 237
    King Lear 9, 135, 144, 146, 147, 151
    Love's Labour's Lost 48, 53
    Macbeth 68, 74
    Othello 25, 26
    Richard II 9, 36, 134, 155, 156, 162
    Romeo and Juliet 25, 26, 150
    The Taming of the Shrew 50
    Troilus and Cressida 42
Shaw, Fiona 9, 153–164, 280, 281, 288
Shaw, George Bernard 202
    Heartbreak House 40
    Joan of Arc 145, 221
Shooting Stars 170
Short, Clare 113
Simon, Josette 7, 45–54, 285
Simone, Nina 274
Smith, Dame Maggie 146, 203
Snow White and the Seven Dwarves 145
Some Kind of Life 72
Spall, Timothy 124, 242
Stafford-Clark, Max 60, 150
Stanwyck, Barbara 214
Staunton, Imelda 9, 118–29, 282, 283,
    285, 286, 287, 291
Steadman, Alison 8, 71, 73, 229, 244–53,
    279, 282, 287, 291

Stevenson, Juliet 9, 124, 130–42, 158, 173, 226, 279, 280, 281, 285, 287
Stewart, Patrick 132
Strand Theatre 186
Streep, Meryl 161
Street-Porter, Janet 113
Strindberg, August 100
  Easter 99
Stubbs, Imogen 7, 35–44, 279, 282, 284, 285, 286, 288, 291
Suchet, David 132
Summer Show 191
Syal, Meera 7, 55–65, 256, 280, 282, 285, 287, 288

Table Occasions 267, 268, 269, 270, 273
Take a Peek! 276
Take It From Here 216
Thatcher, Margaret 124
Theatre, therapeutic role of 154, 156, 223, 227
The Caribbean Mystery 210
The Changeling 183
The Comic Strip 168, 170
The Critic 225
The Divide 101
The Dressmaker 72
The Duchess of Malfi 224
The Maids 31, 49
The Miracle Worker 48
The News Huddlines 209, 213, 214
The Pit, Barbican Theatre 226
The Prime of Miss Jean Brodie 250
The Rainbow 42
The Rose Tattoo 263
The South Bank Show 194
The Vicar of Dibley 169
The Visit 150
The Way of the World 94, 156
The Wind in the Willows 194
Theatr Clwyd 149
Theatre de Complicite 9, 68, 87, 131, 136, 149

Theatre-in-education 223
Thewlis, David 71
Thompson, Emma 123, 126
Thorndike, Sybil 203
Tiresias 156
Tom and Viv 177, 181
Tom Jones 77, 82, 210
Travolta, John 123
Truly, Madly, Deeply 142
Tutin, Dorothy 203

Ullman, Tracey 215
Uses of Enchantment 104

Vita and Virginia 203

Wade, Michelle 145
Wall, Max 203
Walter, Harriet 226
Walters, Julie 8, 63, 64, 215, 254–65, 279, 282, 287, 288, 291
Wanamaker, Zoe 132
Warner, Deborah 124, 154, 155, 161
Waters, Les 150
Wax, Ruby 132
When We Are Married 166, 245, 249
Whitfield, June 208–17, 291
Wilson, Robert 184
Williams, Enyd 210
Wilton, Penelope 198–207, 229, 287
Wood, Peter 237, 238
Wood, Victoria 5, 6, 8, 23, 64, 70, 108, 114, 170, 171, 185–197, 203, 215, 261, 275, 281, 282, 285, 286, 287, 290
Woolf, Virginia 203, 274
Worth, Irene 203
Wycherley, William, *The Country Wife* 202

Young Vic 9, 147

Zetterling, Mai 84